Between Two Worlds

Between Two Worlds

UNDERSTANDING AND MANAGING CLERGY STRESS

ANDREW R. IRVINE

MOWBRAY

Mowbray
A Cassell imprint

Wellington House,
125 Strand,
London WC2R 0BB

PO Box 605, Herndon, VA 20172

First published 1997

British Library Cataloguing-in-Publication Data
A catalogue record for this book is available from the British Library.

ISBN 0-264-67423-5

Typeset by York House Typographic Limited, London.
Printed and bound in Great Britain by
Biddles Ltd, Guildford and King's Lynn

Contents

List of Figures   vii
Foreword by David Lyall   viii
Acknowledgements   x
Introduction   xii

Section One   An historical identity: collective and personal

1. The foundation from which we work   3
   The shapers * The tension of integration * Personal versus
   professional ministry

2. Stress: villain or vital   15
   What is stress? * A definition of stress * Villain or vital *
   Stress factors in ministry * Other concepts in stress research

Section Two   A vocational identity: ministry in a changing world

3. The stress of a lost identity: the societal perspective   49
   'Who do people say that I am?'

4. The stress of a changing identity: the church perspective   65
   'Who do you say that I am?' * A changing role in a traditional
   institution * Belonging to the fraternal

5. The stress of being a woman in ministry: searching to   77
   establish an identity
   Entrance to the profession * Vocational stress and women

Section Three   A relational identity: intimacy sought and avoided

6. The risk of relationships   89
   The minister as relational being: levels of relationships *
   Overcoming a bad theology

7. The problem of isolation   **99**
   Isolation: what does the term mean? * Types of isolation *
   What is the root cause of isolation? * Self-identity,
   wholeness and ministry * Insulation not isolation

8. Ministry, sexuality and identity   **113**
   Sexual misconduct * Dealing with the issue * The sexual
   orientation of clergy

9. Stress in the vicarage: the identity of the family **125**
   General dynamics * Specific issues * The church widow(er) *
   The child(ren) of the vicarage * The church family needs
   a pastor * Removing the family's mask * In commendation
   of clergy parents

Section Four   The quest for identity and wholeness

10. The quest for the grail of wholeness   **145**
   The presence of paradox * Resolving paradox through
   integration * Integrating perspectives: exteriority versus
   interiority * Developing as spiritual being * The
   clutter within * The need for inner housecleaning *
   The act of encounter

11. Models of support   **160**
   System support models * Community based support *
   Personal support structure

12. Making it personal   **180**
   Total assessment concept * Keeping a journal * A final
   comment on balance

Epilogue   198
Bibliography   200
Index   205

Foreword

When I took up a teaching post at St Andrews in 1987 one of my first jobs was to take some responsibility for piloting Andrew Irvine's doctoral thesis through the necessary examination hoops. His thesis on 'Isolation and the parish ministry' was obviously going to be of seminal importance in giving insight into what was actually happening to ministers of the Church of Scotland (and possibly of other denominations) at that time. The doctorate safely awarded, Andrew returned to his native Canada to develop Ministry Studies at Acadia Divinity College, Acadia University in Nova Scotia. It was therefore with anticipation that I was able to welcome him back to Scotland on study leave in the academic year 1995–96 and it has been with pleasure and excitement that I have watched this book grow chapter by chapter and had the privilege of discussing the material with him. While *Between Two Worlds* is in no sense a re-write of his academic thesis, the book is undergirded by that solid, original research to which he has added years of engagement in and reflection upon the practice of ministry.

The title of the book only emerged as the final draft of the manuscript was being completed. Yet *Between Two Worlds* not only encapsulates the theme and the content of the book, it is also, for a number of reasons, an apt description of the distinctive qualities which Andrew brings to its authorship. First, he is equally at ease in the two worlds of Britain and North America, and perhaps more particularly in the two worlds of Scotland and Canada, his own father being among the thousands of Scots who crossed the Atlantic in search of a new way of life. It is because of his familiarity with both cultures that I believe that this book will be found to be a helpful contribution to the debate about ministerial identity and ministerial stress which is taking place on both sides of the Atlantic.

Second, the fact that Andrew, a Baptist minister, undertook his research in a context which is predominantly Presbyterian, brings a particular strength to his work. 'The great thing about you, Andrew', said one senior minister of the Kirk, 'is that you will go away!' People will talk to ministers who are strangers about matters which they would never dream of discussing with a colleague (for reasons to which Andrew alludes and which constitute part of the problem of isolation and stress). And I can imagine that Andrew, being the pastor that he is, will, not infrequently when the 'official' interviews were completed, have been a minister to more than one minister during the course of his research.

Third, a strength of this book is that Andrew is equally at home moving between the two worlds of theology and psychology. Issues of stress and identity are not peculiar to the ordained ministry of the churches. There are few professions whose members are not vulnerable to the kind of stress which leads to distress and breakdown – and there is more than adequate documentation regarding this phenomenon. People break down not because of the stresses of any particular profession, nor because they are especially weak, but because they are human. This book demonstrates an awareness of the general causes of stress but this is set within a theological understanding of the church and its ministry. Whether or not bad theology is a cause of stress, there is no doubt that, as Andrew points out, the two often go together. However eloquent their sermons on the nature of grace, ministers will find no release from the results of stress until grace becomes part of the lived reality which constitutes their own identity both personal and professional.

Fourth, Andrew moves easily between the two worlds of theory and practice and it is this facility which makes the book an important contribution to the contemporary literature of the rediscovered discipline of practical theology. With a wide experience both as social worker and as minister to congregations, and reinforced by the insights gained from supervising a large number of ministers writing Doctor of Ministry dissertations, the author has produced a book which is no mere academic enterprise isolated from the real world of pastoral practice. At the same time, that real world is reflected upon with the kind of academic integrity which constitutes good practical theology.

Finally, Andrew Irvine has written a book which holds together the two worlds of the past and the future. It is not simply an analysis of the problem but provides suggestions for a way forward; its emphasis is not upon the despair generated by an inability to escape from the past, but upon a hope for the future based upon the discovery of an authentic Christian spirituality. I am sure that this book will enable many ministers to find a way of transformation in the midst of stressful situations and, in so doing, find their true identity in being the kind of minister they feel called to be.

David Lyall, Associate Dean, Department of Christian Ethics and
Pastoral Theology, University of Edinburgh

Acknowledgements

During this year of writing I have become increasingly aware of the fact that a book and its writer are but a small outward presentation of the concerted efforts of many. If it were not for those who contributed of themselves through the sharing of life's experiences, insights, wisdom, criticisms, comments and encouragement this effort would have come to nought. Those acknowledged here along with others too numerous to mention have made the efforts of this past year both possible and a rich experience.

To those who serve the church in parish ministry and who have shared with me a little of their journey, I am greatly indebted. Your task in the stress of daily 'front line' service is the reason why this book has been written. Your experiences are what help us to understand better the subject at hand. Thank you for sharing with us. To the Church of Scotland whose breadth and depth I have come to admire greatly and who were willing to support a 'foreigner' in his prodding and probing of its clergy I voice a sincere thank you.

I appreciate the willingness of Acadia Divinity College, Nova Scotia, Canada and my colleagues there for allowing me a sabbatical year for further research and writing. To those who increased their work-load to take up the slack in my absence I am most grateful. I have also appreciated the time at New College, Edinburgh whose faculty has been most gracious in providing a venue for continued research and support during my year here.

The original research into isolation, which provides much of the foundation for this book, would not have been possible without the wisdom and support of The Right Reverend Professor James Whyte, St Mary's College, St Andrews. His valuable input, sincere love of the church and its ministry and his gracious example have and will continue to be an example for all we who were blessed to be his students and friends.

A special word of appreciate is due to Dr David Lyall, Associate

Dean of New College. Through his encouragement I came to spend the year in Edinburgh. He has read the manuscript and has commented, suggesting changes along the way. As a good and 'brutal' friend his input has been of great value. I am honoured by his willingness to write the Foreword for this book.

There is a risk in making acknowledgements that they become limited to the direct project or discipline under consideration. There are many, however, whose support given in the broader context of life is invaluable.

A very special word of appreciation is due to my good friends Margaret and Everett Hill. They have most graciously opened their home in Fife to me during this year, inviting me to make their tranquil setting mine, and to share in their daily life. They have done much to eliminate for me during this year the concepts which we will discuss in this book: stress and isolation. In the year away from home they provided sanctuary, caring and support. Without them this year would not have been possible. Thank you.

During this year in which I have been away I have appreciated the support and understanding of my children at home, Stephen and Sarah. As 'senior' teenagers they have been a great support both to me and to their mother. My son Sandy who is studying at the University of St Andrews here in Scotland has been once again part of my everyday life and in this time I have appreciated his presence, encouragement and the opportunity to share life with a now adult son. Three greater children no parents could ever ask for!

My greatest appreciation is to my wife Suzanne, my beloved partner and co-traveller in life. Throughout the whole endeavour, from the initial research to the final product she has been my greatest supporter, best critic, wisest advisor, personal editor and best friend. While I travelled and lived abroad during this year of writing she held the home in Canada together, cared for the children, now young adults, read and edited drafts of manuscript as well as maintained her own career in teaching. To her, with my deepest love and appreciation, I promise that the next sabbatical we will 'do together'.

Introduction

The history and tradition of the ministry has, throughout the years, denied the priest or minister much of his/her humanity. Beneath the vestige of office the cleric seems at times a non-being, void of the desires, needs, temptations, doubts and fears that afflict all others.

This is not only a phenomenon imposed by history and tradition. Often, caught up in the trappings of office, it is the minister who, forgetting his/her own humanity, imposes the stress of non-being. C. G. Jung, in his two articles on the ego, speaks clearly of the danger of over-identification with the 'role' of an office and, in that act, the forgetting of the identity of the total self with all the intrinsic value of the inner person.

How easy it is to lose sight of one's humanity, suppressing the emotions and denying the factors which, if left unattended, turn healthy stress into excess stress and subsequent distress.

The old English church, its silence broken only by the grand harmony of the organ, offers a sacred ethos of worship. Down the centre aisle the processional moves as though without form of propulsion. The minister, wearing full clerical dress, is almost an unrealistic figure, given the modern bustle of the London streets outside. It is hard to believe that this surreal figure could be invaded by temptations and doubt, or for that matter, could be anything less than the sacred figure he represents.

Consider another scenario. The large, fundamentalist church in an American southern city is full to capacity for a Sunday evening service. The pastor, skilled in communications, presents a 'gospel' characterized by guilt, causing the 'sinners' to squirm with conviction in their seats. With authoritative thunder the demand is made for repentance followed by the 'aisle walk'. It is not possible to dream, even to suspect, that the one who proclaimed the message could in any way be affected by the same 'affliction of sin' which was attributed to the hearers. There is something in that figure which, in the high drama of the moment, seems above the common afflictions of humanity.

So it is that often behind the 'masks' of office hides a person caught in two worlds between the authenticity of personhood and the role and expectation of office. With whom can this tension be shared? To whom can the inner doubts, fears and even 'sins' be disclosed? Are others, whose masks seem more authentic than ours, invaded by these same realities in their lives?

This book will examine the personal world of the clergy and, within it, factors which contribute to a profession fraught with tension and subject to excess stress. The case can be made that all professions in today's society suffer from the curse of excess stress which often drives the professional to what is commonly called 'burnout'. While not denying this commonality, there are within the ministry those dynamics unique to the clergy. Consider but a few:

1. The minister serves in one of the few remaining 'old time' professions which functions predominantly in solo practice.
2. The identity of the minister is affected by society's increasing view of the church and, therefore, those who serve it, as an unnecessary institution and profession. This is confirmed by decreasing church attendance and membership roles.
3. Decreasing rolls of mainline churches and the increasing rise of independent fellowship churches have forced the mainline churches to follow the lead of business and industry in restructuring and realigning the institution if it is to survive in the twenty-first century.
4. The necessity for proof of 'success', in light of the need for accountability and survival, has prompted competition and, with it, the risk of loss of trust and co-operation among those who serve in ministry.
5. The rapid change of societal standards and values has caught the church, and often those who serve, in the stressful dilemma of attempting to move an entrenched institution into a position of relevance in the world. No longer does the authority of the church go unchallenged simply because it has spoken.
6. The decreasing coffers of most ecclesiastical bodies have continued to place the clergy financially behind those of other professions which demand equal preparation for entrance to the profession.

This book will not only raise and explore issues which contribute uniquely to high stress factors among the clergy, but it will also assist the reader in identifying areas of unrealistic demands imposed by both self and others. It is important to recognize that those factors which contribute to excess stress often lie within us and are, in reality, our response to external stimuli. The response is our response. The task of dealing with stress is not, in the first instance, an adjustment of the external 'stressors', but rather an adjustment in the way in which we react internally to them. This book will explore the need to manage the stress factors, first internally, and then externally, and, thus, to move towards a greater sense of wholeness and health.

In Section One consideration is given to those factors which have served to shape ministry itself and our personal understanding and fulfilment of ministry. Chapter 2 reviews current research on stress and application is made to ministry.

In Section Two the question of identity is raised especially as it is shaped by vocation. Examination is made of current societal and church perspectives of the minister in today's world. In the midst of a changing world, how do the perspectives of others affect the self-image of the minister? Chapter 5 in this section is devoted to stress experienced by women in ministry. Little direct research is available relating to this topic. More research has been done in other professions as women move into leadership roles within them and this is valuable to our understanding. Some may consider the value of this chapter lessened because it is written by a male. However, it is written with the conviction that this is a shared problem and that voices need to be heard from persons of both genders. The material has been read by women colleagues in ministry and revised by their collective input.

Section Three examines relationships and the risks that they create. This includes consideration of the levels of relationships and the absence of such, which leads to isolation. A chapter is devoted to sexuality and the profession, an area of great importance in today's climate characterized by scandal. Chapter 9 on the family attempts to provide a voice for many who share in the closeness of family life with the minister but have often missed the strength of intimacy.

Section Four, the final section, considers how the minister, in the activism of modern ministry, may find identity and wholeness in today's world. The search for wholeness and identity is a journey and each step a contribution. No definitive solution is proposed but suggested routes for part of the journey are outlined. Remember, that all journeys require moments of rest beside still waters.

A word about the research which has contributed to this book. Between 1986 and 1989 I conducted research into the phenomenon of isolation as it existed among the clergy of the Church of Scotland. A lengthy psychological study considered the works of such formative thinkers as Sigmund Freud, Alfred Adler, Erich Fromm, Karen Horney, Harry Stack Sullivan, R. D. Laing, Viktor Frankl and C. G. Jung. A theological understanding of the subject was developed primarily from the writings of Paul Tillich and Emil Brunner.

Field research explored the concept of isolation as it was experienced by the ministers of the church. A representative sample group of 200 parish ministers (15.6 per cent) was selected by random process. To each of these was mailed a specially designed questionnaire, supplementary standardized testing and a specific survey form to be completed by the spouse (if such existed) and returned under separate cover. A total response of 85 per cent was received of which 79 per cent were considered adequately completed to constitute a reliable data base. The high level of response is believed indicative of the concern and interest in the subject.

Following the receipt of all responses, 35 direct interviews, chosen by random selection, were conducted. A report was submitted to the Church of Scotland in 1990.

Since then, my own role in teaching in a theological college and in continuing research in ministry has served to stimulate further enquiry. During the past seven years the material has been used in the classroom and in conference and workshop presentations which has prompted constant re-evaluation in light of the response from students and ministers. As director of a professional doctoral programme in ministry, my constant interaction with senior ministers of many denominations has contributed immensely. Utilization of the research in Scotland, Canada and the United States has proven valuable in providing a breadth of insights from ministers on both sides of the Atlantic. During the writing of the book, the opportunity to use the material in conferences in Scotland and in the teaching of a Doctor of Ministry course in Canada has aided in the continuing search for relevance. To all those who have participated in this process, I am greatly indebted.

One further note: all the brief case studies presented are drawn from some phase of the research but have been modified for the sake of confidentiality. In some cases they are simply representative of trends determined by the study. All names are fictitious.

Too often the clergy feel that they are on a journey alone, sheltering within them those doubts and fears, those struggles of their humanness which they think surely afflict no others. This book is intended to demonstrate that we are all on a common journey and en route we all face varying renditions of a similar theme. As we raise the theme together and, at various points and junctures, say our 'Ah, that's me' or 'Oh, yes, that's my situation', and add our story, may the solidarity of common journeyers lend its support one to the other.

Section One

*An historical identity: collective
and personal*

1

The foundation from which we work

> Therefore since through God's mercy we have this ministry, we do not lose heart.
>
> St Paul (2 Cor 4.1)

What is this ministry? From the Apostle Paul to the most recent graduate from theological training the question has been raised. What is it through the centuries that has shaped the profession we call ministry? As we consider ministry at the end of the twentieth century and speculate on what form it will take in the coming century of change, it is hard to imagine that Jesus himself, or for that matter the early church leaders, could have conceived of the profession as we know it today. In fact, the seeming bi-vocational ministry of many of the apostles may well indicate that it was never intended to be a profession at all.

More importantly, the question needs first to be asked: 'What is it that has shaped and given character to our ministry?' As we begin to consider the issues of stress within the profession of ministry, we need to develop some understanding of these factors which, for us, have defined ministry. The definition is twofold. First there are those factors that are part of the 'collective consciousness' of what ministry is or should be. Second, there are those factors that have been, and are, part of our own personal consciousness and experience of ministry. From this foundation – our individual yet composite understanding of ministry – we can determine those issues which, for us, create the stress and potentially the distress experienced in the profession.

Our answer to the question will not be exhaustive, but rather will attempt to lay a simple foundation from which we can consider the subject at hand and apply it to our own individual life situation. For each of us that will be an individual and personal process. We will find that the way in which the defining factors of ministry apply to us individually will present a vast array of combinations and permutations. The following account may seem somewhat of a caricature, but in its extreme we find the point made clear.

> The young man who entered the office seemed somewhat out of place in the relaxed 'free' atmosphere of the theological college. The dress of black 'clerical' garb with Roman collar was somewhat inconsistent with the polished cowboy boots which appeared beneath the sharply creased dress trousers. Around his neck hung a comparatively giant wooden crucifix – a sharp contrast to the bright gold bracelet and rings which dominated the wrist and fingers of his right hand. He appeared at first glance as an odd combination of modesty with clerical dress and the 'collar' of servanthood contrasted with signs of prosperity and the occasional outcropping of the worldly 'western' culture.
>
> He began to tell his story of a rural, non-church upbringing with the only religious influence being the urging of a nominally Roman Catholic mother to 'go to church regularly at Christmas and Easter'. During his later teenage years he came under the influence of a charismatic group, had a 'conversion' experience and subsequently trained and was ordained a minister of that denomination. After serving in this capacity for a number of years his craving for a more formal liturgical pattern of worship led him to seek ordination in a comparatively traditional and formal denomination, where his more charismatic nature caused equal if not greater turmoil than his previous liturgical influence had on the charismatic world. His search continued but was hardly disguised by his appearance or query.

The defining factors are not always as obvious as in the above description. Often those things which have served to shape our specific ministry are deeply rooted and, at times are almost in the unconscious of our being. What are some of these influences? As we raise them, for that is all I will do here, we need to apply them to our ministry and to our understanding of the task to which we are called. Hopefully these will raise others in our thinking, possibly those more specific and influential for us.

The shapers

Biblical understanding

For most, if not all, the Bible is a normative text and source from which to draw patterns and models for faith and practice. Much of our worship, hymnology, prayer and bases for fellowship find root in our biblical understanding. Our mission, evangelism, outreach, social action and speciality ministries of multiple and varied description justify their *raison d'être* somewhere in sacred writ. (There may be good reason to be critical of some of the theology that evolves in that justification but that is another topic.)

It is important to point out here that 'understanding' is a key component. The Bible never 'speaks' save through human thought and interpretation. Therefore the Bible shapes our ministry in a way that is always subject to how we, and influential others, understand and interpret it.

Near where I live two prominent road signs quickly (traffic passes at 100 km/h) give insight to the understanding of the concept of ministry of those in the small church which erected them. One, in bold black and white, says 'Prepare to Meet Thy God', while the other, bordered by swords, adjures the passer-by 'Flee from the wrath to come'. There is little difficulty in determining the biblical understanding of ministry of those who erected the signs.

The predominant public face of a church may speak of issues of justice, equality and liberation, of social action, of things to come, of revivalism, of signs and wonders, to name but a few. All can find a scriptural foundation. Those who serve the church as clergy find their ministry shaped by this biblical understanding.

Shakespeare said: 'The devil can cite Scripture for his purpose.' So it is that what is done in the name of ministry is often wrongly as well as rightly justified by scripture. The Bible becomes not only the seriously sought foundation from which ministry generates (and it often is this) but, at times, the justification for the action of those who fulfil and participate within it.

So the variance in understanding of scripture becomes a primary tension at the very bases of the profession.

Historical imprint

We are the product of our history. It is our story which defines who we are and contributes to the way we act. In the same way the history of the church has served to define ministry. The history of the church, from a Western perspective, has been one of dominance and influence. In the Christendom of the post-Constantine world the church, and those who spoke on its behalf, held considerable sway and power. The once persecuted church became a major player in world affairs. As a dominant social, political and spiritual power, often more the first two than the latter, it helped to shape the Western world which, with its own imperialistic intent, spread Christianity and Christendom further. By holy war, by political and religious dominance and later by missionary fervour, the rule of Christianity came to be seen, by the church and in the Western world, as universal and authoritative.

There is a need for caution here not to stereotype the church as negative in action. The church has throughout history, as it does today, expressed itself in diversity of thought and action. The 'church' which vested itself in the 'system' also produced the William Wilberforces, Dietrich Bonhoeffers and Martin Luther Kings who challenged the system and brought about social reform and balance to the lives of oppressed humanity.

With Christendom came the view of the minister as one of authority and power. This power was not only related to the spiritual but affected all aspects of life, both personal and societal. However, in the twentieth century, as the predominance of the church gave way to the 'new religion' of science and technology, the authority of the clergy gave way to the domination of the scientist, and quantitative materialism replaced the supposed ethereal concepts of religious thought.

In this, the last decade of the twentieth century, we live in the aftermath of Christendom, in what, in reality, is a post-Christian era. Although feeling its effect the church has been slow to accept this and even slower to respond effectively. As long as we go on thinking that Christianity is the dominant power of society we will live in the tension and turmoil created between the expectation that the society will respond because we see ourselves as dominant and authoritative, and the reality of functioning, as Hauerwas and Willimon (1989) describe it, as 'resident aliens' with little influence and authority in a rapidly changing world. All of ministry today is mission. We will look at the tension of leading the church in a post-Christian era in a subsequent chapter.

What has been the response of ministry to the imprint of history? Three types of reactions have generally followed. There has been a continuing and accumulative action; a modifying and accommodating response; or a reactive and redefining movement. The continuing and accumulative action are those things which have been preserved within the church relatively untouched by the passing of time. Such things as the offices of the church, aspects of worship, the creeds and some teaching of the church find root in antiquity and continue relatively unchanged today. The question of the value and place of these continuing functions and rites in a modern and rapidly changing society must be asked, thus creating all the tension such queries raise.

The modifying and accommodating response has been the ongoing attempt to change the ministry of the church to interface with the prevailing time and culture. To some degree this has been evident in the hymnology/music of the church (although for some always a century behind), in worship (the new/alternative order of services) and in the church's attempt to face the issues of the day (gender and inclusive language), to name just a few. To keep the church contemporary is always fraught with strain and tension.

The reactive and redefining responses have called for a reaction against the historical imprint and have demanded something new and different. The action of Luther, the radical reformation of the sixteenth century, subsequent denominationalism in Protestantism, all come from a reaction against the established order and the need for, in some sense, 'new beginnings'. This reactive change is not limited to the past but rather is found in the continuing rise of new expressions of the faith, the modern charismatic movement, The Rave (alternative) Services, the Toronto Blessing and the renewed lay movement which in some expressions raise questions as to the position of the ordained. Many of these, which are viewed with suspicion by the established church today, will become the norm of tomorrow, shaping the church in new and different ways. Change of any sort is always difficult, but the tension increases as constant assessment is made of what is valid as a renewed and renewing expression of the faith.

History, that of world, church and our own personal story, has shaped and continues to shape ministry. We live in the tension between the historical tradition and relevance to a modern world.

The tradition of our Christian faith

Not only our biblical understanding and the broader history of the church, but also the tradition of our specific denomination or group affects our understanding of ministry. From the very founding of a specific denomination to its expression in today's world, the issues which gave rise to its creation continue to influence the ethos in which it functions. It has been tempered by time and the world with which it interfaces, but it continues as an expression of the uniqueness that gave it rise. Issues such as the place of women in ministry, birth control, style and freedom of worship remain contentious matters within specific denominations. It is often the discontent, which gave rise to a new expression in the establishment of the denomination, which continues to present itself as key issues, at times even irrationally, in the modern day. The Plymouth Brethren movement (of which I was once part) in the 1820s separated from the then established church over, among other issues, clericalism and denominationalism and sought a pure worship of regenerate believers without denominational attachment or label. Today the Brethren continue to resist such terms as ordination and church membership while at the same time 'commending' persons to the ministry and requiring persons to be 'in fellowship' to receive what is often still a closed communion.

It is these issues, often unspoken, which can present, for the unsuspecting minister, paths fraught with pitfalls and tension. This is especially true as they are played out in the local church. For me, having ministered in a more ecumenical Canadian church scene, it was rather dismaying and confusing at first as to why there was some resistance to a Christmas Eve candlelight service in the church I served in Scotland. But with a history of tension between the 'Protestants' and the 'Catholics' (RC), the use of candles was still viewed by some as 'papistry'. This was not general, but unique to individuals, and certain groups. So it is that the traditions which gave rise to specific denominations still, in varying ways and degrees, continue to affect the church and its ministry today.

There is a second part to this. We could refer to the larger tradition of the denomination as its large-'T' Tradition. There also exists the small-'t' tradition as found within the local congregation or expression of faith. Each church within any denomination structure also functions with its unique and specific traditions. Such things as the position of the baptismal font, the covering on the communion table and what may properly be placed on the sacred furniture are unique to the local tradition and thinking of the congregation. Add to this the 'theological thinking' of the local congregation, which often is an eclectic mixture of teaching and cultural traditions, and creates what, at times, may well be described as a folk religion. To navigate through these unspoken uncharted waters is both dangerous and stressful.

Societal expectation

There can be no doubt that there is a certain expectation in society in general as to the manner in which a minister should talk, walk and function as minister. Some of the recent scandal around clergy would have been passing coffee chatter in other professions had it not been for the higher standards that society expects of ministers. This is not to justify the inappropriate actions of any, but simply to state that there are higher expectations placed on those who are called to ministry. These expectations are not only within the community of faith, but also within the community at large.

Society has expectations also concerning the ministry itself. Even in our post-Christian society, the church is viewed as an institution in society not unlike other organizations such as school, hospital, city hall and commercial firm. There is a certain 'public ownership' which gives public access when required. For instance, in many places a church wedding is still the norm. It is therefore expected that the church and services of clergy are readily at the call even of those who never attend or support it. Refusal of either (church or clergy), for one reason or another, to be used for this purpose can and does evoke responses of hostility and anger. It is expected that the church and clergy will, upon request, participate in other rites of passage from christening to burial, community activities, public blessings and performances and broader social interaction out of 'duty' with no compensation to either institution or person.

Society has its expectations of the clergy and they, directly or indirectly, affect the way in which we fulfil ministry and contribute to the pressure of the task at hand.

Personal experience and reason

All of the above is tempered and screened through our personal experience and reasoning concerning ministry. Student ministers, as they come to training, often arrive as imitators of ministry and the style of ministry which has most deeply or most recently impacted them. A student in preaching class, having experienced a ministry enamoured with the prophetic teaching of the Old Testament, proclaimed the Word with all the thunder of a latter-day Amos. Moving beyond the duplication of what has been one's experience of ministry, to a personal style and understanding, is one of the most difficult tasks for aspiring ministers.

This difficulty continues with us throughout ministry. We always react, negatively or positively, against those things we have experienced and we continue to shape what we do in ministry by our rational and reasoned thought. Our experience of ministry may have been primarily sacramental. Our reasoning may bring us to an understanding of sacrament beyond the confines of the nave and lead us into a ministry of social action in the world. To hold this in juxtaposition with what has been our experience may, depending on the degree of variance, cause to arise for us all forms of responses from an over-reaction to the personal experience such as James Barr's condemnation of fundamentalism (Barr, 1977, 1984),[1] to assimilation and acceptance of both with moderate adjustment. Regardless of the manner of our response, ministry is shaped and formed by our reasoning.

As we consider these factors which have given rise to ministry as we understand it, it may be helpful to apply a classical form of theological thinking. This approach has been evident in the thinking of many theologians, but for some in the Protestant world, came to light in the four principles foundational to the thinking of the Wesleys (Eayers, 1926, pp. 227ff.). This quadrilateral has been helpful in working with students training for ministry and in application to personal reflection concerning the practice of ministry.

The concept is based on the premise that our thinking and practice concerning issues are influenced by four components of a quadrilateral. Each of the quads informs the other as part of holistic understanding. Collectively they contribute to the thought process. Each of us tends to begin from a preconceived position within one of the quads, judging this 'starting point' as being most important. It is only as we wrestle with the contribution of the others in our thinking that we come to some balance of thought. Each has its unique contribution and each presents valid input for our understanding.

The quadrants are as in Figure 1.1: scripture, tradition, reason and experience. We come to our understanding based on the way in which each informs the subject, and in turn one another. For instance, we come to develop an understanding of baptism based on scripture, the understanding developed and promulgated within the tradition of the church and in particular that within the specific theological school of thought of which we are part, our own reasoned consideration of the matter, and personal experience of it as a foundational part of our faith experience.

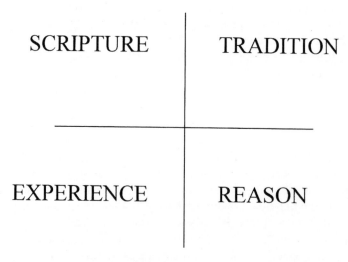

Figure 1.1   A theological quadrilateral

There can be no doubt that each individual, based on their own subjectivity, begins predominantly within a specific quadrant. For instance, the fundamental literalist would consider the contribution of scripture as predominant and would want to begin (and continue) within that range of thought. Similarly, the Catholic movement would rely heavily on tradition while the product of the charismatic movement may lean more toward experientially-based consideration. A well-rounded theological understanding comes as all contribute and inform both the subject and one another.

This offers another way of considering those shaping factors raised in the earlier part of the chapter. We apply our biblical understanding, the tradition of the denomination and the tradition of the denomination of which we are specifically a part. Add to this our personal experience of ministry and the experience of ministry of both the community of faith and the community in general. Finally, add what is our rational, reflective and reasoned consideration of ministry in today's world and we begin to develop a holistic understanding of ministry in these the latter days of the twentieth century.

The tension of integration

What do we mean by the term integration? In simplest terms it means to make into a whole or to draw together into one complete unit. A common use of the term implies the unification of all parts of a society into one whole unit or entity. One has only to think of the racial strife in nations of modern society such as South Africa and the United States of America to recognize that the process of integration is often fraught with tension and turmoil as composite parts negotiate for their position and role within the unified whole.

So it is in the unification of those things which shape the ministry and indeed the minister into a whole or unified entity. The merging of diverse dynamics to form a wholeness centred in ministry causes a tension as the assimilated diversity becomes a functioning viable unit. In the earlier caricature-like description of the young minister we discover aspects of past history and experience which he had difficulty in formulating as a single functioning unit. An attempt to bring them together created friction, both externally and internally, which became evident in the ministry as lived out and experienced by him. His continuing struggle was to bring these components into an integration which could accommodate the divergences of history (personal and otherwise), tradition, experience, scripture and reason. From this there must flow a ministry which finds acceptance in the Christian community or the ministry ceases to be valid or indeed ministry.

There is a sense in which this integration is essential if the task of ministry is going to be fulfilled with the minimum of internal and external conflict and stress. Although the tension of integration is considerable, greater is the stress which generates around a ministry which is disintegrated and fragmented. To provide ministry within such a situation is to be constantly faced with fulfilling a function while lacking a central integrity which brings unity and purpose to the

activity. Ministry without a central integrity is a compilation of happen-
ings which come together to form this thing described as ministry.
Events or activities, some of which may not seem to fit, come together in
a disjointed fashion which is inconsistent with other aspects or parts of
the picture. In contrast ministry with a unified centre and concept
functions from that centre of integration and all that happens is consistent with that central premise. Thus it is consistent or complementary
to all other facets. In reality all are of the same essence, expressions of a
single understanding, for they flow from a central integrity and purpose in ministry.

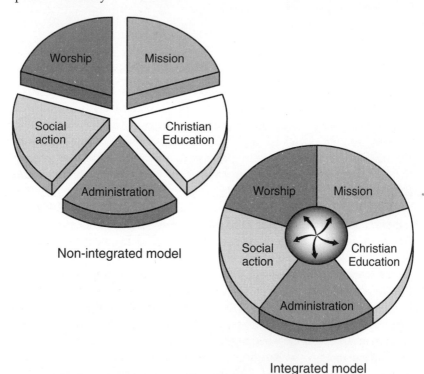

Figure 1.2   Non-integrated and integrated ministry models

Probably one of the greatest sources of frustration and tension for the
minister is ministry which is fragmented or unintentional in its thrust or
focus. There is always the dilemma of trying to hold together those
components which do not seem to fit together or, if they do co-exist
together, seem to have little value one for the other. For instance, one
may have a young persons' group which has a life of its own, but seems
to have little impact on the broader church life. Nor does it seem in any
way to be depend upon the broader faith community for its nurture and

life. The task of ministry is exacerbated by the energy drain that it takes to hold, maintain and justify this within the life of the church.

Throughout this book the word 'integration' will frequently appear. There will be a call for integration as a means of dealing with stress. Integration must be evident within the minister in order that it can be evidenced in the place of ministry. This process, as we will see, is not without its own pain and 'stress'. It is a process which should begin within the earliest days of training and should continue throughout all of ministry and, indeed, life. We will be addressing integration, which is more an ongoing process than a product, at different stages and at different levels. Personal application is left to the individual. There is never a simple formula. Rather integration is the product of prodding, soul-searching, personal assessment and honest enquiry.

Personal versus professional ministry

We began this chapter with the question 'What is this ministry?' It is a question which we have not answered definitively because, in reality, there is no single answer. We could respond in a simplistic manner saying: 'It is the bringing of the gospel to a needy world' or 'It is making the love of Christ evident in the world'. But all of these responses would diminish ministry to a personal perspective, for surely the meaning and working out of these statements would be as diverse as the readers themselves. We live in an age, however, where there is a risk of reducing ministry to a formula, a model for growth, a way to success or maybe even a plan for survival. One has only to read the titles of the many books on pastoral ministry or pastoral theology (sometimes lacking theology) written by the 'successful' minister or expert. For the clergy who do not fit a particular model or who find themselves in a situation where it cannot be implemented, ministry can become frustrating and defeating. Suddenly ministry seems to be 'a model' or 'modular' based, the creation of the professional, the writer, the 'successful' minister who describes it or the seminary which teaches it. It becomes an activity and a task which is the 'professional's' interpretation of what ministry should be and how it should be done. Inability to measure up to someone else's or the system's model may be seen as being less than adequate and an admittance that maybe, just maybe, we are the living reality of probably one of the most feared words in ministry, a failure.

What then can we say to the question 'What is this ministry?'

First, we need to look at our personal understanding of ministry as coming from our journey. We cannot escape those factors which shape us any more than we can escape those genetic factors which make us unique individuals. As we are genetically shaped as a part of humanity, a specific race, a family of origin and unique as individuals, so we are imprinted with those ministry DNA (Dynamics Never Absent) which have shaped and moulded us. This is not to say that we cannot change our understanding or function of ministry, but change needs to recognize those dynamics and to integrate them into who we are and what we do. In the awareness of the dynamics which have given shape we are able to compensate and so to reduce internal conflict and distress. For instance, I find my strong resistance to exclusivism in the church more manageable when I recognize my own history in the exclusiveness of Brethrenism. I understand better my anger with exclusivism and recognize that in my desire for inclusivism I am in reality excluding the exclusivist. Ministry then, as we know and live it, is personal.

Secondly, there is a need to work out what it means to function in ministry. We cannot be so 'personal' in our understanding and fulfilment of ministry as to be unaware and indifferent as to how this interfaces with the local community of faith, the broader church community and the community at large. From the understanding of the 'personal' shaping of ministry comes the need to develop the means and ways by which this connects with the diversity of the church.

Finally, there is a need to think and to rework our theology of ministry. This is a task often left to theological colleges. Hopefully it begins there. However, there is a need for a continual rethinking of our theology of ministry in the light of growth and developing maturity and in the face of a changing world. Our spiritual lives, and therefore our theology, should never be fixed or crystallized. This is indicative of petrifaction or death. Rather there is a need to rethink our theology of ministry, and from this basis to come to a new and fresh approach to ministry and to the knowledge of who we are as persons called to such a task.

Note

1 Barr (1977, 1984) demonstrates this both in content and in the language used.

2

=======

Stress: villain or vital

Stress is becoming an increasing global phenomenon affecting all countries, all professions and all categories of works, families and society in general.

(International Labour Office, 1992)

What do we mean when we talk about stress? The word itself, a technical word commonly used by engineers, doctors, linguists, psychiatrists and other professions, has become commonplace within the vernacular of the everyday person. 'I'm stressed out' says the student studying for exams. The doctor goes to a weekend seminar on stress in the profession and the harried housewife feels stressed by the daily routine of caring for the children, operating the family taxi and a multiplicity of tasks receiving little reward or appreciation. The minister rejoices with a young couple on the birth of their child and then goes to comfort an aged lady as she bids goodbye to a lifelong partner and in that very transition feels the tension of being all things to all people. Stress is a growing global phenomenon affecting all walks of life all aspects of society. But what is it?

In this chapter I will explore some of the more common theories or understandings of stress and apply them to the context of ministry. These definitions I will consider in lay terms for by better understanding the concept we move towards ways of proper stress reduction and management. We cannot manage effectively that which we do not understand. I will attempt to be comprehensive and thorough in the definitions but would ask the stress specialist to be patient with the simplicity of definition for I seek understanding as an outsider to the field. I will then consider some specific dynamics associated with stress which have direct bearing on ministry and the clergy. Finally in this chapter I will look at other concepts evident in stress research which may have special, yet somewhat disturbing, implications for ministry.

What is stress?

For many in today's society the word 'stress' conjures up an image of some large, ominous, inevitable force which invades the lives of individuals bringing with it tension, anxiety, fear and unbearable pressure. There is some justification for thinking of stress in these terms for it is often defined this way. The *Omega Concise English Dictionary* defines stress as 'constraining or impelling force, tension, pressure, violence, weight ... ' Such a definition is only partial and as such is problematic.

To consider stress as an inevitable and ominous force creates several illusions. First, there can develop the assumption that there is little one can do about it. Stress is seen as an unavoidable fact of our society today prompting a fatalistic attitude and approach to it. Secondly, this understanding of stress is totally negative. Stress is always seen as a portending evil, destined to continue and to create ongoing difficulties. Thirdly, this view risks limiting the reaction to stress to the extreme of giving over to it and allowing it to conquer, to retreating into a world of escapism.

I will consider several models of stress which will assist our understanding of the phenomenon. Sutherland and Cooper (1990) give a helpful description of these. The models are: a stimulus-based model; a response-based model; and an interactive model.

A stimulus-based model

Probably one of the most common understandings of stress, and that closest to the populist view given above, is that stress is predominately stimulus based. In other words the individual is constantly the recipient or object of dynamics in life which create tension and strain within their personal world. Stress then becomes an external or environmental phenomenon which is at work in the cosmos and in the personal system of the individual, something with which one must cope or attempt to control. Figure 2.1 is a stimulus-based model showing the individual as recipient or the object of stress.

This view of stress is helpful in understanding the factors which contribute to or cause stress. It is, however, somewhat limiting, taking little account of the person other than as recipient of those factors. There is little place for the response to the external stimuli nor does it place any responsibility on the individual other than to lessen or adjust the external 'stressors'. Similarly, little allowance is made for the coping or tolerance level of the individual. The emphasis in dealing with this understanding of stress is to identify the 'stressors' or stimuli in the

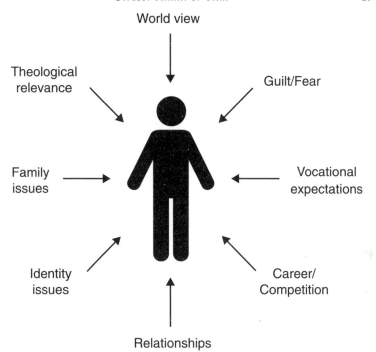

Figure 2.1 Stimulus-based model of stress

lives of the individual and to create the optimum 'stress-free' environ-ment. It seems, to the writer who is not a medical doctor or a psychia-trist, that the rise in the use of Valium and 'soft' tranquillizers in the 1960s and 1970s, and the current rise in the use of Prozac in the 1990s, is an attempt to create the optimum 'stress-free' environment, optimizing the individual perspective of the world around about and creating a level emotional affect, thus reducing the awareness of stress stimuli or stressors. It may be argued that these mood-altering drugs modify response, but since the 'user' is not actively engaged in making this change, it is rather the stimuli effect that is changed.

The stimulus-based model of stress places its emphasis on the ex-ternal factors which create strain or tension in the individual.

The response-based model

The response-based understanding of stress is to some degree the opposite of the stimulus-based model. Here the emphasis is placed on the response of the individual to the external stimuli. This is an attempt to define the abstract phenomenon by that which can be observed or measured, namely the response. For the individual experiencing stress, the description is not of the intangible or abstract phenomenon but rather of the visible and accountable response which they have felt. Such words as 'tense', 'anxious', 'a cold sweat', 'rapid heart beat', 'felt faint' and 'panic' become the description of the concept.

Figure 2.2 may help in our understanding of this model.

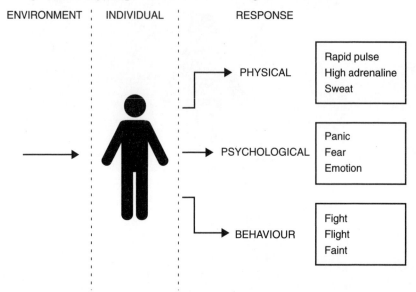

Figure 2.2   Response-based model of stress

This view of stress is helpful in understanding the individual reaction of the person under stress. It takes into account the variety and levels of response allowing examination and understanding of physical, psychological and behavioural action caused by the stress stimulus. The problem inherent within this, as with the stimulus-based model, is that it does not provide a holistic perspective or whole picture of stress. The risk is that the effort in controlling or dealing with the stress is concentrated now on the response of the person making the solution primarily internal and individual. Whereas in the stimulus-based model the effort is made to 'fine-tune' the system for an optimum stress-free environment, in this model the individual is 'fine-tuned' for optimum response reduction to the environment. Both models are helpful but neither model, in and of itself, is complete.

An interactive model

The most widely accepted model for stress in today's research appears to be the interactive model. This model takes into account the stimulus or 'stressors' which contribute to stress, the reaction of the individual, the unique temperament of the person and the way in which these factors interact in specific and ongoing situations. This model is helpful for our understanding and provides a more holistic concept of the phenomenon.

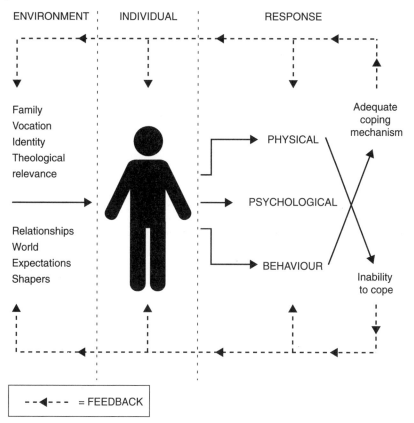

Figure 2.3 Interactive-based model of stress

In this model we can see those factors which contribute to the stress of the individual. These in turn create a response reaction in the person which can be physiological, psychological and/or behavioural. This response either allows the individual to cope with the bombardment of stressors, in which case coping behaviour is learned, or the person is unable to cope, thus precipitating additional reactive responses. From either the coping or the non-coping outcome there is a constant and continuous feedback which informs the individual, influences the way in which response is made, and ultimately modifies the way in which the stimuli themselves are viewed. For the jungle walker who faces a roaring lion, or the minister who faces an irate elder, following the initial response, successful coping will make the next encounter a little less stressful, while inability to cope will make all subsequent meetings with the adversary even more threatening and fearful.

Sutherland and Cooper (1990, p. 20) make the following comment on the interactive model:

> Within the interactive model of stress, it is necessary to consider all three conceptual domains in the stress process:
> 1. Source of stress;
> 2. Mediators of the stress response;
> 3. The manifestation of stress.
> Situations are not inherently stressful, but are potentially stressful.

The interactive model takes account of all aspects of the phenomenon and clearly acknowledges that there is a reactive cyclic pattern of stimulus – response – revised stimulus – revised response, all effected by the unique intra-personal dynamics of the individual.

A definition of stress

We have considered a number of models by which we can consider or examine stress. It is helpful if we can develop a working definition of the concept. In order to do so we need to take into account the medical or physiological definition and then develop a psychosocial definition based on an interactive model. As we consider stress among clergy it is important to recognize that both definitions are important and that one is not mutually exclusive of the other. Eadie (1970) made this evident in his research by pointing out the relationship between physical health and the psychological well-being of clergy in the Church of Scotland.

In *Stress and the Medical Profession* (1992), the British Medical Association indicate the following as physiological responses to stressors:

increased blood flow to the brain
decreased blood flow to the kidneys
increased sweating
increased blood pressure
increased heart rate
slowing of digestion
increased depth and rate of breathing
increased blood flow to the muscles
dilatation of pupils
increased muscle tension
haemoconcentration
diminution of immune response
release of glucose and fats into the blood

reduced blood flow to the gut
dry mouth
hearing more acute. (p. 14)

These are physical 'alarm' responses to the presence of stressors and do not in and of themselves define stress. Ecker (1985, p. 17) in his book *Stress Myth* lists a similar set of responses to stress and indicates by definition that such responses allow the sympathetic nervous system to provide extra activation known as *stress reaction*. He then goes on to use this as a working definition of stress. In so doing he fails to take into account within his definition a more holistic and interactive view of stress which is inclusive of the environment, the individual, response and the ongoing psychosocial effect. The BMA in their report clearly indicate a broader definition of stress beyond a physiological response. It is important for us however to understand the physiological nature of stress and the effect it has on the body. This, in an interactive understanding of stress, is a vital stress indicator.

It becomes clear that no single-based definition of stress is satisfactory. The concept itself is complex, multifaceted, interactive and dynamic in process. The simplistic understanding of machine-like reaction in a stimulus-response is no longer adequate for our understanding. Sutherland and Cooper (1990) demonstrate this when they define stress from *Stedman's Medical Dictionary* (1982, 24th edn) as:

1. The reaction of the animal body to forces of a deleterious nature, infections and various abnormal states that tend to disturb its normal physiologic equilibrium.
2. The resisting force set up in a body as a result of an externally applied force.
3. In psychology, a physical or psychological stimuli which, when impinging upon an individual produces strain of disequilibrium.

They then go on to point out that in their person–environment understanding of stress this definition is in need of elaboration to include these and other dynamics.

We can conclude that there is no simple definition of stress and yet we must attempt to define it despite its complexity. Taking into account the abstraction the term implies it may be best, for our purposes, to consider it both from a phenomenological perspective and as a process.

Phenomenological stress can be defined as a 'perceived imbalance in the interface between an individual and the environment and other individuals' (International Labour Office, 1992). The perceived imbalance implies a discrepancy between demand and capability to respond. It is helpful, in my estimation, to expand the definition to include the intrapersonal dynamic, indicative of the imbalance between the functioning individual and the inner self. Jung would describe this as the awareness between the conscious and the unconscious. This component is implicit in an interactive model and relates to how the individual responds to internal perspectives and self-understanding.

As process Cummings and Cooper (1988) present the following helpful explanation (quoted BMA, 1992, p. 7):

1. Individuals, for the most part, try to keep their thoughts, emotions and relationships with the world in a 'steady state'.
2. Each factor of a person's emotional and physical state has a 'range of stability', in which that person feels comfortable. On the other hand, when forces disrupt one of these factors beyond the range of stability, the individual must act or cope to restore a feeling of comfort.
3. An individual's behaviour aimed at maintaining a steady state make up their 'adjustment process' or coping strategies.

Stress phenomenologically, then, is that which interferes with the equilibrium of the individual (demand versus capacity). Stress as process creates autonomously a series of physical, psychological and behavioural responses in an attempt to return the individual to the familiarity of the 'comfort zone'.

Villain or vital

I began in the early part of this chapter by referring to a popular view of stress as 'some large, ominous, inevitable force which invades the lives of individuals bringing with it tension, anxiety, fear and unbearable pressure'. Is such a view justified? Is stress a villain or is it vital to life and existence?

It would seem as though stress in and of itself possesses the potential for both negative and positive effect. It can be that which is oppressive and ultimately destructive and alternatively it can be that which is releasing and creative. The difference is found in the capability to adjust and to cope with the forces which move us beyond the 'range of stability' or beyond our comfort zone. Consider stress from both a positive and negative perspective.

Stress as positive (vital)

In reality life would be rather boring and flat without stress. Without the challenges and stimulations which move the individual beyond mere existence, life would become bland and unexciting. Yet it is these very challenges which produce sufficient stress for the individual to meet and fulfil the demands placed upon them. From a physiological perspective our very existence owes itself to the 'stress' or 'strain' which keeps the arterial system functioning, the muscles in tone and the digestive system responding to the input and distribution of food and nutrition. Physiologically, without the stress factor the system would quickly become nothing more than a limp, unsustainable conglomerate of collapsed cells.

Similarly, our cognitive capacity is kept sharp by the 'stress' and 'strain' of use and challenge. We can all probably attest to the fact that following a long period of absence from study our minds feel like 'mush', incapable of sustained and disciplined use. The challenge of use beyond that required for mere existence soon sharpens the mind, activating cells we never knew existed. It is this constant challenge to the system which keeps both mental capacity and physical system in tone and prepared to meet the challenge.

Besides its necessity for physical and cognitive survival there are other essential and positive aspects to stress.

1. The 'Fight and Flight' response is one which is familiar to all of us. It is that response which enables the organism to cope with the potential dangers or hazards in life. The increased release of adrenaline and steroids prompted by the stress of driving on the M25 around London at 5:30 in the evening with the result of survival is not unlike the survivalist response of the Arctic explorers who 'mush' their dogs and draw together their sleds in a circle to give protection from the encroaching blizzard. Both are questions of survival.

With no research and little knowledge I attempted to purchase two Siamese fighting fish for a small tropical fish tank. The owner of the pet store, far wiser than I, would only sell me one, indicating that to put two in the same small tank would be disastrous. Curious to see what would happen I held a mirror to the side of the tank. Immediately the fighting fish, suspecting an intruder to personal space, began to swim more rapidly in circles. As the speed increased the head of the fish seemed to enlarge as facial scales stood up and appeared bloated. The colour of the fish changed to a deep blood red and the whole appearance generated a fearsome facade as he prepared to attack his mirror image.

So as individuals, stress generates within us the capability to challenge or fight the factor which invades our world, or it allows us to take flight from the impending challenge and retreat. Stress then becomes a key component in survival.

2. The cautionary response may also be a valuable and positive perspective from which to view stress. Early mechanical understanding of stress, as found in either a stimulus or a response-based model, did not take into account the ability of the individual to determine the onset

of stress and to compensate for its presence. The interactive model clearly indicates that there is ongoing and constant feedback which allows a learned and modified reaction to the stressors. This of course was foreign to the machine-like quality pictured in early definitions which indicated that one more 'straw' would break the camel's back causing collapse or at best an unknown response.

The very fact that the individual is able to recognize the signs of encroaching stress and adjust both the stressor and the response to a more acceptable and beneficial outcome is, in and of itself, positive. The doctor, recognizing the stressors of long intense hours in the surgery, is able both to modify working habits and to manage personal and work lifestyle in a compensatory manor. Such action may offset the dire outcome of severe illness as identified in the BMA (1992) report. That report makes reference to direct causal links between stress and coronary heart disease, cancer, and asthma, let alone the more minor increased risk of respiratory and cold infections (Eadie, 1972).

Viewed from a cautionary perspective, stress and proper reaction to it can prevent or lessen the risk of serious disease.

3. A creative response to stress can help us to understand stress in positive terms. The expressions are often heard 'necessity is the mother of invention' or 'I work best when under pressure'. What is being said is that when the stress of having to produce or the necessity to find a solution to a problem is thrust upon the individual, creative response is the outcome.

For many of us, and the author is included in this, there is a love–hate relationship between the stress of urgency and the creative genesis of the pressured moment. Many a good sermon (don't mention this to the Professor of Homiletics) came into existence in the pressured necessity of a Saturday night. This is not unlike the last-minute preparation of the successful pole vaulter. It is that tensing of intent with all the fear of anticipation which produces the capability not only to clear the bar but to do so with a healthy margin.

Stress viewed from a positive perspective can produce creative and positive response. Hans Selye (Kutash and Schlesinger, 1981), an early pioneer in stress research, describes this form of stress as *eustress* or pleasant and creative stress. This is probably what prompted Lloyd Ogilvie (1984) to write his book *Making Stress Work For You*.

Stress as negative (villain)

How can stress be both positive and negative? The answer is that the difference lies not so much in the stressors themselves as in the way in which we cope or fail to cope with them. Two persons in the same circumstances experiencing the same external pressures will react in two different and individual ways. Their pattern of coping and the ultimate outcome will vary greatly. The problem then seems to lie not so much with the stress or the stressors but with the individual response.

Selye (1950, pp. 9–12) presented an early and mechanical understanding of stress response known as the *general adaption syndrome* which may be helpful here for our consideration. He delineated three stages in the process of stress reaction:

1. The Stage of Alarm Reaction during which the stressor is recognized and there is a response of countershock and the raising of initial defence.
2. The Stage of Resistance is the period during which a more formalized adaption process is developed. During this stage there is an attempt to return the system to its 'range of stability' or normal comfort zone. The continued bombardment of stressor(s) or the weakening of the defence mechanism may lead to inability of the individual to cope.
3. The Stage of Exhaustion occurs when stage two fails in its effort to cope and the system breaks down.

It is in the failure of the second phase and the entrance into the third that stress achieves its most negative quality.

Stress, excess stress and distress

Stress then can be said to produce a diversity of reactions leading to a variety of results. The major difficulty for the individual seems not to lie in initial stress, except in severe cases, but rather in excess stress. By excess stress we mean more stress than the system can cope with or manage. The inability of the system to handle the stress and to return the individual to the comfort zone then leads to distress. Distress, as defined by the *Concise English Dictionary* is 'extreme anguish or pain of mind or body, exhaustion, fatigue, calamity, state of disaster'. Selye (Kutash and Schlesinger, 1981) describes this form of stress that created unpleasantness or disease as 'distress'.

Consider the diagram overleaf (Figure 2.4).

The excess stress may develop for a number of reasons. It may be that the capability of the system is not adequate to handle the level of stress. The minister who faces his own inner unresolved struggle with a terminal disease may have difficulty in providing pastoral care to church members in a palliative care unit. The anticipation of each visit may generate a restless night, physical afflictions and inappropriate

Between two worlds

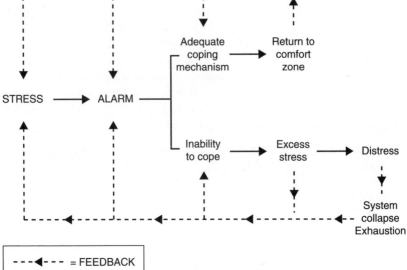

Figure 2.4 Stress – excess stress – distress

emotional outburst such as panic reactions, fear and even misplaced aggression. This distress may lead to the collapse of coping mechanisms and the eventual exhaustion of the system.

The development of excess stress may occur from the continual bombardment of the individual with stressors. The constant presence of the stressor(s) provides no opportunity for the system to move back to a range of stability or a comfort zone. The constant barrage upon the system may weaken it and leave it susceptible to distress and system exhaustion.

It is possible here to apply an interactive understanding of the nature of excess stress and subsequent distress. From the response, either coping or not coping with stress, there is a feedback which may both reinterpret the stressor and modify the alarm. Fear of non-coping may exacerbate the alarm reaction creating excess stress and thus more distress or may prompt a different response leading to better resolution.

The important thing to note here is the need to develop coping mechanisms which can be used in dealing with stress and which will prevent the development of excess stress. When excess stress does develop, and in some cases this appears inevitable to some degree, there is a need to recognize it for what it is and to deal with it in some manner which causes it to be lessened. In so doing distress is prevented from occurring.

Stress factors in ministry

There are a great many factors or stressors which may contribute to the presence of stress within the individual minister. Some of these will be applicable to a broad range of professions while others will be specific to ministry. Dewe (1987, p. 352), in research on stress and coping strategies among clergy in New Zealand, points out the need for both 'global perception' and then more specific, occupational measures. He defined six broad categories: *work overload, role conflict, role ambiguity, dealing with grief and people in need, relationship with parishioners and parish, and self pressure.* Within our discussion we will identify stressors which fit within these categories and will consider the specific factors as they are related to ministry and issues of identity. While recognizing the universality of some and their presence in other professions we will consider all from a ministry base.

The list of stimuli contributing to stress will be divided into two primary categories: internal stimuli and external stimuli. Recognizing that this division is arbitrary, it may aid us in our consideration of the contributing factors from different perspectives. Some factors will appear, at least in similar fashion, in both lists. One enables us to see it from the perspective of an internal stressor while consideration from the other perspective helps to understand it as a stressor applied from without. Some could be in either or both groups but the decision has been made to restrict it to one since that appears to be the predominant source from which the pressure comes.

We will at this point only identify the stressor with a general comment. Many stressors will be mentioned time and time again as we consider the subject in some depth in the subsequent chapters.

Internal stressors

There is a close relationship between stress and emotions or feelings. The suppression or bottling up of feelings in and of itself creates an escalation of anxiety, possibly to the point at which capability to cope is exceeded by demand. This is not unlike the inappropriate use of a pressure cooker. As the steam pressure continues to build inside, proper seals retain the pressure and gauges warn of the potential overload. Failure to take this warning seriously will inevitably lead to the pressure valve blowing and the contents being forced out under great pressure, covering walls, ceiling and floor and anyone who happens to be in the way.

So it is that internal factors and the emotional trauma caused by them can create potential hazard. Consider the following, recognizing that this is not an exhaustive list:

Identity issues

The question of identity is a major one for the clergy in today's society. Jung noted that an individual can become trapped behind the mask of the persona and in so doing 'takes a name, earns a title, represents an office, he is this or that' (Jung, 1953, p. 156, para. 246). The identity of the individual can become to some degree synonymous with the 'role' of office, from which many cannot escape. In all functions of life, at least those visible to the outside observer, the clergy may be 'Reverend So-and-So' or 'the minister at Saint James', the 'woman minister from St David's', and so on. The psychiatrist Robert McAllister (1965) made the following observation:

> The clergyman seems to me to be constantly involved in his
> environment in a way that does not characterize any other profession
> or vocation. He develops an overworked sense of identity with his
> clerical role. He cannot be anything but a clergyman at anytime,
> whether he is on vacation or at work or in the privacy of his room. A
> physician, a lawyer, a bricklayer, a carpenter . . . can be something else,
> can get completely away from his profession or trade.

The identity is assumed both from within and from without. As the church and community served by the clergy often see them in terms of office and role so the clergy see themselves in terms of office. They become even to themselves 'The Reverend . . . ', 'the minister' or 'the pastor from such and such a church' and the name is lost or becomes synonymous with the position. The problem is even greater for the spouse of the clergyperson who becomes a second-string description, 'the husband/wife of the/our minister'.

All of this raises a multiplicity of questions of identity for the clergy. Not least of these questions is how the individual, that person behind the mask/persona, can find true relationship which nurtures and strengthens. In the loss of personal identity which occurs when relationship is predominantly based on office or role there is the anxiety of unfulfilment and the inner self becomes starved for healthy depth interaction. A false identity is established based on role, where in desperation the individual seeks fulfilment and relationship. Not only is the stress of loss of personal identity great in itself, but it disallows opportunity to alleviate pressure through expression of inner need, desires, doubts and fears.

The question of identity is also raised in relationship to the changing role and status in a post-Christian world. The identity of role and office is rapidly changing in a world where the clergy for many have little contribution and a diminished, if any, role or place in society. If the role of the clergy is predominantly one of office and that office in the eyes of the world is diminishing, what is the effect on the clergy's self-esteem and self-image? Identity is a continuing theme throughout this book.

Authority dynamics (control/loss)
Related to the identity issue is the question of power and authority. This is not an easy question to address with clergy, for pietism looks unfavourably on such things in ministry. In spite of that there are those who, like Alfred Adler (1928), would say that all that we do is driven by a 'will for power'. This means not simply the drive for dominant power but the presence of authority for the ultimate good.

If we are honest with ourselves we would have to admit that the desire for power and authority is a part, if not a controlling aspect, of our make-up. The milieu of the Church does not guarantee an exception and, with piety placed aside, human beings are still human beings both within and without the church.

The question then of authority and loss of authority is a major issue for many clergy. This is especially true in a world where more and more people are highly educated, a greater responsibility for decision making is encouraged in the workplace and a more 'businesslike' way of doing things has evaded and in some cases replaced the 'spiritual' procedures of the past. In my own denomination the spiritual search for the calling of a pastor to a local congregation in which only one candidate was considered at a time has in some cases been replaced by an application and hiring practice. Consequently there is a rise of dismissals and firings of ministers and the subsequent court cases that ensue.

The authority, spiritual or otherwise, once enjoyed by the clergy no longer exists. Power and control is diminished and ever decreasing. This, coupled with the whole issue of self-image and self-esteem, creates ever increasing stress for many clergy.

Success issues
How does one measure success within the ministry of the Church? The change in the church to a more businesslike institution has given rise to issues of accountability and success.

There has always been a question of what constitutes success within ministry. The old-time revivalist counted the number of conversions and the evidence of change in the lifestyle (often the level of church attendance) of the 'saved'. Modern-day church growth enthusiasts would see success in terms of percentage of increase in membership or attendance while many churches continue to use the numeric measuring stick of counting pastoral visits, baptisms, funerals, weddings and membership. (You know, the frustrating year-end reports.) But internally, within the thinking of the minister, how is success measured?

There are few standards, other than the quantitative ones mentioned above, that can be used for measuring success. Endless hours of prayer and personal preparation, research and sermon writing, counselling and spiritual guidance, and planning have little way, if any, of being assessed as successful or otherwise. The accounting techniques of a year-end evaluation form have no place or means by which to measure the spiritual growth of a congregation which at this phase in its life cycle is experiencing numeric constancy or even decline. Is then the minister deemed a failure for lack of measurable standards of success?

Too often, the clergy, void of adequate standards of accomplishment and working in the nebulous world of the spiritual, will resort to proving success by working long hours and extending themselves beyond that which is reasonable. For many, the proof of success then becomes the crowded appointment book, the booking of engagements long into the future and the making of this known at every opportunity. The author's research indicated that in a representative sample of clergy, the highest single group, some 28 per cent, had taken no days off in the previous month and an additional 28 per cent had taken one or two days off in the same 31-day time period (Irvine, 1989). Beyond the physical risks, which are great enough, there are the psychosocial risks inherent in this false measurement of success. Pressured by overwork and the stress innate within it, the temptation is to deny personal responsibility and to blame the 'stress' on the church, the task of ministry, inadequate training or the people who just simply demand too much. This creates even greater tension as the discrepancy between driving oneself to prove success is coupled with believing the problem really originates with someone or something else, namely the people or the task. Caught in the dilemma of striving to prove and being driven by what is perceived to be the demands of others, the stressor of success issues becomes critical to the emotional and physical health of the minister. The question of success and its measurement arises frequently as we consider a wide variety of other issues relating to stress.

Sexuality
Issues of sexuality may, for the church, be the key concern of the next decade. Increased awareness and a new openness to gender issues has placed this topic in centre stage for many denominations and individuals. Some have closed their eyes, hoping it will go away by the time they awaken. There are two distinct facets for consideration here.

The first is the sexual identity of the minister. Goodling (1980), dealing with male clergy, indicated that in the ministry where the practitioner is expected to love, nurture, feel deeply the emotions of others and yet, culturally, is expected not to cry and to remain emotionally (male) strong, there is tension of sexuality and role confusion. Writing earlier, McGinnis (1969) spoke of the emasculation of male clergy as they donned the robes of vestment and took on the mothering aspects of pastoral care. It is hoped that to some degree these stereotypes of gender roles have diminished in the passing of years but, unfortunately, they are still evident.

However, the question of the sexual identity of the clergy in this decade has taken on new meaning relating primarily to sexual orientation. The rise of the demand for ordination of persons who are engaged in relationship or live in union with persons of the same gender has presented for the church and for clergy a new challenge in sexual identity. Also, in this day of more outspokenness around sexual issues an increasing number of already ordained clergy are identifying themselves as persons of an alternative sexual lifestyle. As the church deals with what is permissible and acceptable within its understanding and structure, so individual clergy struggle with their identity as they or others they know, and often respect, bring into the public domain their sexual lifestyle.

To deny or denounce this now evident reality of life, as was/is so often done, is simply to reassign all the emotion and stress that it brings with it to the pressure cooker mentioned above. Fletcher (1990) demonstrated clearly the increased stress factor in homosexual clergy. To somehow seek to separate or divide this from the rest of our personhood or the personhood of others, is to bury a whole aspect of our being which in the end will prevent individuals from reaching their fullest potential and fulfilling their highest end in ministry to others (Kelsey, 1991).[1]

There is a need for ministers to recognize those aspects of being within them that are feminine and masculine. (Jung would refer to this as the *anima* and *animus* and would call for the unification of these opposites as a move towards wholeness.) From this broadened understanding of one's sexual identity comes the capability of dealing with the stress of divergent perspectives.

The second part of sexuality which needs to be raised here is a growing awareness of the risk inherent in providing ministry to persons of both the other and, increasingly so, the same gender. In the male-dominated history of the church it was simply assumed that the clergy (male) would deliver pastoral care and spiritual guidance to parishioners female or male. Two things have direct bearing on this assumption in ministry today. First is the rising awareness, as in other professions, of sexual impropriety between clergy and recipients of pastoral care, both female and male (Rutter, 1989). Secondly, there is an increasing awareness that gender plays a role in the individual's under-standing and response to faith issues (Gilligan, 1982). Both of these for the sexually aware minister present ongoing tensions and stress. How does one provide care and counsel and the opportunity for con-fidentiality and privacy while at the same time minimizing the risk of inappropriate sexual encounter or the appearance of it? Then again, to minister in the spiritual realm strictly from a male or female perspective may not be meeting the needs of the opposite gender, thus limiting the impact on the whole people of God. Gender issues will be raised again in the following chapters.

Guilt

Although we are dealing in general with a range of issues which will evoke various strong emotions it is important to draw specific attention to the presence of guilt as an internal stressor of clergy. There are no clear parameters to the task of ministry. A clergy friend once said to me 'I long for the day when I can say "There, that's it, I'm finished" '. It is not possible at the end of a day to say 'I have done all there is to do'. Someone has rightly said the only time of escape from the pending task of ministry is as the minister drives from the parish he/she is leaving to the new one in which he/she is about to begin.

Because there are no clear limits to the task, no adequate measures of accomplishment or success, and little specific accountability, the minis-ter is often driven to measure up to undefined standards. Eadie (1973, p. 30) found this 'intense need to succeed' a major source of stress. Add to this that much of the task of ministry is done in the seclusion of the church or office where no one is observing the work being done and there exists the formula for the minister to be driven by invisible demands prompted by guilt. The minister observes the parishioner who goes off to the office for 8:30 returning at 5:30 and feels guilty strolling the shopping mall or walking in the park if observed on his/ her day off. Similarly to take a morning off, knowing full well of the interminable church meeting scheduled for that evening, creates guilt.

Guilt, however, is more than that which arises from the technical aspect of ministry and the measuring up to invisible and undefined standards. There is a far deeper concept of guilt rooted deeply within one's own identity and perception of the minister. Any emotion or feeling which is deemed unacceptable to the minister and therefore to the individual creates the onslaught of guilt. The presence of anger, hatred, jealousy, rivalries, desire or the sexual attraction of another person all have the potential to generate guilt and the related tension, as the personal system strives to return to its safety or comfort zone.

Although guilt in and of itself is useful in equalizing the system, undue or unjustified guilt is problematic. There is a need to recognize one's humanness and therefore the potential for all of the emotions and responses which may create guilt. In so doing one can deal with the actual situation rather than misdirecting energy to compensate for unrealistic guilt.

Guilt is more than an emotional response. It is a theological issue. Feelings of guilt often arise from a sense of inability to satisfy the demands of another. This is often rooted in the relationship to a parent figure, influential other and inevitably to God. Coate (1989, pp. 154ff.) sees this as being deeply rooted in the Judaic–Christian tradition. Can finite being ever satisfy the infinite? From the inability to satisfy comes guilt. In the following section on theological issues this becomes the question for Cynthia.

Guilt, regardless of source, can become an incredible stress factor for the minister. Driven by this, with no clear delineation of task, the stress of endless hours, restless periods of time off and the constant demand to perform, the system soon becomes incapable of adequate response to the demand and lapses into exhaustion or collapse.

Perfectionism

Only the most egocentric narcissist would make any claims towards perfection. However there is a risk in dealing with the idealism of a perfect faith to set standards too high and to seek too great an excellence. The very holiness nature of the faith creates an idealism which makes anything less that perfection hard to accept, especially within oneself.

Once again, where standards are undefined and success is difficult to determine there is a tendency for ministers to seek a level of perfection which is unrealistic. Giving to God and the church our best is acceptable providing that 'best' is defined in realistic terms.

The demand always to have things done to perfection or at least 'right' may lead to an unwillingness to share the task of ministry with others. After all, 'If you want a task well done, you need to do it yourself'.

Perfectionism places undue demands and creates unreasonable stress.

Theological issues

There is no intention here to deal with a whole range of theology or theological thought. Rather we need to consider the root meaning of the word theology, *theos-logos*, or our thought concerning God.

It seems as though the basic understanding of God, the way in which the Divine acts and relates to humankind, is embodied in the way persons respond to and participate in the ministry of God in church and world. Let me give here a simple illustration and then allow the reader to reflect on their concept of the divine and its implication in their ministry.

> Cynthia was in her second year of theological training and excelled in her academic programme. During the year, supervised field education necessitated her being placed in a church setting for the practice of ministry under the guidance of a senior pastor. As was to be expected she did well in the practical application of ministry, at least from the church's and supervising minister's perspective. Weekly reflection papers completed by Cynthia revealed quite a different viewpoint. In these she expressed dissatisfaction with what she had done, occasional discontent that the supervisor and lay committee had not picked her up on her 'failures' and 'weaknesses' and questioning as to whether she was really called or suited to pastoral ministry. At the end of first term she was asked, along with all the other students, to submit a personal statement of theology of ministry. Her statement was most revealing. In a section on God she revealed an image of God as a demanding Father, awesome and to be feared, who ruled with power and authority from on high. In subsequent interview she revealed that one could never satisfy this God and therefore any attempt was less than adequate.

How God is viewed and understood will affect the way in which the individual lives out ministry. A view of God as a demanding God sets the stage for a ministry driven by unrealistic demands which can never be achieved. From this develops the guilt of never being able to satisfy or appease an exacting God. Similarly a view of a God who makes no demands may create a ministry without direction and purpose. Both extremes present stressors as one seeks to live ministry in the real world.

External stressors

There are also those stressors which generate primarily from external sources. Many of these we will deal with in some detail in the chapters to follow so they will only be raised in categories at this point. In so doing we will give some indication as to the diversity of external stressors.

Vocational demands

Since this is a book about clergy we will begin with a consideration of the occupation and stress. It seems as though for the clergy, as indicated above by McAllister, there is a risk of over-identification with the task of ministry and therefore when considering vocational stress all issues of stress in life become factors. If, as is the case for many ministers, this is an all-consuming task, then issues of family, societal demands and personal requirement intersect and may become overshadowed by the factors of vocation. In recognizing that no factor is mutually exclusive of others there are several which need here to be identified.

The area of *expectations* for most clergy has been a source of conflict. Here we discover at least three separate sets of expectations. First there are the expectations of the church. These are those sets of anticipations which they, the people, have come to expect of the ministry, or more specifically, their clergy. These are based on a similar set of factors which we saw in Chapter 1 to shape the minister. For instance, many traditional, and especially rural based churches, still expect pastor visitation, not only in times of crisis, but as a routine occurrence from their clergy. But a modern, self-sufficient and mobile church member-ship may wish to be left alone, calling for clergy support only as needed. The expectations of the church are diverse, dependent on those things which have served to shape its membership. In fact, the diversity of expectations is so great that the task of fulfilling all, in most cases, would be nigh to humanly impossible. Even the more official expecta-tions of the church, those which originate from the appointed boards of the church, originate from those things which have shaped the board/ committee and their vision for ministry through that church in that community.

The second set of expectations are those which lie within the minister. He/she have their own expectation as to what constitutes ministry and the way in which they see their personal gifts for ministry being utilized specifically within that church and community. Again this originates from those factors which have shaped their vision of ministry and probably to a large degree their training and experience. Returning to our illustration of the church which has the expectation of routine pastoral visit to every member, the minister may understand his/her strength to be in pastoral counselling and therefore devote much of his/ her time to structured and specialized counselling of persons in crisis or with special needs. The stage is set for a contention over ministry based on a conflict of expectations.

The third set of expectations is one which I choose to call *imaginary expectations*. These are the assumed expectations that the clergy thinks the church expects of them. These may be based on the comments or insinuations of a few, an isolated occurrence or may be purely illusory. These are often the factors which drive the clergy the hardest and prompt the comment 'He/she is his/her own worst enemy'.

Other issues come in under vocational factors and need brief mention here. These include the monetary factor which for many clergy is a constant source of frustration and tension. Based on the years required for entrance into the profession, compared to other professions, ministry in most denominations remains one with the poorest financial support. Despite the middle-class nature of the church, the clergy are often placed in a position of living beneath the level of both parishioners and community. The continuing tradition for many churches of provided housing places the minister in the position of having no equity in the real-estate market, often making retirement, and the anxiety of approaching retirement, difficult. The whole monetary aspect of the ministry brings with it considerable difficulty.

There are other vocational stressors including such things as time management, conflict issues, working conditions, administration, acceptance and recognition and interpersonal dynamics all of which arise, directly or indirectly, in subsequent chapters.

Theological issues

There is the constant pressure in ministry of correlating one's theology with the changing world in which we live. That is to ask 'how does one's theology help in creating and recreating a Christian world view which remains relevant to such things as science, technology, ethics and a whole range of modern-day issues'. The average church member/attender is no longer satisfied with a church which deals solely with the spiritual but does not help in the struggle with the problems of everyday life. The clergy are under constant pressure to reinterpret the scriptures and the teaching of the Church for twenty-first-century humanity.

The Roman Catholic church exemplifies this as it grapples with issues of celibacy of clergy and the contentious matter of prohibition on birth control in an over-populated world.

Family issues

We will devote a whole chapter to issues relating to the family. Needless to say this is a major area of stress, especially for those clergy who are married, and additionally for clergy with children.

Several general matters arise at this point. First, there is the matter of division of time between a vocation which can be all consuming and the demands of being a marriage partner and a parent. This is aggravated by the fact that many of the Church's functions occur in the evening and on weekends. The 'off time' convenient for most clergy tends to be during the week, while most evenings and weekends are tied up with church activities.

Secondly, there are issues relating to the position and acceptance of the parsonage/manse family both in the church and in the community. The expectations that we referred to in the section on vocational issues also applies to some degree to the family. There is often a set of expectations that surrounds the family of the clergy which creates additional stress for all involved. These expectations may include such things, such as the role of the spouse, the behaviour of children and the participation of all in the life of the church. There is also a degree to which the pastor and family are viewed, in many church settings, as in the public domain.

Add to this the normal difficulties of being a parent in today's society and the pressure and stress of balancing the task of ministry and the obligations of family become demanding.

Colleague dynamics

The area of collegiality is one of the more ambiguous areas of external stressors since it should be one of the greatest areas of support and mutual care. It becomes, however, an area of mixed blessings. There is no doubt that in some situations and in some ways the fraternal or ministerial association is of some support and provides limited mutual care. This more often occurs on a one-to-one basis outside of the formal structure. In many cases, however, it is the basis for only superficial co-operative effort and more often than not becomes the platform for sharing 'successes' and 'busy schedules' and thus the source of competition. Rarely do they become the source of pastoral care as clergy struggle with their personal difficulties and the difficult task of ministry.

There is also the issue of trust between clergy at the collegial level. In a profession where success is obscure and often measured in numeric terms there is a sense of competition between clergy which propagates diminished trust. This is not only an interdenominational problem but more often an issue between clergy of the same tradition where the identical measuring stick is used as the tool of assessment.

The competition between clergy often goes beyond the fulfilment in local ministry to the level of career and lifelong achievement. There is a degree of careerism as clergy dream and seek moves towards a larger church, an urban church and the recognized choice placement within the system. Of course careerism is frowned upon in the 'call' to ministry and within the idealism of the church. The stress and strain of 'advancement' while 'waiting the call of God' is difficult to live with and hard to justify to others of the profession. We have all heard variations of the story of the minister who sanctimoniously advises his colleagues that he was 'praying' for God's guidance concerning an invitation to a large prosperous parish, while he had left instructions at home for the family to begin packing.

Relational dynamics

A section will be devoted to the risk and the stress inherent with relationship. The very nature of the ministry is that which deals with the inner, personal and often the intimate matters of life. The clergy enter into the affairs of persons in a manner unlike any other profession. They struggle with the pain, suffering and inner turmoil of those who seek solace and spiritual guidance. They hear the confessions of those burdened down with guilt and shame, somehow attempting to lead the individual to the grace of God. They walk with those who struggle through the difficult days of family distress, marriage conflict, divorce and the pain of loss and grief. In all of these they deal with persons at a vulnerable point in life and in so doing make themselves susceptible and open. The very relational nature of ministry creates risk and tension.

Societal pressures

The clergy are public personalities and even in the secularization of today are the leaders of an institution of society. It is still the place, howbeit to a lessening degree, where people come for marriage, funeral rites and in the hour of desperation. The clergy still serve the community as conveyers of grace and distributors of blessing at community and social affairs. From this generates the public ownership of the clergy and the expectation that they will provide a service when asked to do so. With that comes the supposition, as we considered in Chapter 1, that the clergy will fit a certain stereotype both in function and in lifestyle. To walk the tightrope between service to the community and ministry to the Church is often one of difficulty and not without tension.

Personal space

It is important not to leave out of the list of stressors the personal needs of the clergy. Here we refer not to the dreams and aspirations of the person, for these are internal and personal. There is a need for the minister to have personal space to fulfil some of the things that he/she wishes and indeed needs to do. This is the personal time simply to escape or, to use a colloquialism, a time to 'do their thing'. In the pressure exerted by all the above, there is the risk that the area most neglected by many is the area of personal space or time. Many a clergyperson will speak of 'used to go fishing' or 'played this or that sport at one time' or 'have a stamp collection that I will work on when I retire' as indicative of the fact that the pressure to fulfil expectations of church, family, denomination, community and other have robbed them of the personal space and time to do something for themselves, for their personal pleasure. A colleague in ministry expressed to me on one occasion that he enjoyed golf but that on the rare occasion that he actually played, he always felt 'guilty and selfish' by the time he got to the third tee. Guilty, selfish for taking time for himself? The neglect of taking personal time and space creates the stress of an unfulfilled person.

Other concepts in stress research

There are a number of concepts found in stress research which have particular importance for ministry. These are areas raised by various researchers as factors which contribute to stress levels. For our purpose these concepts will be applied specifically to ministry. To aid in our understanding each will be introduced with a case scenario.

Stress and control

The seventh year of ministry in the church had not been particularly an easy one. There appeared to be some dissatisfaction among some church members with the way things were going, although the majority really did not seem to care and were rather apathetic towards all that was happening. From the outside all looked favourable, in fact successful, but internally there was friction and an undercurrent of turmoil. For Tom it was frustrating. There seemed to be no way to identify the source of discontentment or even the cause. He felt helpless to deal with it and the indifference of the majority made things even worse as the vocal minority seemed to rule the day. The dissatisfaction was always attributed to the disgruntled 'they' of the church and Tom could not seem to find a way to face the issue head on and deal with it.

He was honoured when the theological college of the denomination approached him because of, as they expressed it, 'his obvious competence in ministry'. They asked him to become field supervisor for a ministry student who was required to serve in a church during her second year of study. He thought this might be the very thing to help him get his mind off the internal turmoil. Then came the request from the college that as part of the placement he have the church session establish a Lay Intern Committee to meet with the student for support, feedback on her performance from the perspective of laity and as an opportunity to allow her to relate to church people. This was to be a lay committee and was to meet without the influence and possible dominance of the minister. Tom would not allow such a thing. 'No', Tom stated indignantly, 'no meetings of which I am not a part will occur in this parish!'

A predominant factor determining level of stress for Tom was the question of control. This becomes evident in several ways.

Tom felt that he had little or no control over the discontent that was evident in the church. It was evasive and an attempt to confront or deal with it was to no avail. Someone else, the group of other unidentified people, were controlling the current discontent and obviously controlling Tom. Their actions had made his life miserable. Although he rationally could dismiss them as a small yet troublesome minority, their control dominated his thoughts and action and left him feeling angry and manipulated.

The second level of control was that of his own dominance over the affairs of the parish. Arising from his inability to control the discontent in the church and possibly from the insecurity of being manipulated by a few, he exerted extreme control over all other areas where he had the capability to do so. The expenditure of too much emotional energy in so doing further alienated him from the congregation and possibly from the college and the collegial support of another in ministry, howbeit one in training.

Fisher (1986) in her research states the following:

> Stress exists when conditions (internal or external) deemed unpleasant cannot be changed ... An extra element may be the *cost* of exercising control; if there is only a minor imbalance (between demand and capacity) then a person may decide to expend energy because reversibility of the circumstances he dislikes are within reach. On the other hand a larger imbalance may incur too much cost to correct. (p. 12)

The question of control has always been a contentious issue both within the church and therefore in the lives of the clergy. In an organization of volunteers with usually only one paid staff member the question of control is prevalent. How does one lead volunteers who are diverse in role, capabilities, commitment and responsibility? Hulme (1985, p. 11) quotes one frustrated minister who claimed envy for the business world in as much as 'if business employees aren't doing the job they get fired'. The church is established in community with its 'volunteer' officers and personnel while the ministers come and go many times in the lives of the members. The church with its roots in community and its lay leadership to some degree having tenured residency creates an 'us' and 'they' mentality which in spite of surface acceptance still identifies the minister as an outsider. The power base develops and remains in community and often with a select few. Into this enters the minister to exercise leadership, and with that a degree of control.

When control (instrumentality), as in the case of Tom, is beyond the clergy in one circumstance and then exercised in such a way as to utilize too much energy in another, the result is extreme frustration and stress.

The real and the ideal

There also is found in Fisher's (1986) research what she describes as the discrepancy between 'the perception of reality' and 'ambition'. This is related to the above concept of stress and control. When there is a difference between the way an individual would like things to be and the way they really are and there is little or no way of reconciling the two, the end result is that the discrepancy is perceived as loss of control and thus creates stress. There is a difference between what we will call the real and the ideal.

Consider the following:

> Alistair had spent five years in training for ministry and was now in his first placement, a parish in the North of Scotland. In the context of an interview on ministry he spoke of and demonstrated by his emotions great frustration with his current situation. The church he served, and to a large extent the community in which he lived, comprised seniors and much of his time was spent in visitation to the elderly and the ill. In frustration he exclaimed: 'I trained for ministry to help a church to grow and become alive in its ministry. Instead of that, all I do is hold hands and pray in smelly bedrooms, while maintaining the fabric of the parish.' When Alistair went out to prepare coffee the interviewer scanned his bookshelf, to discover numerous books on a California/United States style of church growth.

It is easy to identify with Alistair for we have all experienced similar frustration, possibly over different issues and to varying degree. The ideal perception of ministry is rarely realized and often distorted by the reality of a struggling church in a real world. What was perceived as being 'my' ministry, be it one of pastoral care, effective preaching, revival, social action or as in the case of Alistair, one of growth, is always frustrated by what is actually experienced in ministry. It is this incongruity between the real and the ideal and the lack of control to make the ideal real that for many is the source of constant pressure and stress. This may well relate not only to the actual shape of ministry but also to personal goals and aspirations, marriage and family, relationships, finances and career and many other areas. In all of these situations the attempt is made to resolve the discrepancy and to some degree there is a reconciling of the differences. But where that does not or cannot occur the stress may lead to excess stress beyond the capability to cope, and thus distress.

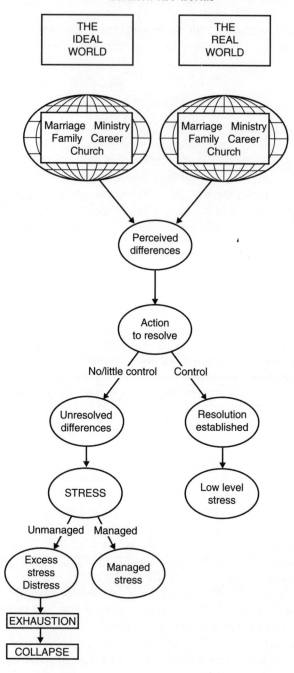

Figure 2.5 The ideal versus the real

The diagram opposite helps to present the concept of the ideal and the real and is an adaptation of a figure from the work of Fisher. The perception between the ideal and the real can and will be resolved in many circumstances. Where the action to resolve leaves a high level of discrepancy the level of stress is high. Unmanaged stress leads to excess stress the ultimate outcome of which is what Selye would describe as exhaustion or collapse. However, resolution of the discrepancy leads to the establishment of control and a low level of stress which is manageable and controlled.

The poor-fit concept

There is evident in some research a concept sometimes called 'poor fit' indicative of a mismatch between a person, his/her environment and the task at hand. Levi (1987) makes the following comments on the 'person–environment' fit concept:

> [I]t is often taken for granted that equal human value means equal ability and needs. This is not so, people differ in all possible respects ... An important task, is to match the components of the ecosystem – i.e., to create opportunity of the right person to find the right job. With the aid of aptitude tests, job analyses, and vocational guidance, every person should be allowed to find the optimum, or at least acceptable, personal 'ecological niche'. ... for example, the majority of a randomly selected population will lack the psychological equipment necessary to become a cabinet minister, a university professor ... the question posed must not, therefore, be whether a person is fit or unfit but rather whether he is fit or unfit for a specific job under specific conditions. (pp. 180–1)

The question is one of fitness for a task within a specific time frame. Despite the belief in the 'call' and within it the action of the Holy Spirit, regardless of the process of the church, there is evident within the church this very concept of poor fit. There is at times a misfit relating to expectations, abilities, training and even theological stance. Sometimes the aspirations of the clergy are too great or too little for the congregation served. These all can and do create undue stress and frustration.

There are times within ministry when the question of the call to the ministry, in general, must be questioned. The privatization of the faith has appeared to lead, in the thinking of some, to the privatization of the call. This is inconsistent with Thomas Oden's (1983) understanding of the three dynamics of the call which includes the inner working of the spirit, the evidence of gifts for ministry and the affirmation of the community of faith for service.

Consider the following case:

> The Reverend Smith was a late comer to ministry. He had for some 25 years served as a police officer in the local police force where he was known as a rigid enforcer of the law allowing little flexibility or grace. He was also know as religious because of his active participation in a local church where he served as elder and, with some oratory ability, as an active lay preacher. Even in this capacity he was recognized for his outspokenness and his criticism of those who might vary in their understanding of the faith or on issues of theology. As an elder he controlled with all due dignity and sobriety of a judge. Frustrated by what he described as the laxness of the law he left the police force to train for ministry. His dominant personality made those who questioned his ability to cope in ministry to render silent consent. He completed his training which was modified because of his age and experience and he was ordained. Now in his second placement, the first having ended in a somewhat unsatisfactory condition, he faced, after six months, strong and open conflict. The current church, used to operating with strong lay leadership, was not prepared to be ruled with an iron fist. The younger generation of church members, while wanting leadership, was not prepared for the authority of an inflexible dictator. Conflict ensued. The pastoral ties were dissolved within a year and for the second time in five years, Revd Smith was without a place of service. The blame of course, according to him, lay with laxness of modern-day Christianity.

Reverend Smith certainly did not fit into the ethos of the latter placement which required the leadership of a co-worker, not the direction of an authority figure. But there is also the issue here relating to the concept of fitness for pastoral ministry and the role of minister within the Church.

Experience demonstrates that there are at times those who are in the pulpit who should be pumping petrol and it is safe to assume, and undoubtedly true, that there are those who are pumping petrol who should be in the pulpit.

To somehow assume, even with all piety, that the Holy Spirit and whatever mechanism the church structure has established, by some act of magic, always create the right fit is to deny the freedom for humanity to interfere and to frustrate the divine intent and will of God. As humans interfere with God's divine will in all other aspects of life so they do in the selection of those who should serve within the church. The act of ordination, a holy and sacred rite within the community of faith, is not above the interference of human beings, leading to the wrong person entering ministry and thus creating the 'poor fit' to which we refer. This becomes a factor in creating the presence of stress in clergy and for that matter equally in the Church. One may well feed off the other.

Unfortunately, in many denominational systems, the examination for 'poor fit' is the test of experience in the church to determine unsuitability. The problem is that often churches are hurt and weakened and the individual minister is embittered and destroyed by the process.

As we come to Chapter 11 of the book and look at models of support, there will be a plea with denominational systems to develop counselling that will help individuals exit the ordained ministry with the saving of face and the re-establishment of meaningful service elsewhere.

Summary

We have within this chapter examined some of the current research and understanding relating to stress. We have presented an understanding of stress as necessary for life providing that the capability to handle the stress is equal to the demand. It is the unresolved stress creating excess stress which often develops into distress.

We have also considered factors, both internal and external, that contribute to the level of stress within individuals in ministry. Many of these we will refer to as we examine more closely some of the outer and inner needs of ministry.

We will now, in the next chapter look at the stress of vocation as we consider the role of clergy in the modern-day church.

Note

1 Morton Kelsey refers to this in his book *Reaching: A Journey to Fulfilment* (1989) as 'Fulfilment as Love', without which there can be no real care for others.

Section Two

A vocational identity: ministry
in a changing world

3

───────────

The stress of a lost identity

The societal perspective

> But self-esteem is not an abstract concept; it is a central theme of a
> person's life, and the particular point marked on a self-esteem scale
> represents an individual's evaluation of his or her own worth as a
> person. Moreover, judgements of self-esteem are not made lightly, but
> are formed from years of experience with other persons. In particular,
> judgements of low self-esteem reflect the consequence of an individual's
> daily interaction with people in the larger society. The effects of low self-
> esteem as a stressor in itself should be seriously considered, because it
> represents an everyday experience of devaluation and rejection in
> interactions with other persons.   (Wills and Langner, 1981)

> What pastors ... need is a theological rationale for ministry so cosmic,
> so eschatological and therefore so countercultural, that they are enabled
> to keep at Christian ministry in a world determined to live as if God
> were dead.   (Hauerwas and Willimon, 1989, p. 145)

In Chapter 1 we have discussed those factors which shape both the
profession of ministry and the way in which individual ministers fulfil
their roles within it. It is the collective coupled with a personal consciousness which has made ministry what it is today and, indeed,
which shapes the multiple sets of expectations which drive ministry. In
Chapter 2 we have examined some current research and theory relating
to stress and have identified, in general terms, factors which, in their
uniqueness to ministry, create stressors for the clergy. In the later part
of the second chapter we considered three stress-related theories which
have some special application for the clergy.

The word 'vocation' or 'calling' speaks of the inner voice which
brings 'divine call or spiritual injunction or guidance to undertake a
duty'. It is in the response to the calling that the task of ministry
becomes more than a profession. It remains a profession in that, as
response to the Divine, it must render to God the highest level of
excellence. It is in this very concept, whether consciously acknowledged or unconsciously sublimated, that clergy struggle to perform at

levels of expectations which are unreal and unattainable. These expectations come both from within the individual and from outside sources.

The divine call is foundational to all that will be said concerning the vocation of ministry. It is only as that call is seen as extending to weak mortal beings with the assurance of sufficient grace for the task that expectations can be placed in a proper perspective. God's call has always been to those who grapple with their own humanity in light of the divine encounter. Consider King David of old who had to contend with his warring spirit and his lustful eye. The words of Psalm 51 rush from a heart of torment, uttered by the lips of the one whom God called a 'man after my own heart' (1 Sam 13.14; Acts 13.22).

Listen to the experience of the apostle Paul, that superior Christian leader, as he came face to face with the stress of encountering his humanity:

> We know what the spiritual law is; but I am unspiritual, sold as a slave to sin. I do not understand what I do. For what I want to do I do not, but what I do I hate to do. And if I do what I do not want to do, I agree the law is good. As it is, it is no longer I myself who do it, but it is sin living in me. I know that nothing good lives in me, that is in my sinful nature. For I have the desire to do good, but I cannot carry it out. For what I do is not the good that I want to do; no the evil I do not want to do – I keep on doing. Now if I do what I do not want to do, it is no longer I who do it, but it is sin living in me that does it … What a wretched man I am! Who will rescue me from this body of death? Thanks be to God – through Jesus Christ our Lord. (Rom 7.14–20, 24, 25 NIV)

For the Apostle Paul there was an all-consuming struggle within, a tension between that which was and that which should have been. The ideal of the spiritual life could not, even for this the most influential of all apostles, keep pace with the reality of a vulnerable human being living in a sinful world. From that humanity there was no escape, not even for the Apostle Paul. Nor can there be an escape for the person ordained to leadership within the Christian community. Ordination does not negate our humanity. We are not, for all our outward piety, any less human and therefore we suffer the turmoil of those factors within us that vie for dominance. So it is that, as the individual seeks to lead the church, all the human dynamics of emotion: the anger, the fear, the desires, the greed, the lust, the competitive spirit, the fear of failure and so many more, are evident and real within. The external factors which drive all other human beings also drive the clergy. This is often forgotten. The human need to express these emotions and inner conflict is suppressed. The identity of the human is eclipsed by the role of divine office. Harbaugh (1984) writes:

> Pastors are persons. Most of the problems pastors experience in the
> parish are not caused by the pastor forgetting he or she is a pastor.
> Most difficulties pastors face in the parish arise when the pastor forgets
> that he or she is a person. (p. 9)

We will now examine in detail some dynamics of ministry which
prompt and promote stress for the clergy at the end of the twentieth
century. As the new millennium dawns upon us so will an era which
will bring with it changing factors. But some of what we face, as
evidenced in the Apostle Paul, was of old and will continue, in various
forms, for many years to come. Similarly not every factor affects all or
produces the same degree of reaction in the lives of each individual.
Readers are asked to reflect openly and honestly on each and to apply
to their own situation as appropriate.

Two important questions must be asked: 'What does it mean to be the
clergy in an increasingly secular society?' and 'What does it mean to
provide leadership in the church which was once a shaper of culture
and now is becoming a minority sub-culture?' As we look at these
questions we will consider the position and role of the church in the
world. At times the focus may seem to be as much or more on the
institution as on the clergy. This is because the two are inextricably
linked. Rediger (1988) commented: 'The health of the clergy is crucial to
the health of the church.' The reverse is equally true. The health of the
church is crucial to the health of the clergy. As the image and identity of
the church goes, so goes the image and identity of the clergy.

'Who do people say that I am?'

When Jesus asked this question of his disciples there was little doubt
that he knew what the rumour mill of the day was saying about him. He
probably smiled inwardly as he heard his disciples try to protect him
from the damning names he was called, as they told only the favourable
comments: 'Some say John the Baptist, or Elijah, Jeremiah or one of the
other great prophets.' They forgot to mention that he was considered by
some a rabble-rousing radical, a religious fanatic, a gluttonous drunk-
ard who hung around with all the wrong people.

What is the world's perspective? The clergy must ask the question for
themselves as they seek to provide a ministry of the Kingdom in today's
world. There is a risk that the question is raised only to hear the positive
comments or that the gracious Christian community only feeds back the
acceptable. 'She is a super person!' or 'He is a great fellow'. Still, deep
inside the clergy lie the knowledge and the fear that they are not well
viewed and, at the least, are considered by many in society with total

indifference. Eadie (1975) found public image and personal identity a significant source of stress for clergy as they continually strive for acceptance. He states:

> He (the minister) therefore develops an idealized image of himself as a loving person in order to gain love, admiration and approval. The clergyman overcomes anxiety associated with isolation by becoming loving and lovable. Here is a point of ambiguity and irony. The clergyman attempts to escape the anxiety of isolation yet his vocation sets him apart and may isolate him from his fellows. (p. 3)

It is in determining the perspective imposed by the culture that clergy struggle with their self-image and identity. McFadyen clearly points out that who we are is determined, in part, by our relationship to others (1990, p. 29).

Leading the church in the post-Christian era

It is a different era. For this generation of clergy the world is radically different from that which the last generation of ministers served. While recognizing the universality found in history, the specific issues which today's clergy face are vastly different. Even such a basic premise as the sanctity of life has been radically altered. At both ends of life the 'God' control has been altered. Medical technology has expanded life expectancy beyond past generations. Prenatal care and diagnostic assessment allow determination of the health of the unborn child which at times leads to the suggestion of abortion of the severely ill or deformed. A process somewhat akin to the creation of a master race of healthy individuals within, what is determined as, the normality of life. Discussion of right to die issues has become predominantly a medical and legal debate. For the minister, as practising theologian, questions which involve the divine factor must be asked: 'Is God still the creator, the giver and taker, the sustainer of life?' 'Can medical interference to extend life be accepted while their expertise in predicting quality of life while the child is still in the womb is denied or ignored?' 'How does the spiritual, and those who represent the Divine, provide guidance in such matters as these?'

The world in which we live is vastly different. Technology has changed the way in which this generation views and experiences its environment. It has reduced the world to a readily accessible community. In this information age the Internet circles the globe, making communication the commodity of the day. Instantaneous access to data is at the fingertips of even the novice through the High Street purchased computer. The visual age which dawned with the availability of the television to every home in the 1950s has led to subsequent generations of interactive graphics which has brought us to the beginning of the age of virtual reality. Not only can persons see and react to the visual, they can actually participate in the process, being a part of both the action and the outcome.

In this rapidly changing society the church often continues in practices of yesteryear. Like a horse and buggy on the information highway it relies on yesterday's technology to interface with today's world. The generation of today are faced with a church which communicates its story through written text, lecture-like sermons and a message often totally void of relevant visual form. Against great odds, the task of making the faith appropriate for the person of this generation falls on the clergy. In *Megatrends*, Naisbitt (1982, p. 54) has called for 'high touch' in a 'high tech world'. How does one, in a comparatively staid traditional institution, provide 'high touch', especially when the 'touch' needs to be part of 'tech' and the majority of providers are not well trained in either? Consider the following dynamics of the faith and the effect these have for those who seek to minister in this generation. Reflect on the stress of being relevant:

Rooted in antiquity

The clergy are seen by many as those who are the perpetuators of a ancient way of seeing life and the conductors of ancient rituals. A recent BBC documentary on circumcision in the Jewish community made this point very clear. Modern Jewish parents were denouncing the rite of male circumcision claiming that their child(ren) could be as much a part of the Jewish faith community without this ancient barbaric mutilation of the flesh. (Descriptive words are theirs not mine.) After all, they claimed, there were no longer actual animal sacrifices and still the Judaic faith remained strong and vibrant. Against this cry on behalf of the infant male child, the orthodox rabbis pleaded for obedience to God, to the act of circumcision, and to the faith.

The modern understanding of ancient faith matters is the same for those living in the post-Christian world. The Christian faith began 2,000 years ago in Palestine, in a world of thought far different from that of today. The understanding of the old order in the light of the cross event is told in the New Testament story of the emerging church as it struggled for its identity. Then the official canon, for much of the church, became closed. In the ensuing silence, the church has sought, in its various expressions, to apply faith to culture and to shape culture by its faith. But, foundational to it, has remained a religion rooted in a 2,000-year-old story.

The world rightly asks: 'Does it have anything to offer the citizen of the twenty-first century?' It may well ask the clergy who lead such a faith questions such as 'How can a world view, which is based on a 2,000-year-old perspective, and which uses as its normative authority an ancient canon of sacred writings, be applicable today?' or 'Does the law, as it related to divorce in the time of Moses, tempered by the "new" understanding of the early church, have significance for today?' or 'Do the codes of sexual law evident in the pages of Holy writ have a place in the ethics of today?' or 'How can issues of human rights be addressed by a faith order which, in its own history, bears record to ethnic cleansing both in the stories of the Old Testament and in the experience of the church?' There are grave matters to be reconciled between a faith set in antiquity and modern thought. Failure to do so leaves the church anachronistic.

Michael Fanstone (1993), in a study of why people left the church, found the number one cause was a lack of relevance to life. If this applies to those who have had some experience of the church, then how much more is it applicable to those who casually or curiously view the church from without? The clergy are the face of an ancient order of belief. As such, they, like the church, struggle with questions of acceptance and outdated thinking, in the fear of criticism and even rejection by a world which wants to get on with modernity unhindered.

Loss of authority

The authority issue was raised in Chapter 2 as an internal stressor. It must also be considered as a sociological dynamic in leading the church in a secular world. The clergy are not unlike all other professions in the apparent loss of authority. The doctor is no longer viewed as god by the majority of the community. Teachers face the challenge of parents who no longer see them as the unquestionable authority in the area of education. This applies to the lawyer, the accountant and all other professional groups.

Clergy, who were at one time viewed by most as equal in authority to the doctor and educator, and by some as superior to these for – after all, they represented the Divine – have been virtually stripped of all influence. This seems especially true of the younger generation who, in the atmosphere created by the anti-establishment ethos of the 1960s and 1970s, have learned to question everything, including the sacred. Writing in the wake of the 1994 Church Census in Scotland, Michael Paterson comments: 'A follow on from this loss of faith in authority is that few churchgoers under 30 assume the preacher in the pulpit is right about anything by virtue of wearing a dog collar' (Paterson, 1995).

But even with the lessening of authority, other professions are still universally seen as being essential to the survival of society and are directly utilized by every person in the street. The doctor is no longer god, but is essential to the well-being of every person, as is the educator and, in this day of increased litigation, the lawyer. All of these are still seen as essential and as having expertise in their discipline, an expertise necessary for the health and continuance of life and society. This is not the case with society's opinion of the clergy.

In an article in the *Herald* (1995) entitled 'Churches reduced to sects?' the question is asked in the light of decreasing relevance of religion: 'Why do we give more attention to the views of clergymen than we do to those of any other poorly paid professional group?'

There was a time in the memory of our generation when the church and its representatives did speak with authority. In a Christian influenced world, whole nations, and all but the most essential labour, came to a halt on the Lord's Day, as enshrined in the church and enacted by parliament or congress. Public gatherings began and ended with nationalist song and with prayer. Schools stood at the opening of the day for a reciting of the Lord's Prayer and many classes began the daily activity with a reading from the Holy Bible. Clergy participated and gave leadership in all aspects of life. There continue to be those, such as the Moral Majority movement in the United States, who seek to restore this 'Christian image' of society, blindly assuming that the Western nations are still Christian. They attempt, through the amalgamation of the religious and the political right-wing factions, to make church and faith once again viable in society. The action is one of power disguised as faith.

However, the church, and its leaders, have ceased to be viewed by society as speaking with authority to or for the majority. When only 14 per cent of the population in Scotland (down from 17 per cent in 1984) (Brierley/MacDonald, 1995), 11 per cent of the population in England (Brierley, 1995, p. 241) and less than 27 per cent of Canadians (Angus Read Poll, 1993) attend church regularly, it is evident that the church, if not the spiritual, is viewed as having little worth hearing on a Sunday morning.

The drive to 'make the church have a voice once again' is a source of extreme tension for the clergy. The sociological manipulation of the church growth movement, the development of the 'user friendly church', the establishment of the alternative service and many more attempts have been made to make the church speak once again. This is not new, for Bultmann, in his demythologization of the faith, attempted to make the message acceptable to the person of the twentieth century. Yet the decline in church attendance continues and its voice is heard less today than in his day. 'Does the church still have a spiritual, moral and relevant voice?' is a question which is, or should be, the struggle enacted in every pastor's study as preparation is made for the act of proclamation. This struggle includes all of what Coate (1989) refers to in her chapter entitled 'The strain of proclaiming' and beyond that, to making what she describes as the 'inner dialogue' interact with the reality of the world in which we live (p. 128).

Historical institution

Despite the seeming avoidance or indifference to the church, it is still viewed by many as a historical institution of society and, as such, available to be enjoyed at the convenience of the user, even at times with a sense of nostalgia. Last year my wife and I visited Quebec City in Canada. In the evening as we approached the beautiful Plains of Abraham, the site where the British, under General Wolfe, and the French, under General Montcalm, fought for the ownership of a nation, we were intrigued by the array of eighteenth-century military tents and hundreds of persons in period dress and uniform. Candles and lanterns glimmered in the doorways, while would-be soldiers in languid posture prepared for what was to follow. A group of historical enactors were there to re-fight the historical battle of the Plains of Abraham that next day. With cannon and gun and sword, these everyday bankers, lawyers, labourers and common folk, who had travelled hundreds and thousands of miles, were, for that moment, part of the history of the nation. Tomorrow, they would return to being whatever life normally was for them.

So it is with much of society's view of the church. When convenient or desired they don the dress of church and appear for a wedding, a special event, a funeral or whatever. Tomorrow (or within the hour) they return from the encounter with the world of the sacred, to the routine of daily life, probably less affected than the would-be soldiers.

This concept of the church as historical institution is viewed by clergy in various ways. For some it is considered a point of contact and a way of demonstrating the continued relevance of the church. For others it is an abuse of the sacred and should be avoided at all costs. In between these extremes the majority continue to struggle with a problem to which there appears to be no definitive answer. Carr (1994), in his book *Brief Encounters*, presents a helpful discussion of this issue in what the Anglican Communion refers to as the 'Occasional Offices' of the church.

A churchless faith

There is no doubt that the statistics on church attendance are not indicative of the number of persons who 'believe' in God, are 'religious' or who are persons of deep spirituality and faith. For many the problem may not be the issue of faith, but rather the institutional church. This, coupled with the rampant rise of individualism in our culture, has led to an increase in the privatization of the faith. No longer is it considered necessary for 'faith' to be reflected in allegiance to the institution called the church. Attendance is not seen as a measure of faith, and membership is viewed as a humanly engineered technique for control. The misuse of 'measurements' of faithfulness and control throughout the centuries may well give some validity to this scepticism.

Privatization of the faith is not new, but has always existed in some form in the church, finding expression with the early dissenters from the established church. The early dissenter John Smyth, in article 84 of his Confession of Faith, called for full and absolute freedom of religion in England (Lumpkin, 1969, p. 140). In the famous *Mistery of Iniquity*, thought to be the earliest treatise on religious liberty, Thomas Helwys appealed to King James I:

> that men should choose their religion themselves, seeing they only
> must stand themselves before the judgement seat of God to answer for
> themselves, when it shall be no excuse for them to say we were
> commanded or compelled to be of this religion by the King or by them
> that had authority from him. (Burgess, 1911, p. 294)

The church's division on questions of doctrine and theology clearly demonstrates to the average citizen that no church has a corner in the truth and raises the question as to whether any has more to offer than another. The reaction of many is to acknowledge belief, but to lose faith in the established institutionalized church. The seeming rise of scandal involving clergy and corruption within the institutional church has done little to restore confidence.

It is difficult to deny the sincerity and genuineness of the faith of many who reject the institutional church. For the clergy this creates difficulties. How does one serve as clergy in an institution which is no longer viewed as essential or contributing to the faith or the religious life of the individual? To the person of churchless faith both the religious institution and the clergy are extraneous.

A faithless Church
The opposite to a churchless faith is a faithless church. Brierley and MacDonald (1995, p. 52) in *Prospects for Scotland 2000* drew comparison between the Scottish study and a recent study conducted in Canada. In light of their comments, which has some validity, we will make a closer comparative examination. Sociologist Reginald Bibby (1990, p. 145), in his book on Canadian culture, stated that 'the country's religious leaders give evidence of being in a remarkable situation. They are

telling Canadians that they need something but cannot verbalize what "it" is.' The church, in its attempt to be relevant, has often reduced the faith to that which it believes can be palatable to the modern mind. On issues of controversy many sections of the church have accepted the prevailing direction of culture, seasoning it with grace and calling it holy. This reductionism has moved the church away, in many cases, from both its normative text and its tradition. Ivor Shapiro (1990) comments in an article entitled 'The benefit of the doubt' that Canada's major Protestant denomination has staked its claim to piety, not on what is believed, but upon that which is accomplished. It is a church caught up in rampant pragmatism. Shapiro says 'Without dogma, the Church has only one dynamic – Social Activism'. What has happened is that this church, with its admirable commitment to the need to care for humanity, has lost its theological integrity to the cultural dynamics of the day. It has, in reality, become disconnected from its historic theological moorings. Shapiro, in his somewhat harsh judgement concerning the Church, says this:

> By choosing to declare its indecision rather than resolve it, the council was declaring the church to be the spiritual home not of pious believers but of relevant explorers. Let other churches flaunt their sacred bodies of doctrine and instruct their members in what to believe about sin and salvation, about the infallibility of the pope or the authority of the Bible. *Doctrine, schmocktrine*, says the United Church: it is acceptable not to know what to believe.
>
> In short, the United Church of Canada is an agnostic church.

How seriously we take Shapiro's criticism is questionable since this is certainly not indicative of the whole church. This may however, to some extent, give evidence of a societal perspective of the faithless church which has no course of action other than that of social action in the world. A minister making the professional transition from ministry to social work advised me that he could do anything in social work that the church could do, except with more money. When the church loses its spiritual and theological foundation it runs the risk of becoming another social organization or agency. Paterson (1995), in the wake of the 1994 Church Census in Scotland with its finding of reduced church attendance, claims the theological blandness of the message has much to do with the results.

> When a young churchgoer is reared in a church without the strongest family links and is fed a diet of sermons stripped of issues like salvation and damnation – and in extreme cases devoid of more than a passing nod to Scripture – a gamut of reactions are possible ... by far the most popular option is giving up in regular church attendance.

This is further borne out by the census which showed that the growth that did occur was primarily in evangelical, charismatic and independent churches, all of which tend to be more explicit in their dogma. For the clergy this becomes somewhat of a Catch-22 situation. The rise of individualism and relativism has made absolutes and beliefs imposed by the church less acceptable to a great part of society. At the same time there is a segment of society, obviously a growing percentage, who are searching for churches which will state uncategorically what it means to be Christian and, in so doing, demand allegiance to a somewhat fixed set of dogma. The clergy stand in the breach between proclaiming without compromise the claims of the gospel while honouring the rights of the individual to engage on a journey in search of faith and, in so doing, to disagree with the accepted norm. It is most difficult, if not impossible, to satisfy both the spiritual journeyer who wants absolutes with no room for variance and the one who honestly struggles with issues of faith, doubting, denying and redefining, in an attempt to make it their own.

A voice among voices

Relativism, in its simplest form, asserts a 'multiplicity of truths corresponding to the multitude of modes of life pursued by human beings' (Devine, 1989, p. xi). Truth, therefore, according to this philosophy, is not a transcendent entity, but rather a relative one, dependent on the cultural, social and personal concept of the individual participants. Values and truth, therefore, are not absolutes, but rather are accommodated as being valid within and from the purview of the specific group or the specific individual. Accordingly, all viewpoints are dependent on background, character and attitudes and are therefore of equal value and importance.

Culturally and sociologically the church interfaces with a world which sees it simply as another voice among voices. For the Western 'Christian' world, and especially for the 'religious' Christian, it has inherent within it the unique claims of the gospel, the risen Christ, and a christianized society has in the past given it a place of superiority among other faith orders. Although other faiths may have been tolerated in an emerging inclusive society, Christianity was still viewed as the normative, formative and dominant religion of the Western world. No longer is this the case. Relativism, given birth by an inclusive world view, has placed Christianity, philosophically and theoretically, on the same basis as all other belief systems.

What does this mean for the clergy? Certainly there is the loss of distinctiveness and the voice of superiority that has been automatic in the Christian world. There is the need to respond to the comparative claims of other major belief systems. There is the requirement, if integrity is to be maintained, to recognize that in all belief systems there exists validity. This recognition does not deny the unique truth claims of the Christian gospel. There is a need to enter into dialogue in order to understand one another better. This is not to be confused with the belief of some that entering into dialogue is primarily an opportunity to promote what they believe. All of these dynamics, and more, face the clergy who now find themselves as ministers of the Christian faith in a world where they are but a voice among voices.

The working out of all this is a daily problem for the front line of the ministry. Along with the inclusive and relative world view has come the concept of political correctness. That is to say that there is a need to act, speak, organize and model the claims of inclusiveness and relativism. Asserting truth claims can elicit charges for the minister of being politically incorrect. Bibby (1990, p. 142) says that, in Canada, the word 'evangelism' is a dirty word that 'smacks of intolerance and bigotry'. In other words, propagation of the unique claims of the Christian gospel is not politically correct in Canada. The clergy live in the tension between being ministers of the Christian gospel and living in a politically correct world. I was asked recently to deliver the opening prayer at a school graduation. I was then instructed that the gathering would include a minority of members of other faiths. Therefore, it would not be called the traditional Prayer of Invocation, but 'Moment of Reflection' and that any mention of God, if necessary, should be considerate of others' perspectives including those who disbelieve. It felt like 'praying to no one about nothing'.

This tension exists around all of the church's activities and the public performances of its clergy. Inclusive language, which once implied gender inclusive, now relates to God issues, faith understanding, race, creed and a multitude of other things. It is not that these are wrong. Surely the church, with the inclusiveness of the gospel, needs to remain in the forefront of being inclusive. But there is a tension for the clergy. The non-inclusive church of the past generation, and even our generation, has shaped us so that using such language is not done easily. Coupled with this is a church, greying in years, that is not used to, and at times resists, the inclusive language of the day. This is especially true as it relates to God. The clergy being 'all things to all people', and not wanting to alienate members of an ever decreasing congregation, are caught in the cross-fire.

Inclusivism, relativism and the working out of these dynamics in a politically correct way leave the clergy vulnerable to accusations for the slightest of errors.

The world of competition

When Christendom ruled supreme, by legality if not by conviction, there was little to compete with the church and its activities, especially on a Sunday. In fact, many of the activities which now compete were under the control of the church as church-sponsored events. These included such things as youth programmes, community events, festivals and, in the town in which I was raised, even the movie theatre. What the church did not directly control it urged government to regulate through such acts as the Lord's Day Act and others which restricted hours of operation and times of activities. Some countries/ regions had sporting laws which eliminated fishing, hunting and other activities on Sunday. Church on Sunday in Christendom was the only sport in town.

A tourist passing through a small Quebec town, amazed by the absence of people at 10:30 on a Sunday morning, asked the local garage attendant where everybody was. With a wink at the Protestant minister and a twinkle in his eye he explained 'The Catholics are all in church and the Protestants are all in bed'. A stereotype observation, which in those days was not far wrong, for there was nothing else to do on a Sunday. Even the 'in bed', if it involved more than sleep, was considered by the religious of the day as an unacceptable activity on the Lord's Day. There was little competition for the cleric other than the apathy of the soul, and he/she was trained to deal with that.

Ask clergy today and they will tell you of the competition of the church in its struggle for a small portion of an individual's time. Against the schedule of the church there are tens and hundreds of activities that vie for that same portion of precious time. The 24-hour scheduling of 180 stations on the satellite television network is secondary to the myriads of opportunities for adults and youth to participate in sports, arts, education, social clubs, organizations and countless entertainment activities. Leisure enterprises have become the cutting edge of modern-day market activities. But still there is more.

The hectic world of earning a living and being successful has robbed the individual of personal time and space. With some justification, the need for personal and family time has presented the church with a major competitor in a paradox which is difficult for the clergy to resolve. The claim of 'I/we need Sunday as a time to be together as a family' is a valid claim. On the other hand, the church, with its segregated (by age and/or sex) programming, has done much to pull the family unit apart. In the busy world of balancing work, success, family, personal needs and all the other demands of daily living, it is deemed by many as unreasonable for the church to demand more than one hour a week. When granted, by a decreasing few, the pressure is on the clergy to perform well or run the risk of losing access to even that meagre portion of time.

Ministers have struggled with ways to compete more effectively. Livelier services, lay involvement, musical attraction, time adjustment, drive in/through churches, user friendly churches are but a few. These things need to be considered in the light of the concept of integrated and non-integrated ministry developed in the first chapter.

A minister told me some time ago that since so many people spend the weekends at the cottage he now offers a full worship service on a Thursday night. He works from the concept that it is better to have them in worship one hour a week than not at all. All of these, and many more, are attempts at overcoming the competition. In the real world competition must be faced or the church is vulnerable to extinction. But in the throes of competition, it is the clergy who are pushed to provide more and more, by a consumer whose time allows them to offer less and less. The Thursday night service is an extra added to the full range of Sunday activities and all the pastoral care and demands of an urban church. All of the church wants or needs to be serviced. In one church the demand to provide a separate 'contemporary' Sunday morning worship experience also brought the demand to provide a 'traditional' Sunday morning service rather than one service which sought to encompass both preferences. The interest groups necessitated diversity of services. All of this places on the clergy extreme pressure to respond to diverse demands.

The seeking of relevance
The world's view of the church and its clergy is that both are lacking in relevance and continue to become more so with the passing of time. The decreasing importance of Christianity, at least in its institutionalized form, in the lives of the general public demonstrates this fact. In the light of this, there appears to be a trend among clergy to seek relevance outside the church and its ministry. For some, this has meant a departure from the ordained ministry, but this is not a new trend.

Some clergy are seeking relevance elsewhere while remaining in the context of the ministry. A large number of clergy find their identity, and therefore their importance and relevance, in activities within the community, not specifically within the church. These activities may be in the form of community action, leadership in community organizations, speciality ministry in counselling, group counselling associations or some other form of external activity. The individual remains as the minister of a local church or parish while exerting much or most of his/ her activity in the context of other organizations in community. The cleric becomes director of a social organization, volunteer padre to the reserve army, president of the local chapter of a service group or member of local community boards or committees. For many, this is justified as a valid form of their ministry and possibly rightly so. However, this action may actually increase the profile of the pastor at the expense of the church. The church, which is struggling for its own relevance and identity, now has as its minister one who devotes much or, in some cases, most of his/her time to activity outside of, and possibly only marginally related to, the church. In the extreme, the weak church continues to weaken. The clergyperson is being fulfilled, not by those to whom he/she is called, but rather by persons and activities outside the church. The church supports financially one who serves as a volunteer elsewhere. They do not provide mutual support for each other.

There are some obvious stress factors within this seeking of relevance outside the church. The pragmatic concern of division of time is clear. The church, which wants to be serviced by the clergy, finds their loyalty divided between it and the outside world. The mere division of time and their accountability to the ones who issue the pay cheque become a stressor.

There is a deeper dilemma which prompts internal stress. The individual, in what we described in the last chapter as the ideal, entered ministry as a vocation, at the urging of the Divine and affirmed by the community of faith. Now the reality of seeking identity and meaning outside of the primary community of faith becomes a stress dynamic. This external finding of oneself is a violation of the ideal of being 'called by God' to the ministry of the church. Rationally dealing with the discrepancy between the ideal and the real brings stress to the clergy. Some may, in light of the ideal, see it to be a continued compromise of what it means to be in the service of the church, as one who brings to community the ministry of Word and Sacrament.

For the clergy all this raises a question of identity. Continued decrease in the size, status, power and relevance of the church is evident. The church, once a force with which to be reckoned, has become a subculture in a post-Christian era. The clergy have moved from a position of considerable status and sway to one of marginal value and importance. The movement from high status with low pay to low status low pay is a change difficult to cope with. The identity of both Church and clergy has been affected by the trends of the transition. In the wake of this movement there remains an ever increasing struggle to regain what has been lost and to re-establish relevance once again. When the identity of the individual is so tied to the profession, as we have proposed is the case with many clergy, the re-establishment of professional relevance in the world is akin to redefining one's personal

4

The stress of a changing identity
The church perspective

One cannot discuss pastors and what they do until one has first
discussed the church, which needs these creatures called pastors . . .
Leaders like pastors have significance only to the degree that their
leadership is appropriate to the needs and goals of the group they lead.
(Hauerwas and Willimon, 1989, pp. 112–13)

Up to this point we have been discussing the point of view from outside
the institution of the Church. It may be asked if the identity of the clergy
cannot be more realistically established and assessed from within the
structure that they are called to serve. Surely the place of the clergy
within the organization they lead is one which would promote a
positive image, a healthy self-identity and, therefore, better emotional
health and less stress. To all of this it would be nice to say 'yes that is the
case' and to leave it there. But unfortunately, the response is not as
simple and clear cut as one may wish. We need to look carefully at the
role of leadership of the institutional church in a post-Christian and
highly individualized society.

'Who do you say that I am?'

Jesus now turned to his disciples and made the question penetrating
and personal. No longer could they enjoy the ease of armchair philoso-
phers speculating on the opinions and thoughts of others. Now they
had to look deeply within themselves to respond to how they viewed
the itinerant prophet from Nazareth. For self-willed Peter, doubting
Thomas, James and John the Sons of Thunder, Judas the betrayer and all
who stood around him that day it must have been a painful moment of
self analysis. Who was he really in the context of their world and more
importantly, their faith?

The clergy must ask the question for themselves as they seek to
provide a ministry in the milieu of the church. In the context of those

whom the clergy serve, lie a series of answers which serve to help shape the changing identity of the minister.

Being leader of a traditional church in transition

There is still a role for the clergy in the church and, to the majority of the decreasing number of the faithful, it is a position of relevance and importance. To most of those within the structure, the minister occupies a biblically, historically and traditionally defined role. That role, however, although finding roots in its past, is one of transition and change. The distinctiveness given to the 'ministry' by the church in the mid-part of this century and earlier does not exist in the same way today. Blizzard's (1956) classically defined roles of ministry in the 1950s are not so apparent today. He defined the six roles, based on a 1953 survey of 690 clergy, in order of importance, as; preacher, pastor, priest, teacher, organizer and administrator. While all of these still are existent, in differing order, within ministry today, they form but a part of the expectations of the modern church. As an increasing number of roles are added, and the order of importance altered, confusion is created in the minds of both the clergy and the laity. 'Who do you say that I am?' may be radically different from 'Who do I say that I am?' A number of factors make this especially stressful for the clergy and, I am sure, for the church.

We have considered how the world views the church and the clergy. The church members are, for the most part, not separate and apart from the world. Those things that we have seen in the world's perspective apply to those who are the faithful, although hopefully to a lesser degree. They see the decreased attendance on a Sunday morning. They too struggle with the application of 2,000-year-old teaching to the maze of modern life. They too, and in increasing numbers, question the authority once given to the institution and the clergy. They seek relevance for their faith in a world in which a majority claim there is no place for matters of the faith or at least the institutional church. They too seek answers to the crisis facing the church.

There is a difference, however. Those within the church have opted, for reasons of faith or with other motivations, to remain and be counted as part of the church. They, for the large part, are the committed. But even that commitment is changing in ways which place increasing pressure on the clergy of the church. These persons, who are to be commended for their commitment, are still persons of the modern age. They, like all others, are the citizens of the emerging twenty-first century, with all of its cultural profile which is so radically different from that of past generations. The post-war baby boomers, with the anti-establishment attitudes of the 1960s, have given birth to the baby-busters of the 1980s and the still undefined Generation X of the closing years of this decade. All of these come with their own orientation, needs, desires and expectations into the historic tradition of the church and its theology. But they do not occupy the pew alone. There is still the pre-boomer generation with commitment to those historic dynamics of denomination and church structure. The clergy is caught in the cross-fire of the church in transition. They, themselves, are members of one of these generations. They too come with their cultural predilections. From internal desires and external expectations they are pressured to provide the leadership which meets the needs of the individuals of a diversifying church.

The matter of authority
No longer is the position of the minister viewed as one of authority. The previous authority varied, based on ecclesiastical system, theological stance and, of course, the personality of the clergy. To say that this is a thing of the past is, to some degree, an untruth for there still exist denominational and theological systems where this is evident, at least in principle. The rise of fundamentalism in America, with an influence on much of the Western world, has created a growing sub-culture within Christianity which has become distinguished by the control of influential religious/political individuals who manipulate outcome by 'block action'. The right-wing Moral Majority has become a powerful political force which demands recognition in the USA. For this group, politics becomes primarily a matter of block religious action as opposed to an individual issue of conscience. I was once told by a member of this group 'No Christian could vote (*naming a political party*)', and that anyone who did vote for that party was 'probably not a Christian'. It is easy to see how the test of the faith is inextricably linked with how one votes. The clergy, in such religious structure, then exercise control as religious/political figures.

For the majority of the Christian world, however, the authority of the structural church and its clergy is decreasing. This was amply evident, even within the Church of England, when attempts were made by the bishop of a diocese to remove a clergyman following a number of marriages, divorces and recent subsequent remarriage. The laity of the church, in support of a vicar they loved, refused to accept the bishop's decision. The dispute between laity and the officialdom of the church soon gave evidence that the formal authority of the church was under challenge.

Similarly, the local clergy are under challenge concerning authority. Grace Davies (1990) points out that the church in Britain is increasingly

a predominantly middle-class institution as urban working-class people become alienated from and suspicious of societal institutions,
including the church. While the working class has become increasingly
critical of the church, the middle class brings to the institution increased
education, expertise, professionalism and the influence of a business
world. Decision making is no longer a predominantly sacred process,
influenced greatly by the spiritual leadership of the clergy. More often
the question is the financial bottom line, the accountability process and
the operational structure. The church, and the leadership of it, once seen
as the exclusive domain of the clergy, are now increasingly under the
influence of others who view the operation through different sets of
lenses.

For some, dare I venture many, this is a threatening adjustment,
bringing with it much tension and stress. Given the nature of training
for ministry and the human limitations of the individual, it quickly
becomes obvious that the laity are far more capable of running the
church than many clergy. The wide diversity of experience and training
in the pew is substantial. Modern, competitive techniques soon make
the structure and functioning of the church, laden down with the
philosophy and technology of yesterday, appear anachronistic. Often
the running of the church soon moves from being clergy dominated and
sacred to being controlled outside the ministerial office.

This is threatening. Clergy have been heard to say in the heat of
church meetings 'I wouldn't go to your office and tell you how to run
your business'. A middle-class laity, which lives and works in the realm
of accountability, soon comes to demand as much of their clergy. The
question of accountability may be viewed by some clergy as imposition
into privacy and interference in the fulfilment of a sacred vocation and
trust. The appearance of 'working for the church as one hired' is seen as
a violation of the concept of the Call to the Ministry of Word and
Sacrament. The attempt is made to live out ministry in the 'freedom' of
yesterday's rarely openly challenged authority. As the loss of authority
fails to allow this to happen, the seeds of conflict, external and internal,
with all the stressors they involve, become a reality in the daily activity
of the minister.

Relativism: theological and lifestyle
As relativism has become evident in society it has developed within the
church. This is evidenced on several levels. There is, even within the
structural church, a relativistic view of the Christian faith in relationship to other faith orders and religious groups. Religious belief is seen
as a matter of personal choice and the opting for an alternative belief
system, a differing form of spirituality, or only those parts of the faith

deemed acceptable to the individual, is acceptable. For example, for some it is not acceptable to evangelize or persuade another of the merits of the Christian faith or certain components within it. It is considered, to some degree, a violation of personal choice and freedom. The role of the clergy, from this perspective, is to nurture the individual in his/her personal spiritual journey, regardless of direction, without interference or imposition of the belief of the clergy.

A second level of relativism is in relationship to theological issues for which the church may or may not stand. What one chooses to believe within the church is seen as a matter of personal opinion. This applies even to major theological positions of the church.

> Pastor Mark was leading a study group in the setting of a conservative church when a middle-aged lady, well respected in the church, stated: 'I don't think that Jesus was God. He was the son of God as we all are children of God, but not God's Son.' Suddenly the whole tradition of the church as it understands the Divinity of Christ, the incarnation, the church's view on scripture and many other issues came into question. Debate around the woman's statement brought out a variety of opinions. Pastor Mark attempted to present an argument, supported by what he felt were scriptural proofs. The discussion ended as the hour drew to a close with the lady gently saying 'I know, Pastor, that is what you think, but I really don't believe that. You are entitled to your opinion and I to mine.'

The above incident points out that what is actually believed, even within the church, can be viewed as a matter of personal option. Relativism, as we have seen, is the concept that there exists no or few absolutes and all viewpoints, which are dependent on the perspective of the individual, are of equal value. Gibbs (1993) listed as one of the six key reasons why those in their twenties are leaving the church: 'I had serious doubts about the christian religion.' This is a statement from those who were in and opted to leave the church. Relativism has given rise to the personalization of what is believed, regardless of who says it.

Relativism also applies to lifestyle in relationship to the faith. Again Gibbs (1990) lists among the key reasons for persons leaving the church, their inability to agree or live by the church's moral teaching. The church, as the transmitter of yesterday's values and standards, is at odds with the reality of the individual's experience. This is amply evident in the area of sexuality. Sipe (1995) states concerning his church's view on sexuality that 'the sexual teaching of the church is not credible' (p. 47) for, he says, 'it is clear that the current Catholic teaching is based on an archaic anthropology' (p. 49). So it is for much of the church which has failed to deal in a credible fashion with the issue of real life. These, with multiple other lifestyle issues, become matters of relativistic thinking simply because the church and its clergy have not provided a realistic position. Pressure is upon the clergy to make the faith livable. There is the stress of having, on one side, an entrenched tradition and on the other, a body of people who believe their individual opinions are equally valid.

Individualism and changing loyalties
Individualism is increasing. The desires and needs of the individual often outweigh those of the group, especially the larger structured group. In the early and middle part of this century people were committed to nation, church and the institutions of society. Then came the anti-establishment movement of the 1960s, the products of which now occupy the leadership and pew of the church. This movement, in most of the Western world, emphasized the place of the individual in society. Human rights, based on the value of the individual, became the rallying point, giving to each the right to exercise personal freedom. Sometimes, in its extreme, the right to freedom was expected with little sense of responsibility, especially to the larger group.

The church today has become the product of this cultural movement. Individual satisfaction within the church often takes precedence over the desires and needs of the larger group. Individual preferences become the basis of loyalty to the group and dissatisfaction becomes the basis for opting out. Going to church is akin to the purchasing of a commercial product. People buy in or buy out based on whether the product satisfies personal needs and the needs of the family.

It is believed, by some, that the twenty-first century will see the demise of denominationalism. This is not implying that denominations will cease to exist as such, but rather that the individual's loyalty to a denomination will not be the governing factor in choice of church. The Angus Reid (1993) poll on religious life in Canada shows considerable movement of persons between the denomination of birth and denomination of affiliation at the time of the poll. No longer is a person Anglican, Methodist or Baptist simply because of birth and tradition. Commitment has moved from loyalty to the church to loyalty to relationships and to issues of world and environment. The 1994 church census in Scotland showed dramatic decrease in mainline churches, while at the same time showing growth in charismatic and independent churches. Obviously this is indicative of a movement based on the satisfaction of the individual consumer's need. Sociologist Bibby (1987) comments concerning the consumer-driven church: 'They have become highly selective consumers ... They pick and choose beliefs, practices, programs and professional services from increasingly diversified religious smorgasbords' (p. 84).

This creates a high degree of stress for the clergy who must deliver the right consumer goods. In order to maintain the church at a functioning level and in a way that is indicative of some level of 'success', the minister must provide for the group, while always aware of the needs and desires of the individual. I was recently walking through a small village. In the town centre was a shop made over to be a 'New Life Christian Church'. On the notice-board in front was the announcement of the regular 7:30 Saturday night Healing Service. Not more than a hundred feet down the road was a parish church. On the front gate was a hand-drawn notice announcing their Healing Service for 7:00 pm that same Saturday. To the sceptical mind, competition for the body and soul of the needy individual was obvious.

The rise of individualism, focused on the needs of the person even over the group, makes the pressure on the clergy to run the full, all-service church a source of stress. This stress is especially evident if, as indicated in Chapter 1, ministry has no centralizing integrity and is simply the combination of disconnected events. Stress is also increased by the lack of co-operative spirit and effort between clergy within the community.

Seeking relevance

This has been raised before and we will only mention it here. Those who attend church seek to have the faith made relevant to their daily life. Fanstone (1993) in a survey determined that some 62 per cent stopped attending church because it was irrelevant to their daily life. Gibbs (1993), in his study, listed among the six reasons why people in their twenties left church the statement that it did not meet their personal/family needs. No longer can the clergy address those who attend church in strictly spiritual terms, out of touch with the reality of daily life. The reverse is also true. No longer can the church address issues of life without invoking the spiritual dynamic. Again the growth in the evangelical, independent and charismatic churches in the recent national church census demonstrates this. Clergy are put in the position of having to make the gospel, theology and tradition of the church/faith relevant for today. This means a struggle with the issues. It requires, as Sipe (1995) has done, a sincere appraisal of the church's teaching around issues considered controversial and judged, by some, best left untouched. To fail to undertake this evaluation is to have the teaching of the church conform to the tradition, knowing full well that it will not be applied or lived out in the lives of most of the faithful who attend. The risk is that the faithful today will be the statistics of loss tomorrow. If the church is to be relevant, the minister becomes the interpreter of the faith for the modern person. This creates for the clergy incredible stressors. There is the need to accommodate the older faithful church attenders, often the majority of a greying church population, who have financially supported the institution and are happy with the church as conveyer of yesterday's standards and values. On the other hand, there is the need to make the teaching relevant to the changing world view of today's generation. The clergy become caught in an intergenerational cross-fire.

Competition for time

As numbers in the average congregation decrease and the demands for full-service churches to satisfy individual needs increase, growing strain is placed on church resources, and especially human resources. More has to be done by fewer committee members. It is often thought that any attempt for recovery requires the providing of all the services the church once offered (and that in their traditional form). Again Gibbs (1993) listed among the six reasons for departure from the church, the expectation by the church that people take on too many commitments.

The church members, however, like all other members of society, are under increasing competition for their time outside of the church as well. Work, school, community, service organizations, recreation, to name but a few, demand time. The church, which can be all-consuming, is now simply another in a long list of demands for time, energy and resources. From the minister's perspective the work of the church must continue, and he/she is increasingly viewed as the one who places demands on the church member for already scarce time. Even the one hour, all the time that is given by many an attender to the church, is recognized as a valued 60 minutes, into which must be crowded all the 'religion' for a week, and sometimes longer. Misuse of this time will soon lead to reduced attendance and discontinued support.

Living in a time warp

A pastor friend of mine stuck his head in my office door recently and exclaimed 'My church is getting so excited. It's getting ready to move into the twentieth century.' Thinking he had spoken in error I responded 'You mean the twenty-first century'. 'No', he said, 'For our church we are just getting ready to enter the twentieth.'

Cynical as it may sound, much of the church, in some ways, is a hundred years behind the rest of society. We have been saying this in different sections and in different ways throughout this book. Here it is worth mentioning, not simply as theory, but in the way that this applies to the clergy who are often the visible face of the church and the ones expected to lead the church in days of transition. It is the pastor who is caught between the tradition of the ancient church and the need to become a modern entity. For the clergy the stress of being caught in a time warp is critical. It is difficult enough to introduce the unchurched mind of the world citizen (we are now entering a second generation of predominantly unchurched society) to the world of the spiritual without having to move them from modernity to antiquity at the same time. Most clergy are aware of this. Yet the church often stands, steadfast and unmovable, in the tradition of the past centuries. How does the conscientious minister deal with this without alienating either the older faithful or the faith seeker of today? Once again, caught in the cross-fire, the clergy is under stressful pressure.

There are a number of apparent stressors of transition:

Service structure: For many churches the structure of worship is a product of past generations. It has become the experience of the pre-boomer generation. The service is sombre, orderly, with stately hymns and expository sermons. It is clergy dominated with little if any lay participation. It possesses a sacred air fully acceptable in the earlier part of this century. But for a participatory generation, anxious to contribute, searching more for application than exposition, looking for joy more than sobriety, affected more by emotion than the cognitive, it does little to nurture a yearning spirituality.

Church music: Probably no issue has been so disruptive in so many churches as music. The question of contemporary versus traditional has haunted the clergy seeking to lead an intergenerational church in worship. The music of English Victorianism and American revivalism may have little meaning or place in the experience of the modern believer. Similarly, the contemporary music, led by the praise band rather than the pipe organ, may have little sense or depth for the traditional church attender. The alternative 'rave' style services are confined to radical groups. The clergy is caught in the tension of the diversity, let alone accommodating his/her own preference.

Clerical dress: When a large number of a traditional clergy ceased to wear the clerical collar in daily dress, a retired minister was heard to say 'You can't tell the saint from the sinner any more'. There is an increasing tension in some churches over clerical dress. The tradition of gown, collar, stole and even suit in the free church movement is, for some, becoming an issue. The clergy, in an attempt to relate to the new generation, are reducing the level of dress to a more casual style. This is true of most professions where the white shirt and tie has been replaced by a more casual shirt and relaxed dress. For the church, however, the issue of dress has been viewed as one of respect, toward both God and members, and change has caused difficulty for some attenders. The reverse is also true and today's generation may see the garb of office, however defined, as archaic and expendable. The minister is again caught in the leadership of a church in transition.

For the modern clergy the stress of fulfilling the expectations of the faithful older generation of the church, while responding to the needs of the modern generation, is intense. The Apostle Paul's image of being all things to 'all people', obviously not a new phenomenon, nevertheless takes on new meaning. Multiple sets of expectations create multiple and diverse demands on the one called as leader in today's church.

A changing role in a traditional institution

Earlier in this chapter I referred to the changing role of the clergy within the church with specific reference to Blizzard (1953). While these still exist today, probably in modified order, the list has grown for most ministers.

In addition to these there is the expectation that the clergy will provide life-relevant counselling for a variety of needs. This involves such things as marriage counselling (pre, present and post), career guidance, parental advice, and grief support to name just a few. The emphasis, certainly in the North American context, on the minister as counsellor has aroused demands for which the pastor is not adequately trained. No professional training in a general programme for entrance into ministry is broad enough for the new counselling role. Ministers are often out of their depth. In a time of increased litigation against those in the helping professions, this is an area of high risk and stress.

Increasingly, the minister is seen as an executive in an institution or small corporation. The role becomes one of administration as opposed to that of spiritual leadership. A survey in the Church of Scotland (Irvine, 1989) found that some 27 per cent of the ministers who responded felt that their role was more one of executive director than pastor. An additional 14 per cent moderately concurred with this, while 9.5 per cent strongly felt this to be the case. The role of the pastor has changed from one of spiritual leader to one of managing director, once again a task for which little formal training is provided. Many people in the pew are often better trained in this capacity. This leaves the minister in an uncomfortable position of being accorded responsibility although often the least capable of fulfilling it.

Culturally, we live in an age of charisma. Politically, the magnetism of the leader has as much to do with the outcome of an electoral decision as does the stance on issues. Many of the best political minds have lost at the polls because of their lack of 'crowd appeal'. The church has not escaped.

Churches want, in a competitive age, the style of leadership that will attract attenders. This is especially true in the 'target' theory of those who hold to church growth principles. The minister must have appeal for the specific target group. The baby-boomer generation, more committed to relationships than the institutional church, must find, in their connection to leadership, that with which they can associate. The image becomes an important part of the attraction to, and therefore, the success of, the church in today's society. Although such charismatic style leadership exists in all cultures, the evidence is most obvious in North American culture. An interesting observation in the study on isolation (Irvine, 1989) was that the Myers–Briggs Type Indicator showed clergy in the Church of Scotland to be primarily of the Introvert (I) preference, while the predominant preference of clergy in the USA is that of Extroversion (E).

There is one final emerging role of the present-day clergy that needs to be mentioned. We will describe it as 'miracle worker'. There is often an expectation that the decrease in church attendance can be solved by simply finding the 'right' person as minister. Little attention is paid to the cultural and societal dynamics affecting the current attendance level and the responsibility is laid at the feet of the clergy. A middle-aged clergyman, with a deep sense of failure, stated 'The criticism I get from the church is that "when Dr Fullpew was our minister there would be a queue at the door on a Sunday night waiting for the doors to be open, while now there is only a handful huddled together for evening worship" '. Dr Fullpew was minister in the post-war period characterized as a time of booming attendance for the church in general, and he was noted as a powerful orator.

Of all the changing roles of the clergy, this is most crucial. It encapsulates the unrealistic expectations of a desperate church afraid to face the issues of relevance in a changing world. It provides a scapegoat which can be, and often is, vicariously sacrificed for the inadequacy of the church to be the people of God in the world. It places blame on the head of one who personalizes and spiritualizes it while soldiering on in ministry, inwardly identified as a failure.

Being the clergy, with multiple roles, is not easy in the transition of society and church.

Today's successful minister needs the healing power of a skilled heart surgeon, the nurturing capacity of Mother Teresa and the miraculous power of God him/herself. This coupled with the intellectual capacity of Stephen Hawking, the oratory ability of Billy Graham, the relational skills of Morton Kelsey, the warmth of the Queen Mother, the singing voice of Cliff Richard, the golfing ability of Nick Faldo and the patience of Job may create some demands. Add to this the ability to negotiate like the late Prime Minister Rabin, fight for social justice as did Martin Luther King and always come out a winner like Richard Branson and the formula for the modern-day minister is complete.

Although I write in jest, there is some underlying truth in this expected image of the clergy today.

Belonging to the fraternal

One final comment on the stress of vocation relates to the formalized structure of the clergy associations, locally known as the fraternal or the ministerial. These exist as a formal gathering of clergy, on either a denominational or an interdenominational basis. Although it could be assumed that such a gathering of persons engaged in the same profession should generate strong collegiality and support, this has not been the case.

In my own research among the clergy of the Church of Scotland, coupled with observation and participation in such groups, and confirmed by the comments of others, it was indicated that fraternal/ ministerial groups serve little purpose other than opportunity for informal fellowship and planning of limited joint ministry efforts. The pastoral care and nurture of one another seemed very limited in the context of the groups. When this did occur it was usually on a one-to-one basis.

While pastoral support was limited, the reverse effect was more evident. Most clergy seemed to withdraw from personal revelation of needs because of lack of trust of others who were present. This was at times more evident in denominationally based groups where, to use one minister's expression, 'all are gauged by the same measuring stick'. The lack of trust is increased as the sessions were described as often being the time for the 'successful' to brag and the struggler to remain silent, feeling like a comparative failure. Competition in these groups runs high. Women did not feel they fit well into this competitive atmosphere and often, where possible, formed their own support system with other women in ministry.

So as not to end on a totally negative note, there was some indication that the fraternal did provide a helpful forum for some clergy. They were seen as a form of co-operation and the opportunity to get to know other clergy who could, and would, form a more supportive network.

5

━━━━━

The stress of being a woman in ministry

Searching to establish an identity

'I will not let you go unless you bless me' cried Jacob as he wrestled
with the Unknown at the brook Jabbok . . . I have sometimes felt rather
like that. My life has been lived in the grip of the Church, from which I
have not felt able to free myself – either by giving up or by going
elsewhere. I have therefore stayed and wrestled and prayed and wept,
until the church of my fathers and mothers has given me her blessing,
accepted my calling and sent me forth.

(Levison, 1992, p. 1)

The assumption is often made that there is little difference between the
stress experienced by men and that experienced by women in ministry.
This understanding of stress is based on a stimulus–response perception of the phenomena. The pressures relating to expectations, time
usage, conflict issues, overcrowded schedules and the busyness of
ministry are considered as being the same regardless of gender. Therefore, what is said concerning stress in ministry is applicable and
complete for clergypersons of either gender. Or is it?

Research in other professions and among white-collar workers has
shown that there are substantial differences in the way that women
experience vocational stress. Studies show that while women experience all the stressors of the workplace along with their male colleagues,
they incur others unique to women. These are often societal and
culturally imposed stressors and cannot simply be reduced or eliminated by the individual's wish or action. Similarly, the management of
the stress which develops is often more complex, dealing with deeply
rooted issues of identity both within the individual and the culture.
There is virtually no stress research conducted specifically among
women in ministry, a fact hardly surprising in a male-dominated
profession. Coger (1985) conducted research among United Methodist
Church (USA) women ministers which, although limited in scope,
confirms findings made in other vocations. Research conducted in other

vocations provides valuable insight from which can be extrapolated dynamics applicable to ministry.

Entrance to the profession

For women, entrance into the profession of ministry has been an issue of considerable tension and conflict. Coate (1989) refers to this but examines few other dynamics of stress unique to women in ministry. The church has been one of the few remaining bastions of male dominance in the professional world. That is not to say that chauvinism does not exist elsewhere, but that its entrenchment has been rarely felt more strongly than in ministry. Justification for this gender bias is often based on biblical and traditional premises and opposing arguments are viewed as against God and the established divine order. Yet, in spite of the male power dominance, the rank and file membership and attenders of the church are female. The Scottish church census (1995) calculated attendance at 39 per cent male and 61 per cent female. Even with the majority of church attenders female, the church is often still averse to giving females full and equal opportunity within its leadership. It was not until recent years that the Church of England permitted the ordination of women for ministry. The Roman Catholic Church, along with numerous conservative Protestant denominations, still does not ordain women. These churches often give secondary entrance to limited areas of service, but retain the central power realm of ministry for the male. With this male control of power, women, on their very entrance to ministry, recognize the stress of having to fight for position and even the very right to be there.

This fight to gain entrance may in the long run prove advantageous. The common battle often serves to unite, and in oppression there arises the dynamic of solidarity. The stress of entrance may help serve to create the proper support network among women in ministry necessary to handle not only this stressor but all others.

Vocational stress and women

Davidson and Cooper (1983) list causes of stress for women in the work environment. These have been identified in numerous research studies. Although this list comes from an office and management environment – therefore a different organizational and relational basis – there are useful similarities for women in ministry. They list the following areas of stress within the working environment:

(1) those intrinsic to the job
(2) role in the organization

(3) relationships at work
(4) organizational structure and career

Two major extra work environment factors they record as:

(1) the home/social environment
(2) individual differences and determinants

As we consider stress among women in ministry, we need to apply each of these areas to the structure of the church, both the local and denominational organization.

Under *those intrinsic to the job* Davidson and Cooper list such things as acquiring skills and performance levels. For women in ministry both of these are problematic. Training for ministry has been based mainly on a male-dominated curriculum. Biblical studies, theology, church history and ethics are subjects primarily of thought development through successive generations of male leadership. It was not until the rise of a feminist theology that this trend began to change and then, in most theological training, only marginally. This male bias is very evident in the area of practical theology and ministry studies. Texts written on these subjects were/are primarily the writings of male theorists and practitioners. The models of ministry presented are predominantly male in origin. Ways of doing and stories of success are based on successful male ministers. Little literature exists, up to now, based on feminine models for ministry.

This applies not only to the texts produced and the written documentation which assists in the attaining of vocational skills. It also applies to the very approach to ministry. Coger (1985) draws attention to a competitive model of training. This, she claims, is not consistent with a more co-operative and collegial approach evident among women in ministry training. Roy Oswald, quoted on the cover of Coger's book, states 'She comes at the task of beginning ministry in a new parish in quite a different way than I perceive a clergyman would. I don't think we males would place so high a value on support ... '

The more collegial/co-operative approach means that the acquiring of job skills in such areas as conflict, power dynamics and issue resolution will be different for women than for men. Stress intrinsic in the job for women in ministry is due in part to basic training which is not modified on a gender basis.

Davidson and Cooper also indicate under this section a higher level of workload for most women compared to male colleagues in the work environment. The claim is made that women often feel, or are led to feel, that they must perform at a higher level in order to gain equality with male counterparts. Frankenhaeuser (1989) found that one-third of the women in her comparative study indicated that they had 'to perform better to be considered equal'. Kanter (1977, p. 212) also presents an excellent section on the pressure of women to excel in performance in the work place. This implies a level of competition that we have said is not so prevalent among women ministers. However, there is the concept of success which is universally important to both men and women in ministry. Coger speaks of 'thriving' in ministry and urges theological colleges to help the student in defining appropriate measures of success. The need to achieve at a level comparable to male clergy may lead some clergywomen to set unrealistic expectations for their own performance in ministry.

The *role in the organization* is also an issue for women in ministry. Again, within the organization, the predominant influence has been male. There are, therefore, few role models within the profession or the institutional structure for the clergywoman to emulate. The leadership role in the church, as Davidson and Cooper indicate is the case for business, is one which is viewed primarily as a male role by both men and women. This leads to the stress of role ambiguity as women enter an organization in which roles are both assumed and modelled as traditionally male. Coger indicates that from the politics of her institution she quickly learned that women were rewarded for 'being one of the guys', a denial of her own basic personhood.

Kanter (1977, pp. 208–9) writes that an organization which has 15 per cent or less women in their employ considers them as a 'token' presence. The 1992 United Kingdom Church Census provides the following statistics.

	Female clergy	Total clergy	%
Anglican Communion	820	13,920	5.9
Methodist	246	2,657	9.2
Baptist	85	2,936	2.9
Presbyterian	345	3,060	11.3
Church of Scotland	123	1,230	10.0

These figures do not reflect the sudden increase in ordination of women in the Church of England following the decision in 1994 to ordain women. The large diaconate of the church comprised many who were waiting for such a decision to be taken and the rapid influx of women into ordained ministry is not indicative of the level at which the church will 'normally' function. Continual assessment of this over the next several years will be most interesting.

The Church of Scotland was identified separately, as well as within the Presbyterian group, because of its history (1968) of ordination of women. In no case did the percentage exceed 15 per cent and, in all but two, it is beneath the 10 per cent level.

It becomes obvious that a primary source of stress for women ministers within the church organization is the token status which often accompanies the position. Coger indicates that this tokenism is evident at both the local and denominational level in a number of ways. First, organization, attempting to prove its inclusiveness and reception of women as clergy, makes the gender of a woman minister obvious in ways not evident in male clergy. There is a *visibility* factor where women are noticed, not solely for their capability, but because they are women. A case in point is a theological college principal's introduction of a clergywoman about to address a group of students as 'One of our most capable women pastors'. The specific gender nature of the statement is based on a desire to make women in ministry visible to a group of students and, thereby, to demonstrate the inclusive nature of the college and denomination. However, by that he indicated that he views the role of a female as different from that of a male in ministry. He would not have said 'One of our most capable men pastors'. Also, whether unwittingly or not, he makes the distinction that she is comparable to other 'women' pastors, not to the general rank and file of pastors. Mary Levison (1992, p. 107) in her own story of ordination, *Wrestling With the Church*, gives evidence of tokenism created by the media on her appointment as one of Her Majesty's Chaplains in Scotland.

Secondly, Davidson and Cooper indicate the token status granted women can use women as a test case. Senior leadership positions may therefore place women under greater scrutiny than if the position were occupied by a male. This places pressure on the women in ministry to perform, or out-perform as previously indicated, a male counterpart.

Thirdly, women in token positions in ministry are isolated, having no role models. The gifts they bring as women to the position are genuine and vital, but different from those of a male. The different approach has, in many circumstances, not been extensively modelled within the setting and, therefore, the clergywoman is walking a new path with no role model by which to assess her achievement. The walk is one alone.

The third category, *relationship at work*, has different implications for women clergy functioning in sole pastorates than for those in joint ministries. In the joint ministry situation the woman is often in an associate or assistant role. Research has shown that women in management, even when of equal status with male counterparts, report that they are not treated as equal. Their input is not taken seriously and there is a patronizing attitude. Rassieur (1982) illustrates that similar experiences occur in ministry, often with the senior male demonstrating control in a way unlike a relationship with a male associate (p. 28). Where the woman is senior in a team ministry there is the risk of the situation presenting a threat to male staff members. In one case a male staff member resigned from a staff position claiming that he took theological issue with women in ministry. Interestingly, he had accepted the position fully aware of the staffing dynamic.

Women in sole pastorates do not face the direct relational problem with a male team member. However, there is often difficulty around collegial relationships between the woman and others in the diocese or presbytery (Rassieur, 1982, p. 29). In an interview conducted during my research, one woman indicated that within the presbytery, in which she was the only woman minister, she was avoided by her colleagues who appeared to be uncomfortable with her outside the formal setting, within which she was apparently accepted and relied upon to fulfil various organizational functions. By this action it becomes evident that they identify her, not primarily as a colleague in ministry, but as a sexual being with all the potential risk inherent in that perspective. Informal opportunity to associate with those in the same profession, with whom she should have worked closely, was non-existent. She further indicated that she felt the spouses of many of her fellow clergy felt threatened by her association with their husbands, even though it was on a very limited basis. She felt very much alone in what she described as a 'subtle form of sexual harassment'.

Within the local church setting there is the risk that gender affects the way in which specific members of the church relate to the women clergy. A probationary on internship in a church expressed concern that a certain older man in the church had developed an uncomfortable patriarchal attitude toward her and her son, making ministry difficult. A conversation with the senior pastor indicated that she had experienced the same thing, often being treated like a daughter, complete with fatherly admonition and advice. Other women report being treated as 'special' by some in their churches, as being 'in need of protection from emotional pressure', 'a little girl', 'dependent', 'unable to fulfil a task without male support' and other, sometimes well-meaning, but discriminatory, attitudes. In all of these the woman minister faces the stress of being considered less than equal to the task because of gender.

Organizational structure and career is identified as a source of stress for women in the work environment. Although women have, on individual basis, advanced to senior church positions, this is still not common. Women are beginning to occupy more middle-level service positions within the denominational structure. This often occurs in the areas of training, Christian education and personnel. Upper-level positions still tend to be male-dominated. In pastoral ministry, the opportunities for women to move beyond positions in mid-size churches are limited. This seems to be particularity true among more conservative church groups where women in ministry are often in associate positions or in smaller church settings.

This systemic stress for women needs to be addressed from an analysis of the system. Challenging this on an individual and incidental basis can create increased stress.

Davidson and Cooper also identified two extra organizational sources of stress for women in the work place. They merit consideration:

The home–social environment has special implications for stress for working women. Studies have shown that married working women, with or without family, tend to have a higher overall work load than their male counterpart. Much of this is due to the expectations that women are still the primary nurturer in the home. The end of the day in the work place may become the beginning of role as wife and mother. Although many modern males share more of the domestic responsibility than past generations, much of the burden still falls to the woman.

This responsibility as mother/wife and career person is particularly true for women clergy (Rassieur, 1982, p. 30). Both home and ministry are highly demanding tasks. The strong family orientation of the church makes both roles vitally important. A study by Shipley and Coats (1992) of dual-role stress and working women noted:

> Employed mothers may experience role conflict and guilt within a culture that espouses the traditional gender divisions of labour and the belief that it is the mother's responsibility to take the primary care of her children. Such conflict may be severe where women have high commitment to both work and family.

The traditional nature of the church, and the factor of high commitment of women clergy in general to both ministry and family, make the risk of stress from role conflict and guilt exceptionally high. The authors went on to point out that the biggest health problem they identified in their study was that of depression.

The dual role placed on women in the work place has significant implications for women coping with stress through 'down time'. Frankenhaeuser (1989), in a gender comparative study which utilizes biomedical as well as social indices, discovered that females have more difficulty 'unwinding' at the end of a normal work day. The production of stress-indicating bodily secretions, which in males drops rapidly at work end, increases substantially in female workers at the end of the work day. Similarly, the blood pressure of female workers remained high after work, while that of male counterparts dropped rapidly at the end of the work day. This, says the researcher, 'reflects their heavy total workload, i.e. the demands they experience from duties at home, often in conflict with demands related to their paid job'.

The second extra-organizational source of stress is what Davidson and Cooper call *individual differences and determinants*. By this they suggest dynamics of gender differences which do exist, often fostered and perpetuated by societal presuppositions and perspectives. This refers to what is sometimes called the 'cultural trap'. Persons function differently based on gender because of sex-role learning. For example, society has taught, and continues to teach, that males will be strong, dominant, emotionally controlled, fulfilling roles of protector, defender, and all that implies. Females, on the other hand, are gentler, less aggressive, dependent, emotional, fulfilling roles of mother, nurturer, supporter and all that implies. Rutter (1989, p. 65) refers to the 'masculine myth of the feminine' which has permeated both males and females of our culture. He refers to three specific manifestations of the myth: in women's deference or submission to male will, women's special powers (nurture, healing and the sexual), and women as dark and destructive or the generator of ill fate in the lives of the male (Eve doing the bidding of the devil in the creation story, the witches in *Macbeth*). These stereotypes are evident in underlying dynamics of our society and culture.

This is especially true of the church. The greying nature of the church means that the values held by the majority of those who occupy the pew are traditional values, instilled by the socialization of past generations. The modern attitude of the broader society is slow to take hold within the church because the high proportion of a former generation continue to uphold and to live by yesterday's sex-role learned perspective of the church, community and society. This is often not an intentional sexual discriminatory view of life, but one that is so deeply rooted that it will take subsequent generations to rectify. In the meantime, women clergy continue to suffer the stress of being viewed with societal expectations and attitudes which are restrictive and limiting as they seek to reach their fullest potential in ministry.

It is evident, from the above short consideration of some research from other disciplines, that there is additional stress for women in the work place because of their gender. The church is no exception. In a faith order and a church which claims 'neither Jew nor Greek, slave or free' there is still substantial 'male and female', with all the discrimination of the tradition still within its doors. Several things must be done. First, the role of women in ministry must be taken seriously and research conducted on gender, stress and ministry. Secondly, and in the meantime, more investigation must be made into stress research and gender comparison of other professions with application made to ministry. Thirdly, training colleges for ministers must develop new, and revise old, curricula to reflect the rising number of women entering ministry. In so doing they will begin to properly train both women and men for ministry.

Section Three

A relational identity: intimacy sought and avoided

6

The risk of relationships

True encounter with persons – divine and human – produces self-
discovery and fulfilment. Our bodies need nourishment lest we die. No
less do we all have the basic need to exist in and on the company of
persons, and without such fellowship, we die a death more painful
than physical death.

(Jabay, 1967, p. 30)

Ministry, modelled on the life of Jesus, is always relational. Among the
rich and the poor, the social elite and the outcast, the self-diagnosed
healthy and the physically and spiritually ill, the believer and the sceptic,
Jesus provided, from the context of relationships, ministry to meet the
needs of all humanity. In these encounters he experienced the pain of the
sufferer, the ridicule of the doubter, the anger of the offended, the sorrow
of the lost, the respect of the follower and the rejection of the majority. All
the human emotions that surface in the context of relationship with
others were part of his earthly experience.

In similar manner, as he had been sent, so he sent his followers into a
world and a ministry fraught with all the difficulties of relationships to
others. In the High Priestly prayer of John 17, having reflected on his
experience of the world, Jesus prayed: 'As you have sent me into the
world, I have sent them into the world.' He sent them into a world of
relationships to experience all the joy and pain that they can bring.

The minister can cope with the diversity of interpersonal relationships without allowing the stress of interaction to become the excess
stress which causes distress, provided that he or she takes seriously
their own personal care and the nurture of their personhood or self.
This means largely the discovering and nurturing of healthy relationships. It involves creating the opportunity to find personal support
within the context of life and ministry. In the fulfilling of their need to
function in a healthy relational environment they can cope in difficult
situations with and for others. Their relationships become the foundation from which they manage effectively. I have intentionally used

words like 'creating', 'nurturing' and 'discovering' because I believe the responsibility lies with the individual. It is the action of the individual which will provide the opportunity for relational support. It takes effort. The system cannot and will not provide adequate supportive networks.

Unfortunately, for many clergy, the opportunity for healthy and meaningful relationship which fulfils them as beings, is lacking. They suffer the stress of being alone and isolated.

The minister as relational being

Levels of relationships

Relationships are a paradox: the greatest source of joy; the greatest source of pain. To say that, for the clergy, relationships are a major source of stress, is to state the obvious. But is it the obvious? To the outsider, looking in, it may not be quite so apparent. The minister is often seen as the one caught up in the joys of fellowship within a community of faith. The minister's smiling face at the church's garden tea and the jovial interaction at the church's family supper hardly portray a person stressed by relationship. The mask of serenity which mounts the steps to the pulpit may well hide the heated argument with the session clerk or the conflict within the home. She greets a hundred smiling people at the church door on a Sunday morning with a vibrant handshake and a personal comment of 'knowing'. Opportunities for relationships are numerous. The apparent joy of the moment may in reality be genuine, but it may also mask a deeper inner turmoil and, at the very root, an unfulfilled need. Consider the following composite of a day in the life of a minister:

> For Sarah Harper it was the end of another day of routine ministry at the First Congregationalist Church. The day had begun in the office with the careful preparation of sermon and the service for this week's special Missions Sunday. Of course that had taken longer than expected, especially with the numerous telephone interruptions. There was Mr J and his concern about shortage of ushers for Sunday, Mrs B who wanted to know about plans for the forthcoming tea and sale. Kristy phoned with the list of youth attending the retreat and then there was Mrs C who just wanted to talk. After lunch there was a trip to the hospital to see Mr P who was to go for surgery tomorrow and who, in obvious fear, held tightly to her hand and asked for prayer. Then it was off to lead the women's missionary group in preparation for their part in this week's service. The young couples' casserole supper had been fun and the time of discussion afterwards had reminded Sarah of how vibrant this group was in the life of the church. Now at ten o'clock, with a cup of tea, she reflected on the day. She had interacted with a lot of

people and shared in their daily life and special needs. She wondered if she had really been of benefit to them. Was this what ministry was all about? There seemed to be a lot of activity, but had anything really happened that could be described as ministry? Little of it seemed to fit the texts on practical theology she had read at seminary. As she sipped her tea she wished she could discuss her own doubts about her ministry with someone. And what about the future . . .

Relationships occur at a number of levels for all, clergy and non-clergy alike. Powell (1978, pp. 50–61) described 'Five Levels of Communication' which are helpful in considering communication but are not adequate for the nature of our study of relationships. The reader may want to look at Powell's levels and consider them additionally to the concept presented here. Relationships are not simply interpersonal but are set in time and space. They take place in the community, the place of work, the context of the job, over coffee and in every aspect of life. The levels of relationships fulfil the needs of an individual to interact in a socially acceptable way appropriate to the situation. Each nurtures a need ranging from simple recognition to intimacy. These levels of interaction are part of a healthy and normal development. All levels have the potential to be positive or negative. Each can progress or digress from one stage to another, although the latter is often more problematic than the first.

Level 1: The Passing Nod
This is the relationship of simple recognition and acknowledgement. We meet the same individual driving to work each morning. Our paths cross, since we are both creatures of habit, at approximately the same time and place. We recognize one another without knowing the other's name or details of life other than what is observable in that shared moment of time and space. However, we become accustomed to one another and, in passing, greet one another with a smile and a wave through the windscreen as we go to our places of employment.

Level 2: The Courteous Exchange
The second level of relationship occurs as we meet face to face with individuals and, in the process of meeting, exchange a courteous greeting. As we wait at the bus-stop or frequent the post-box, we greet one another with a 'Good morning', and a comment about the weather. Since we travel the route regularly we become particularly aware of other regular users and with these we form a 'special' relationship. The absence of one or more of the parties is noticed and the verbal interaction may show special interest and concern when the relationship is

re-established. At this level of relationship it is possible that names are not known but assumed, and getting to know the other's name may be coincidental and often through a third party.

Level 3: The Neighbourly Chatter

At this level of relationship the interaction moves deeper, involving common interests centred around the kinship system of family and community. Questions concerning the welfare of family members or mutually known persons and issues may arise. Matters relating to the general community base may be discussed and shared at some depth. This level of relationship may be found not only within the geographical neighbourhood, but also in places of frequent encounter and relational exchange. For instance, through frequenting the same shop I may get to know the person at the till, being made aware through the ongoing interaction of issues relating to family, plans, habits, concerns and other revealed insights into his/her life. This level of relationship is friendly and makes the daily routine of life enjoyable.

Level 4: The Working Relationship

This level of relationship is usually one of long standing and is continuous in nature. It exists between individuals who work together or who meet in similar situations regularly for a common purpose. In this context people get to know a great deal about one another, both through verbal disclosure and common experience. In the sharing of common space for considerable periods of time, we grow accustomed to one another's traits, moods, reactions and points of concern. At this level we know a considerable amount about one another's private life, if not through personal disclosure, at least through the 'grapevine'. Because the focal point of the interaction is the work place, or the like, there is the potential for competition, groupings and sub-grouping, high emotional interaction and questions concerning trust.

Level 5: The Social Connection

At this level a personal choice is made concerning who enters into a social relationship with the individual. From the range of interactions certain individuals, couples or groups will be identified as having common interests, affable personality and/or other characteristics which lead the individual to want to devote personal and social time to a more meaningful interaction. Here, often in a relaxed atmosphere, relationships mature, trust is developed, barriers to interaction are lowered and a level of 'knowing' one another occurs. Growth of the relationship at this level, as in the previous two, leads to a greater measure of sharing, and a high level of relational needs is met as maturity is achieved.

Level 6: The Depth Interaction

This is a very special level of relationship which develops out of a sense of trust, shared experiences and the assurance of confidentiality. It is at this level that the inner workings of the heart and mind are mutually shared at a level consistent with the above mentioned qualifiers. At this level, more than any of the above, the socially desirable image of office and position is allowed to be relaxed and the inner humanity made evident. Here the doubts, fears, dreams, aspirations, and all those things we hesitate to discuss openly, are made evident with little fear of rejection. A degree of transparency allows for the venting of the system and the re-establishment of a new perspective tempered by the objectivity of others. The number of persons allowed to enter into this level of interaction is limited and they usually do so through trust or necessity.

Level 7: The Intimate Encounter

This is the deepest level of interaction. The term 'intimate' often implies a sexual encounter. That is not the exclusive meaning intended here. It implies a deep spiritual interaction in which progressive self-revelation allows entrance into an ever deepening sphere of relationship. The term *interaction* is significant, in that by it we mean a mutually shared relationship based on equality. This is the level of relationship reserved for the significant other(s) in life. The use of the plural is indicative of the fact that this may well include such persons as a life partner, spiritual guide, parent, or other significant persons in one's life. Interviews with clergy have indicated that this intimate encounter can occur across gender, generation, status, class and education, and among persons of great diversity and experience. It is a spiritual encounter, transcending all barriers, but inherently founded on trust.

Violation of a relationship becomes more traumatic the higher the level in which it occurs. The failure to wave or an angry scowl from the individual in the windscreen encounter of Level 1 is soon forgotten or dismissed. The exposure of confidential material gleaned in Level 6 or the rejection of a significant partner in Level 7 has traumatic and long-term effects on life and being. The further the relationship progresses through the levels, the higher the risk factor.

For Sarah, in the above scenario, interaction had been plentiful, but had remained in the first four levels of relationship. She had been, in the course of the day, surrounded by many people, but not in a way which allowed her needs, as an individual, to be met at the levels of the social, the deep or the intimate. Thus, when the day was over and the process of reflection occurred there was a sense of personal unfulfilment for, indeed, her own relational needs had not been met.

There develops, for the clergy, a discrepancy between the level at which they interact with others and the level at which others interact, or are allowed to interact, within their lives. Ministry, because of its spiritual and personal nature, deals with the innermost needs of individuals. Clergy are called upon to enter into the intimacy of the lives of others, dealing with the deepest of needs in all areas of life. Therefore, ministers struggle with the fears and doubts, the inner turmoil and pain of others' lives – all those things which are often hidden to others. On the one hand the clergy (those who have earned trust) are brought into the lives of others at a Level 7: *The Intimate Encounter*. For Sarah, this may well have occurred in the visit to Mr P, who in facing surgery exposed his fear and need for support from others and, ultimately, from God. On the other hand, only the lower levels of relational needs are met for clergy. Sarah's personal need for relationship was not met beyond Level 4. What appeared as social and intimate encounters had been in the context of work and a part of her duty as pastor of the church. The discussion had centred around others, without attention to her personal needs. No depth or intimate relationship had occurred for her and at the end of the day she was drained and unfulfilled as a relational being. Rediger (1990, p. 82) records from a case study a clergywoman who commented: 'I'm with people a lot, but I need another kind of relationship. I want to be with people who will listen to me instead of me always listening to them.'

Level 1	The Passing Nod
Level 2	The Courteous Exchange
Level 3	The Neighbourly Chatter
Level 4	The Working Relationship
Level 5	The Social Connection
Level 6	The Depth Interaction
Level 7	The Intimate Encounter

Figure 6.1 Levels of relationships

The risk of having relationships

There is always, within any relationship, a potential risk. For the clergy this is especially true. He/she always enters the leadership of a specific parish or congregation as an outsider. It is recognized that ministry, based on the model of Christ, is as an outsider ministry. He who 'came to that which was his own, and his own did not accept him' (John 1.11) was the definitive outsider. This is not to imply that he did not appear at points within his life to find acceptance. Crowds flocked to hear him. The sick were brought to him for healing. Spiritual inquiry was made by even the religious leaders, often more to entrap him than to learn from him. He enjoyed the intimacy of close friends and the inner circle of disciples. Entrance to Jerusalem was akin to the triumphant ascension of a king to the throne as the crowds shouted 'Hosanna to the Son of David! Blessed is he who comes in the name of the Lord!' (Matt 21.9). Accepted for the moment, he was to be rejected in a few short days by the masses and in the moment of greatest need by those closest to him. He who wept over the city died outside its wall, the ultimate outsider.

Clergy enter a new parish or charge as outsiders. Expectation is that the minister, coming as leader of the whole community of faith, will treat all within the church on equal terms. As equalitarian outsider he/ she is unaware of the history, especially the relational and political dynamics, inherent within the group. The historic divisions of the church, by which we mean the natural grouping, as well as the more theological, political and clique-based divisions, become competitive and can quickly attempt to draw the incoming clergy into their camp and cause. These relationships can draw one into conflict in situations where neutrality is required.

Relationships between the minister and individuals or groups within the church can soon be interpreted as favouritism, especially by those who feel themselves outside the favoured circle. Conflict then develops over 'the most favoured' status and even well-motivated interaction with individuals or groups thus can be a source of risk and stress. In the midst of a church conflict a pastor, who met with others on a Friday morning to pray for the church, was accused of gathering his own little support group and taking sides.

There is always the risk with relationships that they will progress into levels which we, or others, deem unacceptable. As friendships become deeper in nature, continued self-revelation may create the reality of the saying 'familiarity breeds contempt'. For many clergy this has been just cause to avoid all 'deeper'-level relationships, except marriage, and to maintain a 'ministerial position' in relationship to persons in church and community. This will be developed further in the section on isolation versus insulation.

Relationships have the potential for getting out of hand. The newspapers these days are full of reports about clergy and others of the helping professions who have entered into relationships, violated trust and ended up in situations of moral failure. Rutter's book (1989) *Sex in The Forbidden Zone* is a good revelation of the movement of relationships from a basis of trust to a scenario of violation and exploitation. The potential for such destructive relationships is always present in situations where one of the parties has a power advantage over another. The risk, as Sipe (1995) implies, is evident in same as well as opposite gender relationships.

For the clergy, dealing in the intimacies of others – for indeed the spiritual is always the intimate – there is the risk of moral transgression or violation of trust. For those who experience high societal and church expectations and play such a public role, the risk is not only of the event occurring, but of the very appearance of impropriety. Integrity must not only be honoured, but it must appear to be honoured.

There is also, for the clergy, the risk of rejection in relationship. As we have said, the minister enters the local church setting as an outsider. He/she has not been a part, until the point of entrance, of the continuing history of the congregation. Although recognized, accepted and even sometimes loved, the minister is, for the most part, considered an outsider. This is especially true in relatively static situations such as rural and small churches. When issues of great consequence arise the historic church as a community of insiders will stand together. During issues of disagreement the clergy, who had in favourable times experienced acceptance, may find their position clearly defined as outsider and, as such, face rejection.

The risk of no relationships

There is also a risk in developing no relationships. This is the risk of separation and isolation, to which we will devote the next chapter. The lack of a relational basis is damaging both for personal development and for the fulfilment of ministry. One cannot be a complete being in either without meaningful relationships.

Avoiding meaningful relationship within the context of ministry declares oneself as either 'super' or 'sub' human. One is superhuman in that the image is created that one can handle the rigours of life without the support of a range of other persons. The superhuman being appears beyond the mundane needs of friendship, functioning on a plain above the average soul. The subhuman image is of one who functions in the fulfilling of the task as though by mechanical action without need for relationship. To deny need for relationship is to place oneself either above or beneath human need. Both are living a lie, for it is in the relational context that fullness of being is discovered. The early creation stories make this clear.

In either case the results are damaging both for the individual and for their ministry. In a generation with stronger loyalties to relationships than to institution, the minister who cannot demonstrate strong relationships simply is seen as 'having never been there' and therefore cannot be perceived as having much to say relevant to life.

Overcoming a bad theology

For most people of my generation, training for ministry involved a discussion of a 'Code of Ministerial Ethics' which provided the dos and don'ts of professional behaviour. Among the list was usually a number relating to relationships in ministry. Several usually went like this:

> Since the minister is called as pastor to the whole community of faith, the minister shall refrain from developing personal relationships within the context of the church and community.

> Upon leaving the church and moving to another charge the minister shall terminate contact with persons of the former charge, thus giving the incumbent opportunity to establish him/herself as the rightful and duly appointed pastor of the church.

The very implication that clergy can turn off and turn on relationships as an act of will, with little or no regard for the emotional and interpersonal dynamics, demonstrates what we have said above about the superhuman or subhuman image of the clergy. Some modern 'Ministerial Ethics' have made marginally more room for relationships in ministry, but the prevailing current against appears to be resistant to change. In my research, ministers between the ages of 20 to 30, while verbally acknowledging to a greater degree that to have friends was permissible, had proportionally fewer friends than their older colleagues. In the 20 to 30 age group, 75 per cent said it was not *right* to have close friendships within the parish compared to 91 per cent of their colleagues between the ages of 30 and 40 (Irvine, 1989).

The concept of clergy as non-relational beings beyond a task-orientated level is founded on the support of a faulty theological understanding. This needs to be corrected if clergy are to permit themselves to become relational people in the context of a relational community.

The bad theology seems to be established on the concept that specific persons, under divine appointment, and with the laying on of hands, are to be 'set apart' for the task of ministry. The setting apart was deemed by the early church as functioning on a different plane of being. This plane was one spiritually, and often authoritatively, above the rest of humanity. The setting apart brought with it a separation from others which was simply seen as 'part of the position of minister'. In some expressions of the Christian church this 'setting apart' became a setting above by creating a pedestal on which the clergy stood. The pedestal was created jointly by the people and the clergy. The clergy placed themselves upon it (possibly a bit like a sacrifice), offering their humanity to God, prepared to suffer the pain of non-relational being. The laity raised the clergy to the pedestal in their need for a human model of the divine life for their example (and perhaps also as vicarious sacrifice). In either case the clergy became not only set apart by divine injunction, but also set aside by human action, aside from deepening and meaningful relationship.

This seems gravely incongruent with the teaching of the apostles and that which was reflected in their ministry. The epistles portray a deeply relational basis to the ministry of the leadership of the early church. The Apostle Paul refers to 'being all things to all people' and developing relationships with the weakest in order to reach their deepest needs (1 Cor 9.19–23). He speaks of the 'opening of his heart' and 'not withholding of our affection' in addressing the church at Corinth (2 Cor 6.11–12). The writer of John's epistles addresses the church with the intimacy of a lover. Peter ends his first writing to the church with the admonition to greet one another with a kiss of love (1 Pet 5.14). The apostles speak often of their deep relational basis with those in the community of faith and those among whom they ministered effectively. There were stringent guidelines or boundaries for their behaviour. However, they were not set aside from the relational basis of life simply because of the divine and unique nature of their calling.

The lack of relationships brings loneliness which in its extreme creates a sense of isolation. 'Loneliness', says Kelsey, 'can destroy people' (Kelsey, 1989, p. 110). This we will now consider.

7

The problem of isolation

If it is the case that our personal identities are moulded through our relationships, then there must be some connection between the quality of those relationships and that of our personhood.

(McFadyen, 1990, p. 18)

Deep satisfaction results from caring for and supporting another person. But as much harm as good is likely to be done by the person who does not first appropriately meet her or his own needs, so that she or he will have energy and confidence to pay attention to the other person's real needs, instead of projecting his own on to her.

(Rediger, 1990, p. 145)

The stress of loneliness is critical for many clergy, for relationships are crucial to identity. There is a deep inner need for relationships which go beyond the surface dynamics of the first four levels of interaction. It is essential that differentiation is made here between a number of terms that are often used indiscriminately in general conversation. These are: alone, solitude, loneliness and isolation. To be alone or to find solitude are neutral terms which mean to be by oneself. This is an essential time for most people, especially in rest from a busy and hectic world. Jesus often sought solitude, a time to be separate and apart. Loneliness, however, implies an emotional quality of longing for the presence of another or for relationship. To be lonely is considered by most people a negative factor in life. For the sake of our discussion here, *isolation* is defined as an acute sense of being alone, beyond the point of but including, loneliness, to the sense of being trapped in this condition.

Isolation: what does the term mean?

In its simplest form isolation implies separation from 'meaningful human interaction'. The emphasis is on the term *meaningful*. For the purpose of our understanding we will utilize a social-psychological definition. The Theodorsons' *Modern Dictionary of Sociology* (1969, p. 216) defines isolation as:

> A degree of separation of individuals or groups from one another in
> terms of interaction, communication, cooperation and social and
> emotional involvement. The prolonged isolation of an individual from
> others usually leads to or is the result of a mental disorder. From a
> social-psychological point of view a person is isolated in a community
> such as a large city if he (she) feels alienated from the people with
> whom he (she) interacts in his (her) neighbourhood or at his (her) job.

The definition indicates the severity of isolation in its reference to the
presence of mental disorder as an effect and, in some cases, a cause of
isolation. The fact that it can be experienced in a thronging urban
context, within the work place and in the neighbourhood implies that
the concept is not based simply on the absence of persons or opportunity for interaction, but rather on a far deeper causal factor. It is the
absence of deep, meaningful relationship.

The same dictionary of sociology defines the person who is isolated
as an *isolate*:

> A person who appears to be a participant in a small group but who
> upon investigation is found to consider no one in the group a friend,
> nor does anyone in the group consider him (her) a friend. The isolate is
> a peripheral member.

At first these definitions appear to create a cold misconception when
applied to ministry. However, in the light of our description of the
minister as an outsider to the church and parish, the terms become more
real. This is more evident when we apply the levels of relationship and
recognize that the interaction which does occur is in the lower levels of
the scale, indicative of the lack of meaningful exchange. The reality of
this is further borne out in my research. First, however, it is important
to identify the types of isolation to which we refer.

Types of isolation

Geographical isolation is the most apparent type when we first raise the
term in relation to ministry. This is imposed by geographical distance
from a major centre or from a primary source of support and interaction. Ministry in the north of Canada or the island ministry of the
Church of Scotland are readily identified as specific examples of this
type of isolation. Oswald (1981) studied this form of isolation. It is
different from the others we will be considering in that it is fundament-
ally physical and may or may not contain within it other types. In my
research some differences were observed between geographically isolated clergy of the islands and those of the mainland parishes (Irvine,
1990).

Professional isolation exists by the very nature of a profession that is based on one person serving alone in the context of a setting. Although larger churches are moving towards multi-staff teams, solo ministry is still the norm (e.g. 82 per cent in the Church of Scotland). Ministry in this sense remains one of the few remaining old-time professions. The medical practitioner today practises within the context of multiple staff surgeries and clinics. Lawyers form partnerships and social workers function out of agencies. Teachers work in multi-teacher schools and accountants work for firms. All of these other professionals have ongoing and continuous opportunity for professional interaction, not only on critical issues, but also in areas of daily interaction. But not so for the minister. As he/she daily faces the pressures of ministry there is rarely anyone with whom ideas can be tested, concepts analysed, actions affirmed or denied or with whom confidences can be shared. Clergy are professionally isolated in two primary ways:

Interdisciplinary isolation is the lack of support from other professionals in the community. Although there may be some commonality in the group served by clergy and other professionals, there is often lack of communication, thus limiting a holistic approach to service. Of the survey conducted some 50 per cent indicated that they felt professionally isolated from other care-givers in the community.

Intradisciplinary isolation is the lack of support from others of the same profession in spite of the common nature and location of service. Over 52 per cent of those surveyed felt professionally alone most of the time. When questioned further concerning various specific interaction, isolation was increasingly evident. Interaction with other clergy was highest (87 per cent) in the professional area, but much of this (83 per cent) occurred within the fraternal. It becomes obvious from the 52 per cent who felt isolated that the level of interaction was not sufficiently satisfactory to offset isolation.

When clergy are deprived of or deprive themselves of meaningful interaction with other professionals they function in a vacuum of professional isolation.

Social isolation occurs when clergy do not have or do not take the opportunity to express themselves within the social context. Too often the minister is viewed by others, and at times by themselves, solely on the basis of their ministerial role, thus preventing a depth of personal and social interaction occurring. In these circumstances it is difficult for the clergy to step aside from their role as clergy and, for lack of a better term, to 'let their hair down'. This is especially true in the context of a church and community where theology and teaching has denied the place of friendship. Although, among the group surveyed, the average stay in a pastoral charge was 8.9 years, 43 per cent indicated they had no close friends within community. Nearly 60 per cent indicated that in the context of 'social evenings' with friends they usually involved themselves in church talk. Moreover, 82 per cent indicated that they were still expected to fulfil their ministerial role even in the context of social events and some 62 per cent felt they were trapped by the expectations of others and needed to 'break loose'.

Much of this may be brought about by the clergy's disposition for overwork. In the month prior to the conducting of the survey, 28 per cent of the clergy had taken no time off and 52 per cent had take only three days or less off in the preceding 30. It becomes obvious that a high proportion of the clergy surveyed were socially isolated, either by their own self-image or by the expectations of others.

Spiritual isolation may best be identified by the response to the question: 'Who ministers to the minister?' The pastor is called upon in his/her ministry to hear the needs of others, to bear their trials and troubles, to mediate the grace of God to the seeker and to share in the struggle of the doubter. But when the pastor suffers these same needs and when their faith falters and they face the Golgotha of their life, who brings to them the comfort, care and the words of assurance which make evident once again the Grace of God? Too often, caught up in the task of ministry to others, the clergy neglect their own spiritual being. The Swiss psychiatrist Paul Tournier, from his extensive practice, commented:

> Carried away in the activism rampant in the church the latter (pastor) holds meeting upon meeting, always preaching, ever in personal conversation, with a program so burdened that he no longer finds time for meditation, never opening the Bible except to find subjects for sermons. One such pastor after several talks with me said abruptly, 'I'm always praying as a pastor, but for a long time now I've never prayed as a man.' (1964, pp. 22–3)

In the survey conducted only 14 per cent of the clergy met with a group of other clergy to provide mutual pastoral care while only 21 per cent indicated that they had a person who served as their spiritual director or guide. Some 69 per cent felt that they had insufficient time for spiritual nurture. When asked to respond to the statement 'I pray with others, but rarely spend time in personal prayer', 15 per cent indicated that this was possibly true, 20 per cent moderately agreed while 5 per cent indicated that this was strongly the case.

The minister who is not spiritually nurtured and receives little ministry from others runs the acute risk of being spiritually isolated.

It is isolation, that separation from meaningful relationships with others, and specifically as found in the later three types, which prevents the minister from being a whole, relational being. Without this wholeness, stress, prompted by separation, is experienced. The inability to handle the stressors which are created leads to the excess of demand over capacity to cope. The accumulated effect is one of distress with the risk of what Selye would identify as *the stage of exhaustion* leading to the inability of the individual to cope and to eventual system breakdown.

What is the root cause of isolation?

What then is the root cause of isolation? The sociological definition looked at earlier indicates that it is not primarily a lack of opportunity for relationship. Sarah Harper had an abundance of relational opportunity. In fact, the presence of too many people made the work of the day, at best, hectic. The levels of relationships make it clear that unless one is barricaded behind closed doors, relationships do develop, at least at the lower levels of the scale. What is it then, that prevents relationships from reaching the depth necessary for meaningful interaction?

The attempt has been made to demonstrate that the very nature of the office of minister is a contributor to isolation. There are those things which historically shape the office in a manner which places the incumbent on a plane separate from others. The concept of the outsider to community, especially that of faith, segregates. The personal nature of the work calls for a confidentiality which hinders a sharing of the difficulties faced, limiting consultation. The solitary nature of the office places the minister in a cycle of isolation. But is this what really lies at the core of isolation or are these contributing factors to a far deeper problem?

In my research it has become apparent that isolation, the inability or reluctance to have meaningful interaction with others, is rooted in the individual's separation from and lack of awareness of their own *self-*identity. Exploration of the works of such formative thinkers as Freud, Jung, Adler, Horney, Stack, Frankl and others, led to the discovery that, although each saw human existence from different perspectives, each understood isolation as not being simply the absence of human interaction. It is evident from the review that the problem lies deep in the nature of humanity and in anthropological history, psycho-development, socialization patterns, religious awareness and the emergence of personhood (Irvine, 1989).[1] Failure to develop an awareness of the *self*, an awareness which establishes a healthy foundation from which to relate to others with a sense of security and confidence, causes relationships to remain at the lower, non-threatening levels of interaction. Here the risk is less and the person is less threatened.

Understanding who we are, or our *self*-understanding, is not a simple

process. Who we perceive the *self* to be results from a complex combination of factors which originate from who we think we are, who we
pretend we are, how others perceive us and how they transmit that
perception back to us. This transmission can be individual and group
based. For instance the minister may receive one set of formative
messages from an individual which may not be consistent with the
response of the group of which that person is a part. All interaction,
given the interpretative component, is subject to distortion. The understanding of the self, even from a cursory glance, is complex. The
concepts as presented here are primarily based on work of the Swiss
psychiatrist C. G. Jung because it has been a major part of my own
journey. The attempt will be made to use as little jargon as possible to
make it more understandable and readable.

Each individual lives in two worlds, or two spheres of existence. Both
of these are equally real to our human existence. There is the outer
world, that sphere in which we physically function, hold office, interact
with the environment, form relationships, establish a role and develop
an observable identity. This is often described as ego development, the
centre of conscious awareness of the individual's functioning in the
outer world. This is the world of doing.

The other sphere is the inner world. This is the world of all those
things which lie within our internal being, sometimes called the psyche.
It is the collection of thought, feeling, emotions, spirit and all that lies at
the root of being. Study of the inner world would indicate that not only
is this a personal inner world but that it is shaped by the collective
contributions of the human journey from the very beginning of time.
This is an unmeasurable concept, as is the very world in which it exists.
This inner world is the world of the spiritual. It is in this inner world, in
what St Augustine referred to as the God-shaped space, that the human
being encounters the Divine through a transcendent experience.

Many of the so-called depth psychologists, those who have advanced
theory on human development and condition, would suggest that all of
life is an attempt to resolve these two worlds. The first half of life is
spent in a striving to separate the ego, or the image of the person in the
outer world, from the inner world; in other words, in the establishing of
a recognizable and unique identity or personality. The second half of
life is spent in the endeavour to try and bring these two worlds back
into harmony or union one with the other.

A brief look at human development would support such a concept.
The child is born with little awareness of the world around him/her. In
the world of the child all functions fulfil primal needs. The cry to be fed,
to be held and to be kept dry is totally oblivious of the needs and
schedules of others. The child's functioning begins as being reactive

and instinctive. It is the centre of its universe. As the child grows he/she becomes more aware of the surrounding world. Interaction with that world becomes important and the child becomes aware of its own existence as an 'I' in the outer world. So the ego development begins. Still firmly rooted in the inner world of needs, the child begins to explore the ways in which it, as an exterior 'I', functions, interacts and influences others in the outer world. Understanding of both worlds grows and develops and the child accepts both as real. The physical world is a real, concrete world. Faith and trust is simple and implicit. This awareness and simple acceptance of both the outer world and the needs of the inner spiritual world probably was congruent with the act of Jesus placing a child in the midst of the disciples and saying 'anyone who will not receive the Kingdom of God like a little child will never enter it' (Matt 18.3).

As the ego develops it takes a stronger shape and, at least in Western culture, becomes the controlling factor. The individual becomes recognizable by the exterior manifestations of who he/she is in the public domain. The adolescent years and early adulthood are spent in a struggle to create a unique image. The image which is placed before the world is in a constant process of being shaped both from without and within. This public face has been called by Jung the *persona*. This is a term taken from Greek and Roman theatre where the actor's role was identified by the mask he wore. This mask or outer skin becomes the means by which the individual is able to face and interact with the outer world. It is the recognizable face to the world and is a healthy part of personal development and growth. Each person has a persona through which interaction occurs. It is the shaping of this persona, prompted by ego development, which the individual spends the first half of life developing. The persona, however, is not the complete self, but simply the facade behind which lies the sum total of the person.

Difficulties develop when the persona, controlled primarily by the ego, begins to become the dominant or sole image of the person. It is understood that the outer mask cannot exist without inner support but it can become the overpowering consideration. The individual is controlled by the projected image he/she creates and all energy goes to the maintaining of that image. The persona can eventually become distorted or fixed in this manner so that it appears to be the real identity of the person.

The risk then is that the individual functions predominantly in the outer world ignoring the needs of the inner world. The persona becomes the mask synonymous with role identity and the ego, now inflated, becomes controller of the individual. With inner needs ignored, it is necessary for the outer conscious sphere to become stronger, for this is now who the individual feels he/she really is. The intrinsic strength of a person, grounded in a healthy symbiotic relationship between both worlds, is lost. As this occurs the person is affirmed by that which complements and strengthens the outer world. Equally, the person is then threatened by anything which may pose a hazard to their outer world. Jealousy, lack of trust of others and intimidation can be prompted by the presence of criticism and even the well-meaning comment, misunderstood. Several things become apparent from this. First, deep and meaningful relationships pose a threat for, by their very definition, they possess a self-revealing and 'spiritual' nature. Entering into relationships at more than a lower level forces one to deal with that which is of the inner being. Secondly, it becomes more obvious as to why the same 'stressors' affect different people in different ways. From the security of an integrated and well-developed *self* the person can experience the stressor, draw on the inner reserve of healing and strength, and cope effectively. The stressor is never allowed to become excessive and lead to distress. However, when the individual functions primarily in the outer world, any stressor which invades that sphere threatens the principal base of identity. There are no inner reserves upon which to draw or, at best, the inner resources are weakened. The very presence of the threat to the individual exposes the poverty of the inner being and, in so doing, creates its own set of stressors.

Edinger (1991, p. 15) points out that this condition, which he calls the state of 'inflation', is at the root of much of the negative factors which exist within the world of the individual. Power motivation, lust and everything which generates from a pure 'pleasure principle' are the product of this sense of inflation. It appears, in the mind of the individual with the inflated ego, as though the world exists for his/her sole purpose and control. All then, including the rights and needs of others, becomes secondary and/or insignificant compared with those of the person with this distorted self view.

Depth relationships, and with them the basis from which to handle stress, are determined on the wholeness of the person and, therefore, the development of a healthy self.

Self-identity, wholeness and ministry

For the minister, the question of self-identity is one of being a whole person in ministry. It lies in recognizing that the real self is not determined solely on exterior perceptions of others, their own cherished self-image or even the mystic image often associated with the office. Rather, it lies in a balancing of these, creating that wholeness or symmetry resulting from an integration between the inner and outer worlds. This is difficult and to achieve it there are risks.

Most, if not all of us, and I include myself as well entrenched in this, have become slaves to the rampant busyness of the modern church world. We have allowed the task to become so demanding that it has moved us away from dealing effectively with our own inner needs, causing us to suppress rather than integrate the diversity within us and to starve our inner and 'spiritual' side of existence.

Now this is hardly surprising, nor am I suggesting that it is all the fault of the pastor. Theologically we have been brought up in a concept that ordination, and for that matter the Christian life, calls for sacrifice and the death to self. Few ordination services will pass without someone reading or quoting 'If anyone would follow me let them deny themselves, pick up their cross and follow me'. Additionally, we have been seduced by a world that has slipped into the church demanding measures of success that are quantitatively obvious and descriptively visible. We live in a world of decreasing church attendance, as we have seen, and in that world we have accepted that success and even survival is based on competition. It follows in our thinking that this competition implies developing a better product than the church next door. Driven to activism we have forgotten who we are as whole being. We have killed the self of wholeness to reward the self of success.

There is no denying the theology of self-denial in Christian life and service, but that does not imply self-neglect. For the Christian, and therefore the clergy, the root of discovering the true *self* lies in the paradox of denial of the old and the rediscovery of the *new self*. Paul stated 'If any person be in Christ he/she is a new creation' (2 Cor 5.17). When Christ issued the statement 'If anyone would follow me, let them deny themselves, pick up their cross and follow me', he was not referring to that which makes the *self* less, but rather that which makes it more. The new *self* finds its roots in a relationship to the Divine and, in that new context, begins as a relational being with the Christ as centre of all life. Christ becomes the reconciling centre of integration. The denial of self is a dying process (for as with Paul it never dies) of the old inner nature in order to allow the divine action of redefining *self* as a new nature founded in God-centred being. The act of denial does not imply neglect of *self* for in so doing the individual would deny the biblical injunction of care and stewardship over creation, of which the whole person is a part.

Jesus becomes the model. His human will became ultimately submissive to the divine will of the heavenly parent. Yet he never ceased to nurture the human entity, his earthly being. He cared for his whole being, physically through food and drink and nurture. He developed deep and meaningful relationships with his disciples and those who were closest to him. He cared for the spiritual through mountain-top meditation, prayer, fasting and the corporate act of public worship in the temple. He debated with the wise. He relaxed with the rich. He cared for the needy. He walked with the poor. He lived a balanced life in a real world. Yet he died to the self in the submission of the will to the heavenly Father and, in that act, became the exalted of God. The Apostle Paul calls us to this model when he says 'Let this mind be in you which was also in Christ Jesus' (Phil 2.5). It is in this paradoxical act that the old self is emptied and the new *self* is refilled as new creation (2 Cor 5.17).

As I have said, this involves risk. For many of us the controller has extensively been not a Christ-centred *self*, but an ego-driven persona which functions in the outer world of action, far away from the spiritual needs and healing centre of the inner being. We have found our identity in doing, not being, and behind the persona controlled by the inflation of the ego lies a withering and impoverished spiritual self. The persona or mask becomes thickened and fixed. The primary flow of energy moves towards strengthening this public face or image. The person becomes recognized by others on the basis of this outer image and indeed may really believe that this is his/her identity. Driven to sustain this image, the inner world with all its needs becomes neglected and energy to nourish it is diverted outward. This energy is directed towards that which is not real or intrinsic to the person. Jung says:

> Fundamentally the persona is nothing real: it is a compromise between
> individual and society as to what a person should appear to be. He
> (she) takes a name, earns a title, represents an office, he (she) is this or
> that. In a certain sense all this is real, yet in relationship to the essential
> individuality of the person concerned it is only secondary reality, a
> product of compromise, in making what others often have a greater
> share in than he (she). (Jung, 1953, para. 246, p. 156)

Figure 7.1 may be helpful to those, like myself, who understand best with aid of the visible. As with all models this is only a line construct and so therefore falls short of the complexity of the concept.

The persona, which interfaces with the world around about us, becomes thickened and fixed in place, strengthened by strong role identity and perceived strong character identity. To maintain this draws the majority of energy, especially if this 'image' is to grow successfully. Deprived of energy, the inner world of the individual is starved of nurture, suppressed and becomes weakened.

This needs to be applied in a very direct manner to ministry. The generalization which follows may not apply to all in its acute form. It is important, however, that direct application be made and this can only occur first in this sweeping universalization. With primary identity in the outer world the minister is affected by all that is affirming or critical as it relates to the role. When things go 'well' in the context of ministry then the minister, for he/she so identifies with role, feels 'well', as though they personally have found accomplishment. When things do not appear to be functioning satisfactorily or apparently negative comments arise, then these are internalized and the minister senses personal criticism. All that affects ministry affects the person of ministry. When attendance is up, the minister is up and conversely so.

This need not always be as direct as implied here. Comments made in a constructive manner become, in the mind of the inflated-ego minister, threatening. Delegation of ministry and shared leadership with others, often laity, become a threat to control. Interaction with other ministers in community becomes competitive, for success in ministry, and therefore personal success, is paramount. Relationships remain on a surface level, for self-revelation may jeopardize image.

As Edinger has indicated, such things as power-motivated action, anger (suppressed and otherwise), desire for control and sexual dominance all generate from the inflation of the ego. There is a sense in which the inflation not only drives the action but in turn feeds the ego

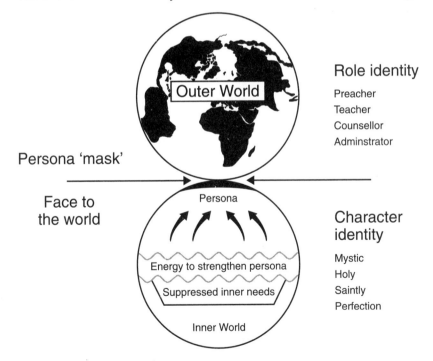

Figure 7.1 Ego inflation control of clergy

thus making it more inflated and dominant. The alienation from the inner world becomes greater as the energy continues to feed the outer world of image.

This broad generalization does not apply to all. There is, however, a sense in which there is a little of this in all of us. In careful self-reflection we may discover that not all of our motives are as altruistic as they would seem. There is a degree to which the image, be it one of strong role or character identity, drives our action.

The need is for each individual to examine his/her understanding of the *self* and once again to seek integration through journeying into the world of being. This seeking of balance will mean a redirecting of energy from sustaining the outer image to nurturing the inner world. To do so will mean that something must be relinquished. The world of action must decrease so the world of being can increase. The 'too busy to pray' must be rectified to some degree by 'too prayerful to be as busy'.

As we have said, there are risks. The drop in action, in the eyes of a world and church which gauges success by quantitative measure, runs the risk of appearing to 'have lost it' and to have become a failure. The return to wholeness can, therefore, be painful. The temptation, when faced with pain, is to turn back to the familiar and to do it more zealously, for there is comfort in the known. In so doing the offering of ourselves as 'living sacrifices' becomes the presentation of dead offerings: burnt-out ministers, dead tired servants and spiritually emaciated beings.

The onward journey also brings other risks. The *self*, as integrated being, becomes the spiritual centre in which the individual can encounter God and others. It allows for upper-level relationships even to that of Intimate Encounter, a spiritual encounter, transcendent of all barriers, but inherently founded on trust. Isolation can only be offset when a full range of relationships is allowed to develop and to grow. For some clergy this becomes threatening. The intimacy of encounter brings with it the additional risk. Scarred by past encounters, and acting to protect themselves and those close to them, they make isolation a deliberate act, which we will define as *insulation*. This is understandable, but dangerous for personhood and ministry.

Insulation not isolation

The *Concise Oxford English Dictionary* defines 'to insulate' as 'to make into an island by surrounding with water; to cause (a thing, person, etc.) to stand detached from its surroundings, to separate from the rest; to place apart, to isolate'. Research has shown that there is often the deliberate act by clergy to separate themselves from deep interaction in a conscious and, at times, in an unconscious fashion. Consider the case study of Tom Walls:

> For the Reverend Tom Walls the last year in the previous charge had been most difficult. After a number of good years of effective ministry a growing number of persons discontent with his emphasis on ministry to the physically and emotionally needy of the community had gained more control in the church. For some church members, who viewed the church as one of status, this sort of direction was unacceptable. 'After all', was the claim, 'these people are a drain on the finances and they contribute nothing.' They could have lived with just one or two 'marginal' people, but under the influence of Pastor Walls more and more of 'this type of people' were attending. The last months had been hard. Even those whom he felt were his friends had become silenced by the powerful influence of a few. In fact, some had even turned against him, saying that maybe this type of ministry should be left to the Salvation Army. So Tom had been moved out of his charge and now was resettled in a new community minded church setting.
>
> Badly hurt by the past church into which he had placed so much effort, he had commented to Joan, his wife, as they arrived in the new settlement, that he would do things differently here. He wouldn't let people get close enough to hurt him in the same way as had his 'friends' in the past church. Now that he had been here a year and a half he was beginning to feel more comfortable and trusting. He was feeling once again close to the people when Joan commented one night 'Tom, you still have a barrier around you. You never allow people to get too close. Never close enough to really know you.'

For many clergy injured by church relationships there is a temptation to build around themselves a barrier of protection. This wall is a partial wall of glass. It allows visual contact and some interaction around the margins. Sound is heard, but there is no opportunity to move past the wall into direct contact with the person inside, the clergyperson. As friction, or the risk of friction, becomes obvious the wall is drawn higher, and greater protection afforded. The clergy can be seen in action, in the pulpit, in visitation and in the function of ministerial office, but the person of the pastor is untouchable. Isolation now takes on the form of insulation. The clergyperson has insulated him/herself from the dangers of being hurt once again by 'them'.

For many clergy, after continual relational injury within ministry, the wall is erected permanently, barring some catastrophic event which levels the barrier and provides opportunity for healing and wholeness. Scepticism develops concerning the sincerity of others in relationships and any desire to establish normal relationships is suppressed. The 'relationships' within ministry – for they must exist to some extent – are relationships of role and function, lacking the intrinsic dimensions necessary for deep interaction. The ministerial ethics to which I referred earlier and the busyness of the church become convenient excuses for the separation. Ministry continues as if this were normal for relationships between clergy and parishioners.

People like Tom, however, desire to establish relational ministry founded on good and healthy interaction. His style of ministry is getting to know people and sharing in their spiritual journeys. The decision to 'do things differently' is a common response to protect a wound, as is the gradual return to 'normal' as the wound begins to heal. The problem is the deep-seated scar which, as Joan pointed out, 'prevents people from getting too close'. If this inner scar is not recognized and treated it continues to exist and relations are never quite as open and free as before. Joan's astute observation may be sufficient to force recognition and resolution of the problem. However, there may be need for some professional counselling or therapy.

These barriers can be established not only to prevent the closeness of persons within the church, but with all other relationships as well. Distrust of colleagues, other professionals and those who present other relational basis will cause the same insulation to be established. This then becomes evident in professional, social and spiritual types of isolation.

Be it isolation or insulation the outcome is the same. The clergyperson is cut off from a primary means of support and, therefore, faces the daily task of ministry alone. Relationships, so essential for healthy well-being, are non-existent (isolation) or rejected (insulation). The stressors of the task of ministry, and for that matter daily life, have little opportunity for expression or objective evaluation. Suppressed within the individual they become potential roots for excess stress and, at worst, distress.

Note

1 A fuller study of this can be found in my doctoral dissertation 'Isolation in the parish ministry' (Irvine, 1989).

8

Ministry, sexuality and identity

> We have seen that passion for work may come from a fear of
> relationship or a fear of genital sexuality. It can be an escape, a
> compensation for anguish. It springs from isolation and leads to
> isolation. When individuals have no confidence in being unique in
> love, they seek to be unique in power and domination.
>
> (Vanier, 1986, p. 72)

It is not possible to write a book on clergy stress without commenting
on the tension around sexuality, a matter, as Vanier has expressed,
relating directly to identity and power. For the clergy it is evident that
this is a subject of increasing importance and one creating great stress.
Clergy often dare not speak about this problem, but suppression does
not provide a solution. It only increases inner turmoil and distress.

There are two major issues which I will raise and on which comment
will be made. The first of these is relating to sexual misconduct between
clergy and those persons to whom they minister. The second will raise
the issue of the sexual orientation of the minister. Complete books
could be, and have been, written on both subjects, so the focus here will
be in relationship to the theme of this book, vocational stress.

Sexual misconduct

There appears to be an escalation in the number of incidents of sexual
impropriety between clergy and those to whom ministry is provided.
Headlines such as 'Sex Cult Rocks Church', 'Minister Charged With
Four Counts of Sexual Abuse against Minors' and 'Christian Brothers
Charged With Sexual Molestation' are commonplace today. It is difficult to tell whether the frequency of such events is increasing or if it is
in the actual level of reporting that there is increase. This question is
further complicated by the number of alleged occurrences which often
stem back ten to 25 years, clearly indicating that this is not a problem
solely of this decade. Needless to say the question of increase is

academic. The occurrence, regardless of frequency, is the real issue.

The fact, however, that such incidents are receiving higher public awareness and scrutiny has served to heighten clergy awareness of the problem and helped them to exercise, in most cases, a more precautionary approach. There is, however, the risk of developing a paranoia around the subject, as evidenced by the male minister who refuses to counsel any female without his wife present or the student for ministry who is afraid to make afternoon visitation for fear of entrapment. Such fear can paralyse ministry and, in the process, make the supposed 'coping method' develop, in and of itself, excessive stress. Nor is this problem confined to situations of ministry with persons of the opposite gender. The increasing awareness of sexual encounters between clergy and persons of the same gender have made all relationships, especially where there is an inequity of power, potentially dangerous. This vulnerability places relationships and relational ministry at risk.

There is also the potential for stress to develop between the clergy's cherished self-images, both personal and collective for the profession, and the reality of how they think, feel, fantasize and react. Rutter (1989, p. 25), in his important study on sex between professionals such as doctors, teachers, lawyers or clergy and those they serve, indicates the prevalence of exploitive relationships. He would imply that the male fantasy, which is the product of a cultural myth relating to sexuality and women, is universal and often involves the area of the forbidden zone. It is important to recognize that Rutter in using this terminology refers specifically to exploitive sex between professional males in power, and women. Application to females in power and, in this context, to clergywomen is not found in his study or, to the author's knowledge, in other research. This section may be considered by some as applicable solely to clergymen. Rediger (1990, p. 2) does indicate that his extensive caseload primarily involves males and presents only two case studies involving female clergy. The 1994 movie *Disclosure*, based on a novel by Michael Crichton, portrays a woman in power seeking control over a male employee by exploitive sex. The plot is hardly indicative of the normative gender role in Western culture. The reader will have to decide for him/herself. Be that as it may, the discrepancy between the rationalized ideal image of 'minister' and the real creates stress, especially if the differences are not resolvable. Consider the following account of the Reverend Frederick Marshall, pastor of St James Church.

> It had been a restless night. Unable to sleep, all sorts of thoughts raced through his mind provoking a range of emotions. He, as Sally Jones' pastor, had been providing counsel and support while she went through a difficult period of separation from her abusive husband. It

was a trying time as this 28-year-old woman faced the reality of her husband's neglect of her, his infidelity and then, when discovered, his accusations creating verbal and psychological abuse. For a number of months now Fred had comforted her, encouraged her and helped her through some difficult days. And then it happened. Yesterday as she was leaving, she paused before opening the door to his office, threw her arms around him and held on to him tightly. Without saying a word she kissed him and then rushed out of the office. The problem for Fred was that, as she held him close, he felt sexually aroused and his hands seemed to have a mind of their own as they slid down her back sensing the warmth underneath.

Now Fred panicked, flooded with conflicting thoughts. Why had he responded that way? Nothing like this had happened before. It was one thing for the episode to happen, but it was quite another that he had experienced physical signs of arousal. Had she sensed his response? It just was not right that a minister of his experience should have allowed this to happen. Should he tell someone? He didn't think his colleagues would understand. They would probably be shocked. Maybe he should talk to Pam, his wife. After 15 years of marriage maybe she could help. No, things had been tense between them since he took on the additional responsibility of the fraternal secretary when she thought he should be cutting back. How was he going to face Sally again?

The thing that bothered him most was that during the past month, as she struggled with the pain of rejection and neglect, he had thought that what she really needed was someone to take her in their arms and give her the love she deserved. To be honest he had even thought about doing it and wondered how she would react to his approach. She was very attractive and so much in need of someone's care and love.

'O God! Why did you let this happen? What about the strength you promised? I'm not fit to be a minister.'

Frederick Marshall found himself caught between his idealized world of being a minister, his humanity and the reality of his actual response. Failure, guilt, anger and betrayal, coupled with the fear of the ramifications of the relationship, dominated his thinking. This was intensified by the fact that in his thoughts, the world of his dreams, such a happening had already begun to unfold. It was almost as if the dream was being fulfilled, and this scared him. He was really uncertain as to his feelings for her, and the swing of emotions ranged from anger to feelings of infatuation. Pervading all this was the nagging thought that he was now unfit, after seven years of training and fifteen years of experience, to serve a congregation as minister. He had failed his calling.

Central to this event is the fact that Fred had forgotten his humanity, that part of him which made him react like every other human being. He had entered into a counselling situation cognizant of the risk, but, like the smoker faced with the warning of cancer on the cigarette package, felt 'It can never happen to me'. That very denial created the potential for crisis. Rutter (1989) states:

> Even men who conduct themselves according to the highest ethical standards of their professions can admit that underlying erotic fantasies may have played a part in their choice (of profession). They must realize that the inherent conditions of the forbidden zone place them at risk of feeling erotically intoxicated by the women they serve.
>
> Being honest with yourself means simply this: Do not hide from the fact that something in your own nature has led you into having intimate contact with women in the forbidden zone ... The more you acknowledge what is inside, the better prepared you will be to find the help you need when you need it, to avoid betraying the trust placed in you. (p. 203)

When the embrace and kiss occurred, maybe wholly innocent of sexual intent, and he reacted in response to suppressed and unresolved thoughts, he was surprised by his own humanity. Now he faced the excess stress, unresolved in the sleepless night, of his own sexuality.

Rutter points out that the fulfilment of sexual fantasy in the forbidden zone is always the product of an inequity of power (p. 68). It is the dominance of the professional care giver over a vulnerable recipient of that care. The imbalance places the recipient, in Rutter's book always the female, in a position of threatened compliance. Immobilized by the power base, even supposed consensual sex is exploitive and, as such, destructive of the individual. Rediger (1990) and Sipe (1995) would make it clear that such abusive sexual control can and does also occur in the forbidden zone between persons of the same gender.

For Pastor Marshall the potential for the episode to progress, or more appropriately digress, to a full sexual liaison is great. He has become, for Sally, a person of power. He has made the pain of a bad relationship become bearable and she has developed a dependency upon him. She equated survival with him and the loss of the relationship would be a considerable loss. He, revealed by his own fantasy of providing the love he senses she needs, has put on the 'mask' of messiah, seeing himself as the saviour of this needy and hurt individual. As 'messiah' he, in turn, has developed a dependency on Sally who reaffirms this role for him. A messiah can only be a messiah if there are souls to save. Sally, by putting him in the role of messiah, may well be providing a means by which he can deal with inadequacies in his own life. This in Rutter's theory is akin to the concept of woman as healer (p. 80).

The guilt created in the minister is great. The action, despite all his/her rationalization, is at odds with the assumed ethics of the profession and with the historic theology of the church. To live with/in the dichotomy between faith and practice is to live with the constant need to justify action, modify faith or both. The justification can take the form of 'she needed that' or 'she asked for that' or 'this was necessary for healing' or 'this would not have happened if sexual satisfaction was found at home'. A change in faith may be to develop such a rationale as 'all God created was good and therefore this is good', 'God wants all people to enjoy life' or 'the Christian view on sexual behaviour is an out-of-date document'. All of these rationalizations – and these are but a sample – place the blame for action outside the responsibility of the individual involved in the act. Responsibility is with someone else, including the victim. This avoids ownership, which calls for personal accountability.

Dealing with the issue

The way in which the church has dealt with the increase of sexual misconduct has varied. Recent events in the history of some denominations have prompted the creation of guidelines for ethical behaviour in providing pastoral care when minister and parishioner are of different genders. It seems as though most of these miss the key issue of sexuality. Such guidelines as 'never counsel a woman without having another woman present' or 'do not sit close to the person being counselled, but maintain a professional position across a desk or table' or 'fit offices with glass doors so that what is happening is clearly visible to your secretary' are superficial and situational. If such guidelines are needed, unless we are prepared to accept the myth that women are seductive and dangerous (Sipe, 1995, p. 120), there is a deeper underlying issue of human sexuality relating to the minister, which must be addressed. To simply provide guidelines and ignore the central precipitating issue is to guarantee a continuing history of sexual impropriety and abuse. They will not deal with the inner tension clergy experience around the core issue of sexuality.

There are a number of things which must happen as the church comes to grips with the issue if the tension for clergy is to be made manageable.

The first is the creation and establishment of a *theology of personhood*. Although we all (or most) affirm the value of the individual, there is a risk in pastoral situations that, consciously or unconsciously, a power imbalance is created, making the personhood of the person in need or in crisis less than that of the care giver. The needs and susceptibility of persons make them of no less value or worth and it is essential that this equality be recognized and maintained. The Apostle Paul, in his imagery of the church as the Body of Christ, pointed out that the 'parts which seem weakest are *essential* to the life of the body' (1 Cor 12.22).

Although there is a risk of a power imbalance in caring relationships for all professions, it can be a greater problem for clergy. Because the clergy are seen as representative of the Divine, there is an automatic tendency among the 'religious' to hold them in a place of importance and trust. This trust can be betrayed under guise of the spiritual, as has been the case in several recent incidents in both the UK and North America. The rationalization by clergy for their own inappropriate sexual behaviour, as reported by Rutter (1989), Rediger (1990) and Sipe (1995), demonstrates a way of thinking that lacks a healthy under-standing and theology of personhood. This, coupled with the abuse later inflicted in many cases, and the rationalization by self and others to cover the act, makes it very clear that there is a great need for a theology of personhood which not only upholds but demands the sanctity of each individual regardless of position, status and need.

Secondly, there is a need for a *theology of sexuality*. Sipe, in his book on sexuality in the Roman Catholic Church, points out two major defi-ciencies: 'the failure to understand and embrace the true sexual nature of humanity, and the resultant lack of a theology of sex in any Christian tradition' (p. 56). He further indicates that in his tradition, and this may well be applied to Protestant denominations, matters of sexuality are not taught. There seems to be a lack of current thought in the area of a theology of sexuality. McFadyen (1990) presents an understanding of wholeness based on trinitarian principle. In so doing he includes a very helpful section on sexuality. This is not to say that there are not other books and guidelines relating to sex and sexual issues. Most of these, however, are pragmatic and based on the traditional understanding of sexuality.

Sipe makes an interesting point which he gleaned from conversation with Margaret Mead. He says the teaching of his church is based on an 'archaic anthropology'. This claim, based on Mead's own view of Freud's oedipal theory as being based on a prehistoric anthropology, makes the church's teaching on sexuality, in Sipe's view, 'echoes of inherent truth, but its view of *human nature* is not validated as experi-enced and lived by reasonable and informed Christians today' (p. 50).

Sipe challenges his church to rethink its understanding and theology of sexuality and, in so doing, issues a summons to all churches to do likewise. In correspondence and conversation with a number of na-tional church leaders concerning this matter, I have often received the response 'we base our understanding on the Bible' or 'the tradition of the church'. To which the response can be given, 'Which is *what*?' To avoid the issue of sexuality in the modern world by a defence of biblicism or traditionalism is to miss the issue. The discrepancy between such thinking and the reality of modern life presents a conflict for pastors. It is to this generation that the clergy and the church must provide a ministry. The absolutism of theology/theory is at great variance with the modern reality of life. For example, many clergy would, on the basis of biblical teaching and within the tradition of their church, oppose premarital sex. However, increasing numbers coming to the church for marriage not only have experienced premarital sex, but are living together. The conflict this presents for the minister or priest is difficult to resolve.

I am not implying here that the sexual stance of society be simply moved within the gate of theological thought, baptized and sprinkled with sacred words of Grace, to make the church's thinking new, modern and acceptable. What is being called for is a dialogue out of which can come clear, but realistic, theological thought, which is understandable to the thinking and practising Christian. This applies to laity and to clergy.

The Board of Social Responsibility of the Church of England has, through its Working Party, produced an excellent discussion relating to the family, changing values and the church. In *Something to Celebrate* (1995) a careful balance is maintained between the traditional and theological stance of the church and the reality of social trends today. An example of this is the very helpful discussion of cohabitation prior to and often instead of marriage. The Working Party calls for a 'both-and' approach in recognizing that cohabitation is a step along the way in their personal journey for many people while at the same time urging Christians to hold fast to the centrality of marriage as the ideal of 'the church's understanding of how the love of God is made manifest in the sexual companionship of a man and woman' (pp. 109–18). The church, which has often been judgemental and censorious, must keep central its role as agency of reconciliation. This report is most helpful and should be carefully read by both clergy and laity.

Thirdly, there is a need to *establish clear professional ethics* which include the area of sexual behaviour between clergy and those to whom ministry is rendered. Rutter (1989) points out that ministry, unlike some other professions, does not have such a standardized code of ethics (p. 186). He attributes this primarily to two things: the fragmentation of the profession in multiple judicatory bodies, and the desire of the church to deal with ethical issues out of the public eye. There seems to be another reason, however, and one probably more germane to the problem. There is a general overall unwillingness to admit that there is a need for such guidelines and a hope that it will 'just go away'. The thought seems to be that all 'called to ministry' know that it is wrong in the eyes of God, the church and the profession and, therefore, nothing more need be said. The truth is that ministerial ethical codes, which apply to other issues but avoid this one, speak volumes by their silence. The silence implies an unwillingness to treat the matter seriously, an aversion to even raising the subject of sexuality and the hope that if it does occur, it is limited to the exceptional few.

It needs to be noted here that some church bodies have begun the process of developing guidelines. The Methodist Church (UK) has produced a helpful discussion document entitled *Some Elements of Pastoral Practice*. This paper among other things points out the vulnerability of both the person to whom ministry is provided and the minister. Being aware of this, directions are given to provide ministry with appropriate professionalism. The Diocese of Oxford (1995) has also produced a valuable *Code of Ministerial Practice* much of which is 'practical and common sense, intending to ensure there is no blurring of the professional boundaries that should be maintained in counselling and pastoral situations'. This document clearly points out the issue of power held by clergy vested in their role as 'pastor, spiritual guide and representative of the faith'. The Church of Scotland in its 1995 book of reports to the General Assembly has presented a *Code of Professional Conduct* of which only one line makes reference to 'exploit(ation) of pastoral relationships for either sexual gratification or monetary gain'.

Fourthly, there is the need to *establish boundaries* between the personal practice and lives of professionals and those they serve. Rutter (1989) and Lyall (1995) call for the establishment of such boundaries. By boundaries is meant the line or borders within a relationship which define the extremes within the range of acceptable male–female behaviour. Such boundaries when related to *space* can be clearly defined and entrance of another into 'personal space' is measurable by distance. The distance affects behaviour (Marsh, 1990, p. 44). In male–female relationships these boundaries of *behaviour* need to be defined and defended taking into consideration biblical, theological, traditional, legal and moral dynamics. It is not sufficient, as some do, simply to state biblical directives without consideration of these other factors. The boundaries must exist for both the clergy and the parishioner, although the responsibility of the minister as professional to establish and maintain such boundaries is paramount.

Clergy, having established such boundaries within their ministry, must clearly recognize when such boundaries are at risk, and when revision and modification of relationships are necessary. I use the term modification, for the minister who is called to the ministry of the whole church cannot simply transfer someone out of the church or parish because his/her boundaries are threatened. A doctor or a therapist can refer a patient to another and terminate the relationship, but this is not normally possible for the clergy. However, revision of the area in which the potential danger is apparent can be the means of defending the boundary. Fred Marshall, recognizing his own fantasy and the dependency developing in Sally, could have sought others as the primary providers of care and support, thus lessening the risk of inappropriate behaviour and yet remaining as pastor and spiritual leader for her.

Boundaries, therefore, need to be rooted in the context of a broader relationship for the clergy than for other professions. Such boundaries need to demonstrate an awareness of the holistic being of both clergy and parishioner, and thus of the multiplicity of needs which lie within each, as their boundaries come together in relationship. These boundaries, such as those which we all acknowledge exist between a father and a daughter and a mother and a son, need to be so firmly rooted that they become a natural part of interaction, without the threat of constant challenge. The foundations for healthy and natural boundaries will develop from sound theologies of personhood and sexuality.

Ultimately, there is a need for the religious world to *face the issue of sexuality* without defensiveness or our present practice of avoidance. We, the church, have avoided the issues of sexual impropriety, cringing when the press has dragged it into the public domain. In facing the issue the church, as institution, must look at its own repressive attitudes toward issues of gender and sexuality. Much of this has been generated out of power dynamics and control rather than from a theological position. This necessitates looking at the systemic problem of sexuality within the church world. This includes such issues as the stance of the church to women in ministry, the opportunity provided for female as well as male clergy within the church organization, the overcoming of deep-rooted gender stereotypes and the doing away with what still remains as 'the old boys club'. In so doing, positive progress will be made towards reducing gender oppression and the creating of a church characterized by equality.

It is imperative that as individuals we face this issue. The recognition of the problem within each one of us opens the lines of communication which enables clergy to seek help, find support and cease struggling alone with their own inner feelings of guilt and turmoil. We who serve the church are not exempt from the problem. Our humanity and, therefore, our sexuality, have not been cancelled by the call to service or the ordination by the church. In fact, it is only as we acknowledge our humanity that the ministry we offer becomes believable and valuable to others. Sipe (1995) comments 'If religion cannot tell the truth about itself, it has nothing to say' (p. 45). The writer of the letter to the

Hebrews stresses the humanity and the temptation of Christ, seeing it as the basis for effective ministry to his followers:

> For this reason he had to be made like his brothers in every way, in order that he might become a merciful and faithful high priest in service to God, and that he might make atonement for the sins of his people. Because he himself suffered when he was tempted, he is able to help those who are being tempted. (Heb 2.17–18 NIV)

The sexual orientation of clergy

The matter of ordination of gay and lesbian persons to ministry has dominated the thinking of many denominations in recent years and will be a key issue of debate for most church bodies into the next decade. This debate involves biblical understanding, theological thought, legal rights of the individual and the implication for the long-standing tradition of the church. Biblical proof-texting occurs on both sides of the debate. In addition to the diversity of theological thought, the appeal to civil and church courts over what is viewed as violation of human rights, and the claim that in its history the church has always, wittingly or unwittingly, ordained gay ministers have entered the debate. There is no intent here to deliberate on either side of the argument. The question posed here relates to the stress inherent for clergy in general and those who are gay, lesbian or bisexual. The latter, according to Kelsey (1989, p. 109), are, in the general population, the least understood and supported group. We could probably assume, therefore, that they are also the most under stress.

In the general clergy population emotions around this issue run high. They are fuelled by the changes of attitude in other professions towards individuals of same sex preference. There was a time in my own career in social work that a homosexual person in that profession would resist chance of exposure for fear of professional repercussions. During that time a male teacher suspected of homosexual behaviour was dismissed from the school system. Although recent court cases in Britain have seen similar occurrences in the Armed Forces, in a generally more inclusive society such events are not as obvious. Open admission of homosexuality among doctors, lawyers, teachers and entertainers have given almost hero status to those who dare 'exit the closet' and make their sexuality known. For clergy in general there is the tension of rethinking presuppositions concerning sexuality and, in the course of debate, the discovery that those whom they know and admire are on the opposite side of the issue. For some in denominations that declare openness to the ordination of homosexuals, the tension has proven too much. Disillusioned, a number of clergy have simply left the ministry of major denominations which have taken such a stance in recent years. New and growing denominations and churches have sprung up primarily as a reaction against gay/lesbian ordination. This heated issue, with changing thinking and theology, coupled with the human dimension of each revelation, prompts a stress reaction for all.

Studies show, however, that those who are gay and lesbian clergy have a higher level of stress than their heterosexual colleagues. Fletcher (1990, pp. 47–51) discovered a substantially higher level of stress among homosexuals than among the general population of the clergy of the Church of England. In that study, he identified four major areas in which stress was experienced by this group of clergy. These included:

(1) *Increased risk of psychopathology*: Although evidence is scarce as to whether homosexual men are more prone to psychiatric disorders, there was evidence of increased levels of depression and a higher incidence of stress. It is not certain if this is caused by a predisposition towards depression and stress or if it is precipitated by relational dynamics, not the least of which is coping in a predominantly heterosexual world.

(2) *Lack of adequate control and social support structures*: The lack of the support of a life partner and the structural support readily available to other clergy may cause increased tension, greater sense of being alone, and stress.

(3) *Particular risk due to religious vocation*: Ambiguity around identity may arise from biblical and theological understanding. Additionally, the conservative nature of the church may mean homosexual clergy are called to serve in a community of faith which has radically different values and norms.

(4) *Prejudice in the community*: Social pressures brought to bear by a community which is, in general, unsympathetic to homosexuals will precipitate tension and isolation.

The previous discussion of levels of relationships and isolation becomes relevant here. There can be little doubt concerning the increased isolation experienced by homosexual clergy. This was made clear by a minister who disclosed his homosexuality in an interview conducted during my research. Separated from family, he did not feel he could share his personal struggle with colleagues. He feared rejection by the parish, if discovered, and had no confidence in the reaction of his denomination. He acknowledged the fear of suicide, the constant need for psychiatric care and the lonely travail of a tormented soul. He was alone.

All of this acknowledges the increased stress gay and lesbian clergy face. Rediger (1990) gives a number of case studies with helpful evaluations. In all of these, the tension arising from issues of identity, guilt, isolation and sexual frustration is evident. For clergy who are homosexual, or bisexual in orientation, stress is a critical factor. They experience little opportunity for support. They walk alone with their inextricable burden. It is essential that the church, in dealing with this difficult issue, recognizes this need in the lives of their clergy and provides the pastoral support and care worthy of the love it professes.

9

![black bars]

Stress in the vicarage

The identity of the family

The fact that there is today a crisis of marriage and the family and that neurosis is constantly on the increase can no longer be ignored ... Love is lacking everywhere and cannot be evoked by an act of will. People who have no proper home in childhood go through life with an unsettled account ...

Any solution must be based on a realization of the changed situation that has arisen ... this means reexamining our attitudes to others, especially the opposite sex, as well as the forces of destiny which govern us and even to God.   (Jacobi, 1976, pp. 75, 76)

This chapter is about the silent victims of stress. They are the ones who share the space closest to the minister, the home. It is about the spouse and children of the clergy. The term silent is not used because they have failed to raise their voices, but rather because they have often not been heard. Sometimes the cry of desperation to be heard and taken seriously has been so loud that the term rebellious and unmanageable has been applied. The plea for attention as individuals in their own right has often been missed, creating great pain for all involved. Much has been written about ministers, the ministry, the stress and strain of office and other facets of the profession. Little has been said about the stress of those who make up the family of the clergy, the first family of the church.

The integrated unit of the pastoral home is as one. Those things which affect the minister affect the family. That which impacts the family will have ramifications for the minister and ministry. Although the reactive nature of the relationship is evident, the way in which the stress of the family plays into the equation is often ignored. The emphasis and concern is placed primarily on, or for, the ministers. The way in which any pressure affects them becomes the focus of attention. But what about the family? The way in which they, the clergy, affect the stress levels of their spouse, children and collective household is not given equal space. While conducting my research among the clergy of

125

the Church of Scotland the question was often raised by spouses and by families: 'What about us? Are you going to look at the isolation factor and stress of the family?' A separate section of the study was devoted to the family and spouse and interviews, where possible, involved the spouse. This was admittedly inadequate, as will be the coverage I can give in this section. I will, however, consider some issues, raising flags of concern and pointing to the mutual effects of tension on both family and pastor.

Davidson and Cooper (1983), in their comparative study of stress in the work place, identified the home and partner relationship as the third highest ranked stressor for women and the seventh highest for men. In this study issues of nurture of relationship with a spouse or partner, care of children, maintenance of a home, and family communication were seen as sources of tension and anxiety. We have seen in the section on women in ministry and stress that this has an effect on women in ministry consistent with the study mentioned above. It may not, however, be as representative of men in ministry. The nature of the position, as one who stands for the high priority and sanctity of marriage and the family, places the issue in a far more central position in their thought and action. Secondly, faced with the pastoral care of families in crisis and individuals with marital conflict and distress, the minister is constantly confronted by his/her own situation, as though, somehow, in the lives of others, seeing his/her life mirrored. This, coupled with having their time preoccupied with the demands of others, as most clergy are apt to have, presents a scenario where little control seems possible. Loss of control, as we have seen in Chapter 2, brings with it its own dynamic of stress. For the family of clergy, spouse and children, the same is true. Being a part of the clergy home and closely associated with the church can be a source of constant stress and one, which for them also, seems outside their direct control.

We will consider some general dynamics which contribute to the equation followed by more specific factors which are applicable.

General dynamics

Tension of balance

Clergy are usually very committed people. They have strong commitments to the God who calls them, the church they serve and the family of which they are a part. Bowman (1996) in a preliminary report on his study of clergy stress within a specific diocese comments:

> Clergy tend to have strong assumptions of what a good husband should be like. The turbulence begins when a priest feels that the demands and expectations placed on him by his work are making it

increasingly hard for him to live according to his assumptions of what he or she should be like as a good husband and father, or wife and mother.

The creating of an equable balance between these commitments presents problems. The demands of the church can be all-consuming. The call to the bedside of a dying parishioner, to intervene in a family conflict or to provide help to a school as a class of children cope with the sudden death of a classmate cannot be ignored or delayed. Similarly, the needs of one's own family create the experiences common to all, of rides to band practice, medical emergencies, school concerts and a spouse who, tired after his/her own day, needs fellowship and support. How does one find a balance?

In the last chapter we considered the identity of the clergy. We noted the risk of an identity which is established in the external world, predominantly as 'minister' centred in the tasks of ministry. This identity demands that one be seen in a strong role as priest, preacher, pastor, counsellor, scholar and other such areas. These can become, in his/her thinking, validations of success, and hence the primary drivers in life. Inadequacy in these roles would be, in their thinking and as they perceive in the thinking of others, symptomatic of failure. Balance then between the various demands of life becomes difficult for these primary drivers making all other factors, including spouse and family, secondary. Many a minister blames their own over-intensity in ministry and the drive to succeed for the loss of in-depth relationships with their child(ren) and the child's subsequent departure from the church. This realization often comes too late and the 'if I had to do it again ... ' becomes indicative of opportunities in life which pass but once.

It is not that the clergy would choose a secondary role for the family, but rather that it becomes the easiest, in some ways, to sacrifice on the altar of success. The thought is always there that the family somehow will hold together and be more easily restored by acts of attention. These often come too late and offer too little.

Managing time and energy

A balanced strong commitment to ministry, marriage and family calls for a *stewardship of time and energy*. To act with stewardship can be difficult and frustrating. There are no limits to the task of ministry and therefore there is rarely a time when the minister is free from responsibilities, at least so he/she thinks. If it is not the activity of meeting upon meeting or appointment upon appointment there is the need to prepare for a service or study for a sermon. Equally there are no time or energy limits to being a spouse and parent. This of course could be said of any profession or job as it relates to the maintaining of a marriage and the raising of a family. However, there are some unique factors to the stewardship of time and energy as it relates to the homes of the clergy.

Probably the greatest dilemma is the synchronization of the tasks of ministry and the raising of a family. Societal scheduling tends to function primarily on a daytime activity of work which begins on a Monday morning and ends on a Friday afternoon. The TGIF (Thank God It's Friday) syndrome, predominant in the work world, is exemplified by the Friday 5:30 exodus from the work place to the rejoicing of the 'Happy Hour' in the local establishments of libation. School is over for another week and children look forward to a weekend of fun and activities. Families leave for a weekend outing, camping or visiting grandparents. But what about the home of the clergy?

For them the sabbath rest is broken by a parent who works what is his/her hardest and most stressful day of the week. There is little or no opportunity for those special outings or family events. For the clergy these are the days of working with the church, that volunteer organization, whose members work the rest of the week. These days become the times for special activities, church conferences, training sessions, bazaars or group outings.

The times when the children and family of the clergy are most available are also the times when the church family is most available for activities as a church unit. This applies to the nights for meetings, the weekends for events and the special holidays such as Christmas and Easter, which become a pressure-packed flurry of activity for the clergy and, often, their family. Activities, which may involve the family, also involve others, allowing little personal or private time for the intimacy of relationship.

Stewardship of time and energy becomes difficult for another reason. The task of ministry, with its intersection with the intimate lives of others, is energy draining. Even if time can be scheduled there is the question of energy. Drained by demands of office, the further involvement with family may call for more energy than is readily available. Family times can be short changed by the minister still working over in his/her mind Sunday's sermon, the trauma of a parishioner, or the conflict with a church board or leader. The times of 'together' may be so drained of energy that they become negative, not happy moments to be remembered.

Appropriate stewardship of time and energy is a major issue and often a point of marital conflict. The desire for it may lead to the establishment of, what has been termed by some, quality time. This is often short (quality as opposed to quantity) times of what is deemed, often by the parent, as meaningful activity. However, often children want parents simply to be, not do, and thus, by their presence, establish for the child a sense of their own value and worth. The response of a parent to the child's accusation 'you were never there for us' is 'look at all the things we did' (naming special activities and events). What the child is referring to, however, is not the quality of short-term interaction, but the security of an ongoing presence found in a healthy parent–child relationship.

Maintaining the image

There is a need to create and maintain an image appropriate to the family of the minister. This, however, can become not a real, but an idealized image. As I have maintained from the very beginning, the identity of the clergy is wrapped up in the idealized concept imposed by both those things which have shaped their personal history and those which are imposed by external sources. So it is with the idea of the family. The 'image' of the family is idealized to be one which is consistent with that which the clergy imposes upon him/herself. Standards of behaviour, participation in church activities, creating a priority in life which gives a primary place to the religious, and the avoidance of 'misbehaviour' become issues evaluated as much by their image potential as by their inherent correctness. These issues are important for many Christian parents who want their children to become good 'Christian' citizens. But the demands sometimes imposed by the clergy upon their own families can be, and often are, greater than those for others. The dress code of torn blue jeans and sweatshirt may be acceptable for the rebellious child of a parishioner simply because it is good to see him/her in church. For the children of the clergy, however, traditionally acceptable dress is expected. For the clergy's children, this maintaining of an image gives an air of hypocrisy to the religious, the church and even family life as they have experienced it.

It is important that we recognize that this is an 'idealized' image. It is a view of the clergy family not shared by all within the church. The imaginary nature, which I identified in Chapter 2, of some expectations must also be applied to the pastors' view of what others expect of their family. Again, the diversity of the church and its aging population may mean that concepts of family and child-rearing held by some, even the majority, of the church are different from current practices. However, those church members who are at the stage of parenting similar to the clergy may see things radically differently. As their loyalties have shifted from institution to relationships, as is characteristic of the postwar generation, so they see their children and those of the clergy as having greater need of relational activity rather than simply of loyalty to the church and its activities. For instance it may be better to allow a child to attend an activity in the community with friends rather than insisting on attendance at a church function where no other children of his/her age are present.

Attributing the power

A fourth issue is that of *power dynamics: visible and invisible.* The *visible* power is often centred around the clergyperson and the need to control what is seen as an affront to his/her position and identity. This control often is exercised unilaterally and with strictness which may be inconsistent with that of the child's peer group. This phenomenon can exist for the whole family in the demand for a standard 'different' from that of others.

> For Stephen, as pastor of a small evangelical church, it was important that his daughter dress appropriately and frequent places which he believed were fitting the child of a minister. When his 16-year-old daughter, Susan, bounced down the stairs in a miniskirt and makeup and announced that she was off to the school dance his reaction was explosive. No daughter of his was going out like that let alone to a 'dance'. It was even worse when Cheryl, his wife, defended Susan with comments that this dress was in style, the dance was well chaperoned and that the young friend with whom she was going was from the youth group of St John's church. The night ended with Stephen shouting, Susan crying in her room and Cheryl trying to establish reconciliation (a theological term sometimes forgotten in the clergy home).

Stephen demonstrated a rigidity in his demands which was not shared by any others of the household. Ignoring the need for Susan to participate in 'normal' teenage experiences, the perspective of Cheryl, and the quality of the escort, he acted as the unquestionable centre of control. All involved needed to respond to his demands in order to maintain what he felt was 'fitting the child of a minister'.

Specific to the minister's home is the additional dynamic of the *invisible* power which relates to the 'God' factor in the actions of many clergy. Actions of busyness, church responsibility at the expense of home and family, uprooting of family through transfer, and control over family and individual are because of the demand of 'God' as ultimate authority. This sometimes is a spoken control, but, more often, is simply implied. The very priority of church (God) affairs over activities of family, implies that 'His' demands are more important, and therefore more powerful, than any earthly demands. When the minister is driven by some invisible force, resulting in insufficient energy remaining to fulfil the important role of mother or father, God is interpreted as being the compelling power. This is especially true around the 'call' to or relocation in a new church.

All of this illustrates that the power dynamics, which should be resident within the family unit, shared by husband and wife and released to children as they mature, remain predominantly with an individual and attributed to a power beyond the control of any. The healthy sharing of control, which creates an environment conducive for familial growth and development, cannot exist. For the clergy, the tension of the family environment, coupled with increasing guilt and the overall feeling that things are beyond control, may create a primary source of stress.

Specific issues

We have looked at some general factors which influence the clergy family and which, in so doing, present the risk of tension and conflict. These are stressors which are more evident for the clergy than for other professionals because they are rooted in image, appearance and control. There are some specific factors which have been recurrent themes in my research and in broader based conversations with clergy and their family. These may not apply to all clergy families.

Living in a goldfish bowl

Traditionally the parsonage (vicarage or manse) was built adjacent to the church, often in a prominent location near the centre of the community. Here the minister was close to his (it was at that time always male) work and he could service the needs of the community from a central location. The prestigious location provided both high visibility and support for the image of the clergy as shaper of community and, to some degree, resident authority. This high visibility, for many clergy families, presented a problem relating to privacy and 'ownership' of their place of residence. It, for many, ceased to be the private domain of the family.

This became evident in a number of ways. For some families there was always the risk of intrusion, if not into the heart of the home, at least to the boundaries. Clergy and their families commented in the research on such simple things as gardening, sunbathing and playing sports with the children raising comments from 'observers'. Some comments were simply small talk, others in jest, while some generated out of a sense that the activity of the family violated their 'idealized' perspective of how parsonage families should function. One minister commented how he would not put in a garden – gardening was one of his favourite activities – because of the constant joking he received from some members of his predominantly farming community church. Another family ceased to sunbathe in 'their' backyard because 'observers' thought this was unsuitable for the minister's family. These, of course, are extremes, but do point to the invasion of privacy,

It is fine to say that a stiff upper lip and fortitude is needed to stand against this invasion of privacy, but when it is constant it becomes a very wearing experience. Even the opportunity to enjoy a family barbecue in the backyard presents the risk that the boundary will be violated and that someone will opt to enter into the property to which they claim ownership. For the family of the clergy, there can be no claim of 'this is our home' for it lacks the privacy which means that within 'our home' I/we can act as I/we see appropriate.

Fortunately, the trend away from church-owned houses is overcoming this difficulty. The rationale given for private home ownership by the clergy is the value of entering the market thus allowing the development of a housing equity. Although this is a valid reason it seems that the opportunity to overcome the difficulty of 'living in someone else's housing' is a far greater justification. To live in a home where walls can be painted purple or psychedelic without permission of a board or fear of criticism serves to establish a family unit which has a place to call its own. You may not do it, but you need to have the right. But for many in the traditional church, ownership by others continues to be reality. For the household of the clergy it becomes a source of frustration and tension.

Public family and private life

Being the clergy family in the community is a little like being one of the Royals. Not that there are photographers and journalists who follow the family, but that, for some reason, the business of the clergy family is public domain and open for public approval or criticism. Of the 131 spouses surveyed in the study of the Church of Scotland some 62 per cent indicated they felt, to varying degrees, that their family was treated differently because they were viewed as being the clergy family. Again it is important to point out that the average stay of this group of clergy and family in a community was 8.9 years, which should have allowed sufficient time for assimilation into the community. This 'difference' was primarily related to differing expectations.

Public ownership of the clergy family has been evidenced in a number of different ways. This may range from the indirect criticism of the children or child-rearing practices to direct disciplinary comments to the children themselves. It is akin to the interference of grandparents in child-rearing situations, except without the family ties. The concept that, somehow, a group of people outside the immediate family have any say in the way in which the family operates or deems what is appropriate behaviour, is the primary cause of stress.

Equally, this affects the way in which the spouses of the clergy are viewed within church and community. The report by the United Reformed Church, *Stress in the Ministry* (1987, p. 12), made the following statement: 'The spouse of the minister cannot be just an ordinary member of the congregation. Everyone has feelings about how the minister's wife should behave or be involved in the church.' The same report goes on to speak of the minister's family as being 'idealized ... the public image is that of all sweetness and light ... no conflict ... a commendable attitude of service to everyone. The family is about the Lord's business therefore the highest standards have to be maintained' (p. 19). There is little wonder that the family of the minister feel like public property, shaped by the expectations of others.

The church widow(er)

A minister's wife commented 'Tom is married to the church. I never see him any more.' The term 'widow' or 'widower' here does not imply the actual death of the minister partner, but rather a neglect of the marriage and a preoccupation with other activity. (The term 'golf widow' is often heard.) Again the nature of ministry, which consumes days, evenings and weekends, accentuates the times of separation and the aloneness of the spouse. In the study 9 per cent of the clergy said they spent no evenings at home, while 46 per cent said they spent only one evening a week at home with their family. The sense of aloneness was often commented on by younger clergy families where the spouse needed to remain home with a young family.

It is important to note here that a considerable number of ministers expressed open concern for the isolation and aloneness experienced by their family. They indicated that the demands on their time prevented them from having sufficient private time with their marriage partner and with the children. The number of nights spent on church work prevented them from participating in the raising of the family, especially during the developmental years. These concerns, accompanied by what the ministers viewed as unrealistic expectations, placed on the spouse by the church, were obviously a source of stress for them.

Robbed of relationship
We have already noted above the lack of adequate time and opportunity for the development of relationship which often plagues the

minister and his/her spouse. The marital relationship, which should exist within Level 7, the Intimate Encounter, is in danger of regressing to a lower level, losing the intimate and spiritual dynamic. Bowman in his preliminary report noted that vicars' wives suffered loneliness and unsatisfactory love lives. More than 60 per cent of the respondents in his study indicated that their work-load interfered with their love life (Bowman, 1996). Such loss of relationship is tragic and affects the personhood of both partners, the family unit, children as individuals, and life and ministry in general. The greatest gift that parents can give to their children is a happy marriage.

The minister's spouse may also lack opportunity for meaningful relationships at other levels. A number of respondents during the study indicated that they felt more isolated than their minister partner. This view was justified by the fact that the minister was involved in relational activity in his/her work, while the spouse was isolated within the home. This, coupled with the caution that even for the spouse to have close friends may be interpreted as favouritism, prevented healthy relationships from developing.

Again it is important to indicate that we are referring to the concept of 'close' friendships as in the fifth, sixth and seventh levels of relationship. For the spouse, as with the minister, much activity can occur within the Level 4 range of work and church. These can be friendly, regular, varied and even enjoyable. The difficulty occurs in the lack of meaningful relationships which permit the inner personal needs to be explored without fear or loss. The question was asked as to whether they (the spouses), because of their position, found it difficult to make close personal friends in the community. Of the 131 spouses who responded to the questionnaire, 26 per cent strongly agreed that this was the case, while an additional 28 per cent gave moderate agreement.

A large portion of the respondents, some 71 per cent, felt it may be the case that most people only made the effort to know them as the 'minister's spouse' rather than as individuals. This allowed for little opportunity to establish a personal identity other than that attached to the office of the minister. It becomes obvious that for many husbands and wives of the clergy, relationships are difficult to establish and hard to maintain because of their position.

The brunt of frustrations
I have referred above to the possible loss of intimacy within the marriage. There is a further step which presents difficulty within the relationship: negative intimacy. I have already pointed out that the clergy, lacking their own deep relationships, have little opportunity to

vent their inner emotions. Fears, frustrations, anxieties, doubts and even anger can become suppressed beneath the image (persona) presented in the public domain. These, and other emotions, cannot always be expressed in the context of work. The spouse and the family may become the recipients as transference of these emotions occurs within what is viewed as the 'safety' of the home. This misdirected reaction within the home caused by what has happened in the work place destroys intimacy, leaving the recipient(s) victimized emotionally, if not physically.

There is an additional underlying effect of this problem of transference. The spouse, aware of the frustration of his/her partner, may seek to protect her/him from the additional problems of family and home. Sensing the pressures of ministry, he/she may seek to bear alone the difficulties that they face daily within their lives. Lacking his/her own adequate levels of relationship and support, the spouse internalizes both the emotional frustration of the partner and the pressures of all that they face within daily life. The problem becomes compounded, and in the extreme, collapse of the system, personal and family, may well occur.

Church expectations
There has been within the tradition of many churches an expectation around the 'role' of the minister's spouse. This may vary from simply an open supportive role of their spouse's ministry to specific functions or offices within the church. Much of this seems to have developed out of the traditional role of the 'minister's wife' as President of the Missionary Society (or some such church organization) and convener of social activities within the church.

Fortunately, most, if not all, of these stereotypes around the role of the minister's spouse are gone or greatly diminished in today's church world. However, there may well remain a subtle residue. There is still the expectation among many church members that the family, and especially the spouse, should participate fully in all functions of church life. Each, of course, sees this from their own limited participation in the life of the church and applies it specifically to that domain. The Sunday School Superintendent needs a teacher. The choir director needs an alto. The social convener needs a cake baked. The missionary society needs a president and the youth leaders think it would be great if the pastor and his/her spouse were involved in their programme. So it goes on. Given, however, the diversity of the ministry of most churches today, this may well place undue expectations on the minister's partner. All of these expectations show little or no awareness of the intense supportive role played by the marriage partner of the minister who is often chief confidant, advisor, emotional and physical supporter, as well as primary care giver in the home and with the family.

Tangled emotions
In the study, many of the respondents expressed satisfaction and joy in being part of a shared calling. These respondents recognized the difficulties of the task which both they and their partners encountered in ministry and faced them with realism. Both the questionnaire responses and the interviews revealed, as is common to all, a range of mixed emotions: joy, sadness, frustration, hope, loneliness – sometimes to the point of isolation, fear and, at times, anger. Most, if not all, seemed to be able to cope well in spite of all of these.

It is recognized that all persons in their daily life have a similar range of feelings and emotions. However, several things become evident. The intimate and personal nature of ministry often makes these emotions more intense for the minister and, therefore, for his/her spouse. Furthermore, the minister and, therefore, his/her spouse become the focal point for most, if not all, that occurs in the community of faith and, to some degree, in the broader community. This, coupled with the lack of relational support, can make the tangle of emotions difficult to manage and, in some instances, hard to resolve. Many of the respondents expressed their need and stated they would appreciate pastoral care and advice.

A career outside the home
It became evident during the review of the questionnaire responses as well as during the interviews that an increasing number of clergy spouses are involved in their own career outside the home. This gave some interesting insight into isolation as it related to the spouse of the minister. A number stated clearly that isolation had been a problem prior to their working career. This had been partially caused by what they perceived as a lack of personal identity. They felt the church viewed them primarily in the traditional role as the minister's spouse.

Working spouses indicated that having their own career gave them a greater sense of identity. One respondent stated she had 'become recognized in my own right at work and this has been my salvation'. One who had left a career to minister with her husband indicated that she 'suffered a severe loss of identity' and that 'all normal, mutually supportive meetings of professions are now closed to me'.

A career also provided working spouses with a circle of friends not associated with the church. This allowed for varying depths of relationship without the normal difficulties of church relationships. Some also stated that their work career outside the parish gave them a more objective view of parish life, thus allowing them to adjust better both in the home and church.

The child(ren) of the vicarage

I write this section from three perspectives: having been one, raised three, and talked to many. In my own tradition the child of the parsonage was called a PK (preacher's kid) and we often hung around together to share our difficulties and brag about our (mis)adventures. (After all we had to give some credence to the rhyme: 'Elder's daughter and preacher's son, the worst devils which ever did run.')

It is difficult being the child of such a public family. This is especially true in smaller communities where anonymity is limited or impossible. In such communities news of misbehaviour often made it home before the child did. As stated above there is a certain public ownership of the family of the minister and the standards applied are sometimes inconsistent with those applied to other children of the community. The expectation or the assumption that the minister's child should always be participant in the activity of the church places undue expectations on the individual. When the minister's son or daughter misses a youth group on a specific night because it conflicts with a sport practice the absence often is not readily accepted and the question of priorities is raised. The pressure on the child may be from both the minister parent, who wants to maintain a positive image, and the church members/ leadership, who think the child of their pastor should be setting an example in establishing priorities. Living within these expectations may lead to a childhood deprived of normal participation in the broader activities of the community.

However, there is a counterbalance to this public ownership and expectations. There comes with being the child of the minister a special status prompted by recognition and identity. The child moves into the community of faith as someone 'special' and is quickly recognized as such. He/she may receive special attention, be given special privileges and is certainly seem by his/her peer group as an 'insider' to the functioning of the church. All of this brings status and identity which may not be afforded others within the peer group. This identity, of course, at other levels is lost when the child is not recognized as John or Jane in their own right, but simply as the minister's son or daughter.

There are several issues which consistently are reported as problematic for the child of the minister.

Moving and lost relationships

Loss of relationships through moving and resettlement are difficult for all, adult and child alike. For the children of the clergy this is no less the case. The transitory nature of ministry in many, if not most, denominations means that the children of the minister experience a number of such moves within their childhood and youth. These moves involve the terminating or changing of relationships which are vitally important in the lives and development of young people. Friendships which have deepened and have become meaningful are radically altered and, at times, lost.

The decision to move has traditionally been based on the 'call' or 'appointment' to another charge sensed or experienced by, primarily, the minister. At times, little or no consultation has been made with the children (or for that matter the spouse). For the child, the move and subsequent loss of relationship is beyond their control. They are not 'called' or under the directive of 'appointment' and in their perspective they become the victim of yet another move. This is especially tragic in some denominations in North America where the average stay in a charge is under two years. In situations where God is seen as the primary issuer of the 'call', the child may well develop an anger and distrust towards one who would destroy their relationships and take away their friends. This is not different from the blaming of God for the death of a loved one.

There is a need to recognize the trauma for the child(ren) of the minister each time a move occurs. Children need to be part of the decision-making process. This calls for sensitive consultation, honest appraisal of the situation, and the openness to allow the dismay, anger and sadness to be displayed. There is the need to help the child(ren) through the grieving process. With grief there comes a deep sense of loss which may precipitate depression (Hart, 1984, pp. 55ff.). There may be need for pastoral care from someone they feel they can trust outside the family system.

Availability

A second matter of concern often expressed by the child of the parsonage relates to the availability of the father or mother who is the minister. As we have seen the schedule of the minister is inconsistent with family life. Evenings and days off may not coincide with the time children are home from school and desirous of their parent's attention. The statements are often heard, 'Dad/mom was never there for me' or 'They were always so busy with the church'. The report *Stress in the Ministry* comments 'When the family does come together "church talk" dominates the conversation. "Dad never switches off." ' (Pratt, 1987, p. 20).

There is a need for both the intensity of those 'special' times and the simple presence and availability of the parent figure. It is often in the closeness of 'being' that the intimacies of inner thoughts and curious questions are disclosed. The structured 'quality time', often based more on action than on being, is hardly conducive to these moments. There is also the need to recognize that family activities with the minister parent often, of necessity, occur in the church setting. When this happens interaction is at the relational Level 4 (the Working Encounter). The minister is performing a part of his/her responsibility and the family, like all others, is a recipient of that action. The family has no more, and maybe even less, ownership of the minister than anyone else present. In relational activities, more attention may be paid to others than to members of the family. While the child and minister are participating in the same event the relationship is not equal to that of other parents and children. I was surprised when my adult son said to me recently 'Dad, what I wanted most on a Sunday morning was for you to come and sit with me'. Although both of us recognized the near impossibility of this occurring more than a couple of times a year, it is indicative of a child's need simply to be with a parent.

For the most part I, as an active clergyman – and I am sure this applies to many others – spent too little time with my children during their growing-up years. As important as the task of ministry is, the responsibility to the family is greater. If both are granted to an individual under the providence of God, then the need to hold them in a healthy balance is not only necessary, but paramount.

The insider's view

As was said in the beginning of this chapter, those who share the home with the minister see him/her in a different manner from those outside the home. The persona, evident to the church and community, is not as clearly evident within the safe atmosphere of the home. This is not to imply a Jekyll-and-Hyde dynamic to the clergy, but as we have seen, the socially acceptable image maintained in the public domain is not always consistent with that of the private domain. This is consistent with people in general although the difference may be more pronounced because of the sacred image of the clergy which sometimes sacrifices their humanity. The 'Could we have quietness?' in the church meeting may be a 'SHUT-UP' in the home or the slip on the church step which produces an 'Oops' may become a 'Damn' in the parsonage.

The above illustrations offered in half jest are not often major. There can, however, be major areas of differences which are difficult for a child to comprehend. Conflict, common to every home and marriage, needs to be tucked behind a mask as the family goes to church and one of the parents leads the congregation in worship and praise. Now other families in the church experience similar masking of emotions, but for the child of the minister the change is greater and more pronounced as his/her parent becomes the representative of God and proclaimer of the ideal Christian life. At times, even the words spoken in worship and in proclamation appear inconsistent with what has occurred before in the home and will probably continue shortly thereafter. Recently the divorced wife of a former minister related the story of how, on a Sunday morning, after a traumatic experience in the home which included physical abuse, her husband preached a sermon entitled 'The Christian home'. Although this hopefully is a rare and extreme case the transference of frustrations and emotions within the home can at time create, in the eyes of the child(ren), an inconsistency that is difficult to reconcile. The 'realness' of both the individual and what they stand for may be held in question.

It is necessary to acknowledge that, to some degree, this occurs in all of our homes. It is a fact of life and is often not so much a question of integrity as it is of our humanness. There is a need to be open and honest with those who share our most intimate space, the home. Voicing of emotions, even anger, is not wrong, but healthy. For our children to experience the fact that we, the clergy, are emotional beings like all others makes us real. To help children cope with emotions is a healthy part of growth and development. We need, however, to be honest when transference occurs and frustrations and emotions are misdirected. Working this through with those in the home, admitting wrong, and seeking forgiveness is all part of a healthy development and totally consistent with the very nature of the gospel we seek to proclaim.

The church family needs a pastor

What has become obvious through the study is that the home of the minister may well be the only one within the church without a pastor. The minister may be priest, in the sense of leading his/her family in spiritual matters, but it is not possible for them to be a pastor to their own family. A doctor cannot and does not treat family members. A psychiatrist does not act as therapist to relatives. A lawyer loses perspective in representing a member of the family. The loss of objectivity and the need for all parties involved to have open freedom of expression without fear of repercussions within the home make this equally true for the clergy. The clergy family must have the opportunity to seek pastoral care and advice from a source which they perceive as objective and without bias. They, like all others, need to have one who cares for them as their pastor, not confusing that care with that of spouse or parent. They must have the opportunity to seek advice which may well pertain to relationships within marriage and the home. They, too, require a confidant with whom they can share their inner joys, doubts, fears and the innermost needs of their being.

It is important that those of the minister's household be encouraged to find their pastoral care giver in someone other than their partner or parent. Opportunity to seek objective guidance at this level may well prevent crisis at another.

Removing the family's mask

A family, like an individual, has a persona which it presents in the public domain. This we could call a collective persona, one which is jointly shaped and worn by the family unit. As with the individual, the persona is not, in and of itself, a negative phenomenon. The difficulty occurs when it becomes shaped more by the outer world of demands and less by the inner world of emotions and spiritual relationships. When the family must always present a 'mask' to the world, regardless of what is happening at its soul, there is a risk that the persona will become fixed and hardened. Little care is then given to the inner collective being or to the needs of individuals within the family.

For the families of the clergy, as with the clergy themselves, there is a considerable risk of this occurring. The need to set examples and to model behaviour can place, wittingly or unwittingly, demands upon the family to conform to externally set standards. This collective persona for the clergyperson's family is shaped not only by the church's expectations, but also by his/her perception of what is expected. This is not negative except when the concern for 'image' jeopardizes or risks the inner dynamics of emotion and spirit.

We who are clergy must help our families to recognize the family persona and to be real within it. Our homes experience all the same dynamics as any family coping in a rapidly changing world. The requirements of our children are no different from those of any others in church or community. Our children must be allowed to grow up in a real world in which the church is a part, but not the only shaper of life.

In commendation of clergy parents

This chapter, for me, has been the most difficult to write. While working on it I had the feeling that I was constantly being negative and that readers would think all clergy families were in trouble.

There are many clergy families who are enjoying happy family life, developing with healthy perspectives and who have found their own and real identity as a family. To these there is a resounding 'Congratulations' for a job well done and for creating a balance in life. It is my sincere hope that this extends to the majority of families.

This chapter has developed out of the concerns voiced to me by many: respondents during the conducting of the study; pastors encountered on a regular basis; and the children of clergy who struggle with their faith and who, in some cases, have opted to leave it behind. In hearing their cry and, indeed, their most inner concern I have sought here to raise their issues. It is hoped that by increasing an awareness of the need solutions to the difficulties will be sought and found. A greater degree of sensitivity, I believe, is needed by all of us, as we seek to raise a family within the church and world. The needs of the family are equally as important, if not more so, than any need we face within the church. Yet, too often, our busyness in serving others eclipses our availability and care of our own families.

The church will be there long after the family nest is empty. Enjoy the time while they are present and cement strong relationships for the future.

Section Four

The quest for identity and wholeness

10

The quest for the grail of wholeness

> The saints proved themselves as such, not so much by their doing as by
> their being, as men who lived from the love of Christ and in His love.
> What makes us true saints is not our action.
>
> (E. Brunner, *Dogmatics*, III, p. 303)

Where does the search for wholeness begin? We have considered the
dynamics of ministry in this latter end of the twentieth century. The
demise of the church seems inevitable, at least as an institution of
central importance and significance to the prevailing culture of the day.
Its role as a sub-culture, and even as counter-culture, is hardly one it
accepts easily and for much of the church there is still the devitalizing
attempt to regain the glory of yesterday. This struggle, with all its
pressure for the clergy to do the miraculous, creates a demoralizing
effect as the grandeur of the past can never be reclaimed, except in
embellished memory.

How then, in the light of a role identity of diminishing importance
and relevance can the minister begin to move toward wholeness that is
real and not simply rationalization? The risk as we have seen is to be
driven to do the impossible, and, even in the light of our inability to
succeed, to take comfort in the brilliancy of the attempt.

Up to this point, however, we have considered primarily the minister
and his/her role and identity from a sociological perspective. Even our
theological considerations have been in terms as they are influenced by
and in turn apply to society. We must now consider the inner journey
towards wholeness and a growing spiritual identity. Secular humanism
would have us believe that the former can be gained without the latter.
The converse of that is the belief that if one becomes 'Christian' a
healing occurs which brings with it total wholeness. Neither of the
extremes appears correct. Wholeness is a journey involving all of being.
It is not a destination to be reached but one which can be approximated
at various times and for varying duration. If, however, these approx-
imations of whole feeling, which are brief moments in time and space,

become fixed they cause stagnancy. This fixed view of wholeness then becomes a source of tension as it tries to relate to the changing diversity of life. The United Reformed Church report *Stress in Ministry* (Pratt, 1987) cited as one of the apparent causes an attitude that was fixed and rigid. This usually generates from an attitude of arrival at a destination in growth rather than an outlook based on onward movement in personal development and growth. Kelsey, seeing this movement towards wholeness as a journey, comments:

> The journey towards wholeness involves bringing all of ourselves –
> both our conscious life in the ordinary world and the depth of our
> psyches and our experience of the spiritual world – to all of the divine
> reality we can know. As we grow in knowledge of ourselves and the
> Holy, our practices will change. (1989, p. 84)

Consider the journey through the following phases.

The presence of paradox

As we have been considering throughout these pages, the life of the minister is based on a series of paradoxical concepts. These relate to the understanding of person, role, status and position in the sociological and greater cosmic order. Add to this the theological diversity which has been historically established, traditionally transmitted, continually modified as denominationally and politically expedient, and the constant interface of faith with changing culture and the perception becomes even more complex. To attempt to live within this diversity is to be pulled by polarized forces which are fractional rather than integrative to a sense of wholeness. It is out of this potential fragmentation and ambiguity of identity, both personal and role, that stress is experienced.

The road to wholeness begins with a recognition of these diversities and the establishment of the process to integrate them into a reconciled state within us. It is helpful at this point, as we discuss the journey to wholeness, to bring into sharper focus some of the primary paradoxes already raised. In so doing we set the stage for resolution.

There exists the tension between *doing and being*. The function of ministry as an outer-world experience can create a busyness which denies the satisfaction of the inner being. This, as we have seen, is the root of separation from professional co-operation, relational support, and places at risk the basis for spiritual nurture. Ministry is increasingly defined as a 'doing' profession in today's world of activism and productivity.

This gives rise to the dichotomy between the *secular and the sacred*. The 'other worldliness' of the role of the minister appears at time in conflict with the physical and rationalistic world which predominates in modern thinking, especially in Western civilization. Kelsey (1989, p. 24) points out that most ministers are trained in rationalism and that the struggle between this and belief is assured to create neurotic problems. To say the least the balance of these two is a constant source of anxiety.

This leads to the paradox between ministry viewed as a *call or a career*. The 'call' of ministry viewed as the urging of the Spirit affirmed by the community of faith has been to some degree replaced by a professional careerism. This is evident both in the understanding of ministers and in the secularization of the position by the consumer. Ministers are often viewed as 'employees' of the church or denomination and as such subject to evaluative process similar to all other 'employees' in the marketplace. This *call versus career* divide also creates tension around advancement in the profession, often understood as moving from the small to the large and even from the parish to a systems position.

There exists within the historic position of the minister, factors which are diametrical and stress creating. Not least among these is the movement of the church and therefore its clergy from a position of *shaper of society* to an increasingly *irrelevance within society*. I considered this at some length in Chapter 3 and suffice it to say here that the transition is one of difficulty for many within the church and especially for its clergy. This is so not only in the recognition of the transition, but also in adapting to an understanding of modern-day ministry as mission from the sub-culture of the church, in a post-Christian era. The church brings the gospel to a culture that, for several generations, is often religiously and biblically illiterate and unchurched. The church continues to function as though it were a principal component in the lives of the majority of society.

A major contributor to this transition has been the tension between a *faith system rooted in antiquity and modernity*. It is essential in order to understand this dichotomy that we recognize that the term modernity is not simply 'of the modern' but implies a freedom of thought and a willingness to accept criticism and research as it relates to a world view and especially religious thought. The people of today have no difficulty raising questions which challenge the faith, and which demand of antiquated faith concepts, responses applicable to the modern world. The church has had greater difficulty in providing a relevant but faith-based reply.

There are other factors which create tensions. There is the discrepancy between the forming of *relationships and the concept of isolation*. Inherent in the task are those factors which appear to separate and isolate. Ministry is relational but the level of the relationships, as we

have seen, is not sufficient to fulfil the requirement for healthy development and maintenance of a well rounded psyche. Isolated from meaningful interaction in relationships which are often asymmetrical the
clergy have little opportunity to deal healthily and effectively with
issues which contribute to tension and stress.

Implicit in this is a *rise in functional and technical relationships at the
expense of intimacy*. There develops an appearance of normal interaction
but the level is predominately at a 'work' or Level 4. There fail to
develop levels of intimacy which deal with the inner dynamic of the
minister. This ultimately affects such variables as *power and servanthood*,
distorting the very nature and essence of gospel and faith based on the
concept of a suffering servant and a crucified messiah. This creates the
potentiality for distorted relationships evidenced in transference, sexual impropriety and violation of power.

Resolving paradox through integration

The key word for the resolution of paradox is *integration*. There always
exists the risk of moving towards any given side of the polarities and in
so doing losing the value of the other. By this is simply meant that it is
not a question of choosing one side or the other or that one is right and
the other wrong. Although our thinking has often been so divided, this
always creates an incomplete picture of reality. For instance, the question of 'doing and being' if decided on one side or the other would be
dangerous. The constant activist is as much at risk as is the reclusive
mystic although possibly for different reasons. In the same way, the
divide between the 'secular' and the 'sacred' may deny the commonality
found in a God-Creator, regardless of our belief in scientific principles
found in theistic evolution or literal creationism. This applies equally to
the diversity of polar forces found in our psychic nature as we strive
towards wholeness. There are those dynamics within us, at the very
centre of our psyche, which are paradoxical and contrary to one another
and the way we perceive ourselves. These, left unacknowledged and
with no attempt to move towards integration, prevent fullness of being.
In fact, these issues left unresolved will present difficulties. Probably a
good example of this is found in the matter of gender.

The Christian creation story as found in Genesis clearly demonstrated the existence of the two, femininity and masculinity, within the
unity of a single being. The creation of human beings according to the
Genesis 5 description was of both male and female in the likeness of
God. This implies both male and female nature as being found in the
Creator God. It was not that man was fashioned in divine image and
that woman was separately and apart fashioned on the model of man.

Rather both female and male found prototype in the God-Creator and, in that re-creation in the image of God, both took the feminine and masculine into single created being (Gen 5.1–2). The separately created being (man and woman) found wholeness in union (Gen 4.1) and in that wholeness an act of procreation gave birth to other human forms, both male and female, as they themselves had been created. So within each lies the God image of the feminine and the masculine, each coming to fullness in union as clearly indicated in the teaching of the Christ as the 'two becoming one flesh'. It needs to be recognized here that there are other more traditional and paternalistic understandings of the biblical creation story. However, even the creation of woman from the rib of man (Gen 2.21) implies that original man, created in God's image, had within him the feminine characteristics from which woman could be formed. John Sanford's book on the presence of the masculine and feminine within marriage entitled *The Invisible Partners* (1980) is an excellent exploration of this concept not only as it is found in Christian teaching but in early folklore and other forms of spirituality.

The case could be made that denial of the opposite which lies within each person is the setting of the stage for difficulties. As we considered in Chapter 7, the inflated ego, according to Edinger, is the source of such negative behaviour as power-motivated action, anger and lust. If the inflated ego, for instance, involves extreme maleness (sometimes a macho image) then the recognition of the feminine aspect of being is problematic. Resistance may arise to any presence of the feminine in the 'role' which in the person's thinking is a 'male' role. For the male minister this may affect the way in which he cares for others and his approach to nurture and loving support. He is threatened by these 'non-male' traits. Similarly, the acceptance of women into ordained ministry, which, in their thinking, is a 'male role', will be resisted and resented.[1] If a form of acceptance does occur or is imposed, it may well reflect male dominance and superiority. Refusal to accept the feminine which lies within may even, prompted by what Rutter calls 'the male myth of femininity', lead to power-based sexual improprieties with women they encounter within the context of ministry. This is an attitude and response based on an inflated ego.

Similarly the case can be made for women who deny the masculine side of their being. In Chapter 5 we considered the problem of what has been described as the cultural trap. The prevailing cultural stereotype is of women as being gentler, less aggressive, dependent, emotional, fulfilling roles of mother, nurturer, supporter and all that may imply. Rutter would indicate that these cultural perceptions have permeated both males and females through the socialization process. Women, reliant on the feminine and denying the masculine, may develop coping mechanisms which play into the cultural stereotype. They may exhibit deference to the male counterpart, non-aggressive action, emotive response and in the end fulfil the role dictated by the cultural trap. This 'role play' prevents the development of a wholeness which encompasses all dynamics of gender behaviour allowing a rounded fullness of being to occur.

This is not to say that the integration process does not create both tension and stress as they interact one with the other. The move towards wholeness is always one of discomfort in that the contradictions of the opposites always translate into incongruity in actions from a cultural perspective.

There is no attempt here to prove the cases outlined above. The illustration, recognizing its controversial nature, was simply to demonstrate that the case could be stated and supported by others, that at the roots of some of our most difficult contemporary problems lies the need to reconcile our inner diversity with who we are as whole beings. How we relate to others depends on how we see ourselves, and are secure, in our own being, a part of which is our sexuality. If we are comfortable in our own male or female being then we neither are threatened by the presence of the other nor view the other as a object to be controlled thus demonstrating our own sexual prowess. What lies at the root of our own thinking and action is the reflection of how we have resolved these issues within our own psyche.

This applies to all other areas of life. There is a need to integrate and unify the opposites that exist in life. Sometimes, as we have seen, these are those which exist in our outer world. Others lie within the inner world. The journey towards wholeness begins with identifying and resolving these differences.

Integrating perspectives: exteriority versus interiority

As we consider within this chapter the concept of wholeness in the lives of the clergy it is essential that we apply the concept of the integration to two primary sources by which we discover our identity. These are our perceptions gained by our exteriority and interiority. By the term exteriority is meant the degree to which we realize who we are by outward form or influence. Conversely, interiority is the realization of who we are from the internal source.

As we have seen in earlier chapters the influence on the identity of the clergyperson is effected by the external societal and church perspective of the office of minister. Correspondingly, the self-image of the minister is generated from interior sources of understanding their personhood and the role of office. This book, although recognizing and considering both directions of influence, has tended to indicate that the primary source is external. There is the risk of being inordinately controlled or swayed by what others think and say. The view of society which indicates the irrelevance of church and clergy by sheer numbers of non-attenders is bound to undermine the self-image of the clergy. The rise of effective lay leadership in the church, coupled with the relativistic thinking and individualist consumer attitude towards the church, creates questions of identity for the clergy. The lack of 'success markers' in ministry causes the exterior quantitative indices to be the primary way of assessing self-worth and value. In addition the minister, as we have seen, is often viewed on the basis of role rather than who he or she is as a person. If McFadyen (1990, pp. 69ff.) is right in the degree to which interaction with others influences how we see and understand ourselves then the external source is, in reality, primary.

There is also the identity gained by interior or self-perspective. There is personal experience of ministry, as we have seen in Chapter 1, which shapes our self-understanding. There are all the emotions coupled with feelings of worth and value, which affect the esteem with which we see ourselves. Centrally, for many, there is an understanding of self as it relates to the divine (or fails to relate) which affects understanding.

The necessity, as we consider the journey towards wholeness, is that both the exterior and the interior influences must be accounted for and held in some form of equilibrium. That which informs identity must take into account both how we understand ourselves and how we are perceived by others. It may be possible here to make a case, as Mc-Fadyen (1990) appears to do, that personhood is only (or primarily) realized in social relationship. Equally, it may be argued that one must first understand oneself before identity can be established that allows interaction with and influence by others. Both, however, do and will influence how a person understands their identity and therefore both must be recognized for their contribution. To be controlled exclusively by one or the other would be disastrous. Exterior control over image would be influenced by every change in prevailing trends in ministry and every interaction good or bad. This would drive the individual to be chameleon-like in identity, always reflecting the prevailing exterior influence. The interior control if predominant would develop an identity which is governed by subjectivity and one which is emotive in nature. Both are essential for balanced self-understanding and the movement towards wholeness.

Again the process is one of integration. Merton comments: 'The path to final integration for the individual, and for the community lies, in any case, beyond the dictates and programs of any culture (Christian culture included)' (1971, p. 217).

Developing as spiritual being

We have seen that ministers, who are called to give spiritual leadership
to the community of faith and to the broader world, often lack spiritual
nurture. Probably one of the greatest changes in the role of the minister
has been away from spiritual leadership to one of managing director of
the institution called church. The role has correspondingly moved from
a contemplative one characterized by prayer and meditation to one of
busyness and activism. In the study over half of those surveyed felt to
varying degrees more like the Executive Director (managing director)
than the Pastor. Correspondingly over 50 per cent also felt that to some
degree people in the church wanted someone to run the show, not
provide spiritual leadership. Over 70 per cent felt they had insufficient
time for personal spiritual nurture and some 65 per cent indicated that
to some degree they were often expected to give to others what they
themselves lacked.

It seems appropriate then that those who are 'called' to the service of
the Divine need to begin the reconstruction of identity with a redefined
and healthy place for the spiritual. Simply put, the spiritual component
must be given place in the identity of the minister. This calls for an
understanding of ministry not solely as a 'task' orientated profession
but as a 'spiritual' role which places value equally on being and doing.
The contemplative times are equally a part of the life of the minister, as
are the physically active times of leadership in worship, pastoral
visitation, administration and all those things which are countable on
an assessment sheet.

This calls for a view of the world which gives equal care to the outer
world of the physical and to the inner world of the psyche and the other
world of the spiritual, and to respect that balance. There have existed in
the history of the church those who in their extremes have, like the
gnostic, denied the flesh and exalted the spiritual. Equally, antinomian-
ism has indulged the physical as an expression of freedom, often at the
expense of the spiritual. There needs to be a balance of these dynamics
in some form of harmony.

In practical terms the development of the spiritual is difficult for the
clergy. They are often so busy doing that the addition of more devo-
tional activity seems impossible. To return to Tournier's comments, the
activism prevalent in the schedule of the clergyperson allows time only
for prayer with others as part of the job and for scripture study in a
search for fodder for the sermon process. For some this 'needed'
discipline of prayer and searching scripture may in and of itself provide
some spiritual nurture. More often than not however, it becomes a
means to an end. The attempt to define more time for personal spiritual

nurture for many simply adds more stress, and, in the end, the inability to maintain the discipline adds to the distress of failure.

The clutter within

The need is not for more activity, even spiritual activity, but rather the realignment of existing action to allow space for the spiritual. The clamour of activism in the outer physical world, prompted by the clutter of unresolved issues in the inner world, prevents the development and nurture of the spiritual which must transcend both worlds. There is a need to remove the clutter so that in the midst of all of life the transcendent spirit can be experienced.

Several years ago I was presented with a graphic illustration of this fact. I was given a tour of a historic church building of a denomination that practises believers' baptism by immersion. As we moved through the building the guide opened a side door into the baptismal tank to show its size and construction. A rich velvet curtain covered an opening through which the congregation could watch the baptism from the main sanctuary of the church. In the tank lay an immense collection of clutter. Old deacon benches, broken chairs, an historic church sign, and numerous religious articles no longer in use but too 'precious' to throw out, lay there joined together by cobwebs and the common practice of collecting dust. When I asked as to when the last baptism was held, the guide had difficulty recalling. Assurances were given however that the 'historic collection' in the baptistery could quickly be removed if the need arose.

Often our lives are reflected in that old church. We have the trappings of spirituality but the inner sanctum is crowded with historic artefacts, deemed too precious to throw out but of no current use. Some of the treasures are religious in nature, carried forward as we saw in Chapter 1 by the historic and personal baggage we carry. These 'sacred' relics become as demanding of space as any other dynamics within us and maybe even more so because of the 'holy' nature of their presence. (It's easier to throw out a tattered-beyond-use book of Shaw's plays than an equally used Bible.) The unifying of the Spirit has been replaced by the tying together of cobwebs and the collecting of dust. Regardless, the place in our lives that, like the baptistery, should be the sacramental centre of our spiritual life is filled with other things, even the religious, which prevents the spiritual from transcending our being.

Brother Ramon, commenting on the works of Thomas Merton, points out that all of humankind is compelled by 'a tyranny of subconscious drives and compulsions in which man [woman] is so often governed by the blind needs and compulsive demands of passion' (1989, p. 97). Why are we compelled to perfectionism, or to unrealistic standards of success, or to appeasement of others at all cost, or to excess work? What is it that drives us? What are those things that keep us firmly riveted in the world of action, neglecting the inner spiritual cravings? Within all of us, there are those subconscious artefacts which clutter the space and prevent the spiritual growth towards healing and wholeness. This is not to say that all within is negative or that which impedes growth. Much that has shaped us is positive and needs retention. There is a need, however, to examine and reinterpret what lies within in light of our unique place in time and space on our journey.

The need for inner housecleaning

The problem then of establishing a meaningful spiritual identity is not simply one of placing an overlay or veneer of the spiritual over the already existing clutter of the inner being. The vacation of the minister spent in the Christian Conference Centre or the Harvest Festival, where one goes to the day and evening session with notebook and pen in hand to learn the secrets of 'being more spiritual', may be of little value. In fact, it may exacerbate the problem. The end product of such an activity may produce more guilt because of the unattainable demands to yet another exercise, be it spiritual. This is not to dismiss and reject out of hand such activities.

There is a need first for the process of deconstruction prior to the process of reconstruction. The first calls for a taking apart of what is currently there. Some things may be kept, others modified and some rejected or retired from service. All are reinterpreted in the light of their contribution to a developing part of identity. This brings into question the appropriateness of busyness and the stress of accomplishment and fulfilling unrealistically high demands of office. It examines all the factors, theological, sociological, psychological, spiritual and others, which drive our actions. The recreation of spiritual identity then comes through the continuing action of reconciling all that is within, with all that is without. Although this affects both the inner and outer world it is predominantly an interior-based process for it is driven by personal perceptions and motivations. It may necessitate the modification of exterior action and perspective but must be based within.

Inner housekeeping produces the space in which the spiritual can exist and grow. C. S. Lewis gives a simple but charming parable, which he borrowed from George MacDonald, of this as it affected his own life:

> Imagine yourself as a living house. God comes to rebuild that house. At first, perhaps, you can understand what he is doing. He is getting the

drains right and stopping the leak in the roof and so on: you knew these jobs needed doing and so you are not surprised. But suddenly he starts knocking the house about in a way that hurts abominably and does not seem to make sense. What on earth is he up to? The explanation is that He is building quite a different house from the one you thought – throwing up a new wing here, putting on an extra floor there, running up towers, making a courtyard. You thought you were going to be made into a decent little cottage: but He is building a palace. He intends to come and live in it Himself. (1955, p. 171)

The act of encounter

Although it is called here an *act of encounter* it is not a single event and is both act and process. It does not occur as an end result of dealing with inner matters but rather becomes both the enabler by which the process can occur as well as a growing reality within the individual. Although consideration will be given to a tri-directional encounter it is recognized that all can and may occur simultaneously. In fact, all must occur in relationship one to the other if wholeness is to be experienced.

Encounter with the Divine

As we have seen above, the role of the clergy is often other than spiritual. Not only is this a reality but the activities of the role and the church may block the personal encounter of the individual with God. Hands and Fehr comment:

> The alienation from God is concealed by the cleric's immersion in 'the things of God' – teaching, preaching, visiting the sick, praying with others, presiding at liturgy. While sincere this kind of activity can coexist with an almost complete absence of private, personal presence to God. (1993, p. 54)

Creating the space for the encounter and intimacy with the Divine is a movement away from the rampant activism so prevalent in life and growing towards what Brunner describes in the quote at the beginning of this chapter as 'being, as men [people] who lived from the love of Christ and in His love'. Many of us have lost the art of being and of living from the love of Christ. Rather we have honed the skills of doing, living more from our ability than from Christ's love and grace. The journey towards wholeness is a journey back to a personal encounter with Creator-God who is, as Tillich would describe, the Ground of all being.

How do we begin the process of encountering the Divine in a

personal and deeper way? Throughout the history of Christianity this
has been a major question. Early church Fathers and Mothers have
developed and promoted spiritual exercise and devotion in an attempt
to facilitate the drawing closer to God. Much is of value for our
understanding in their writings and the model of their lives. Some, as is
evident in all movements of awakening or renewal, is extreme in its
isolation from the world and culture. One common thread which seems
present in most early spiritual thought is the need and value of personal
contemplation. It is in this act of reflection and meditation that life and
all action of life can be understood and reinterpreted in a context of
wholeness. It is this which allows the placing of individual segments of
the journey into the larger picture. My father would often wisely
comment on an incident or problematic event by asking: 'What is the
significance of this in the light of eternity?' In that very question he did
not erase the significance of the event or dismiss it in 'other worldliness'
but placed it in a far larger and whole context. Contemplation allows
this reflective act to occur and to attribute true significance.

The act of contemplation is more than rationalization or a cognitive
reworking of life's events. It is and must be the encountering of God
acting in and through the event to impact the life of the individual. The
late Thomas Merton, a modern-day contemplative, in his book *Seeds of
Contemplation* establishes the act of contemplation in the Divine as
Source:

> It [contemplation] is that life itself, fully awake, fully active, fully aware
> that it is alive. It is spiritual wonder. It is spontaneous awe at the
> sacredness of life, of being. It is a vivid realization of the fact that all
> life and being in us proceeds from an invisible, transcendent and
> infinitely abundant Source. Contemplation is, above all, awareness of
> the reality of that Source. It *knows* the Source, obscurely, inexplicable,
> but with certitude that goes beyond reason and beyond simple faith.
> (1961, p. 1)

The encounter with the Divine becomes personal in the awareness of
the transient reality of God as the origin of all of life and action. It is
from this foundation that action in life draws meaning and purpose.
Other motivations, although ever there by the very presence of our
humanness, are no longer primary. This is not to say that they do not
and should not exist but rather that they become part of a much larger
picture, one of Divine origin.

As part of the act of contemplation there is place for spiritual
direction. By this is meant the guidance of an individual by a director in
spiritual growth and understanding especially as expressed in a life of
prayer and meditation. The value of such a person who has training in
the art of leading others is found not only in their understanding of the

subject and especially the process but in the objectivity of their presence. Alternatively, and possibly more acceptable in this day of greater
personal independence, is the model of the development through
finding a companion for the journey. Tilden Edwards in his book
Spiritual Friend (1980) sees the direction coming through a deep spiritual companionship which comes from another, not primarily director
but as both friend and director walking with the person for a part of
life's journey. His book is excellent in raising again the need for such
growth partners and for its practical guidance in implementation of
what he describes as 'the gift of spiritual friendship' (p. 9).

Either model of guidance calls for the act of participation with others.
Spiritual development when viewed, as it is so often today, as personal
and private is prone to much subjectivity. The comfortable 'spirit
encounters' are most frequently made. The more difficult and often
painful challenges to how life is lived in the presence of the Divine are
avoided or softened. There is a call for the objectivity of another or
others.

Thornton (1984) laments the fact that in theological education today
much effort is taken in training for the fulfilment of worship and
preaching but little attention is given to personal development. The
study which I conducted in the Scottish church indicated that only 21
per cent acknowledge having a spiritual father/mother confessor or
spiritual director with whom spiritual needs could be shared. The
evidence of spiritual isolation and the crying need to develop a disciplined spiritual direction make the role of the director in such a
process ever more evident. A helpful and practical exposition of this
can be found in the book by Thornton.

In contemplation and spiritual direction there is the implicit need for
the definition of a time and space for Divine encounter. The complexity
of today's world, with its activism, is a thief of time. Much of life is spent
in the dull roar of the bustle, making the tranquillity and silence of
being still, at times, unbearable. It is like trying to sleep in a remote rural
location after living in the heart of a constantly moving and noisy city.
The silence becomes deafening and almost unbearable. For the busy
minister to step apart from activity and to be quiet and still in meditation is difficult. Into the thought processes rush all past activity, anxiety
over what needs to be accomplished and the consideration of sermons
yet to be delivered. With so much to be done and so little time, being
still seems simply to raise the level of anxiety. The defining of a time
and space in which meditation and quietness can occur is an act of
discipline. The Psalmist (46) exhorts that in the chaos and upheaval of
life there is a need to be still and to know that God is God. In that
stillness God gets our attention and we experience Divine encounter.

Encounter with the self

In the discussion of the clutter within and the need for an inner housekeeping, we have considered the need to encounter the self at a new level of self-awareness. It could be claimed that this appears as a psychological process and that it can exist without a spiritual dynamic. Although some would see this to be possible and would claim that even Jung understood the spiritual and God in psychological terms, this is not the case here. There is a difference between a purely psychological understanding of self and the understanding of self as a whole entity. The totality of the person or the self is more than a single perception be it psychological, ontological, philosophical, physical or spiritual. Rather, it is in a composite of all that progression is made toward selfhood and wholeness.[2] A concept of wholeness that allows only for a single dimension of being is not what it professes to be. It is, however, in what Tillich calls 'the multi-dimensional unity of life' that we see 'a unity and relation of the dimensions and realms of life' in which we can 'analyse the existential ambiguities of all life processes correctly and express the quest for unambiguous or eternal life adequately' (1968, vol. 3, pp. 12–13).

For the minister then the process of self-encounter or intimacy with self, as one of knowing oneself from the multitude of dimensions, is essential. Merton comments that 'He who attempts to act and do things for others or for the world without deepening his own self-understanding, freedom, integrity and capacity for love, will have nothing to give others' (1971, p. 164). This is not simply a psychological process, or for that matter a spiritual understanding, but a composite of all possible perspectives. In order to find this intimacy with the self there is the need to be open to the enquiry which brings about an awakening self-awareness of psychological or physical or spiritual needs. No single understanding can bring healing and wholeness in all dimensions. We have, however, in this section begun with the Divine encounter for, as with Brunner who sees 'no real existence of the Self apart from fellowship with God' (1937, p. 302), Christianity gives pre-eminent place to God. The Apostle Paul quoting the Cretan philosopher Epimenides stated that it is 'In him we live and move and have being' (Acts 17:28).

Encounter with others

I have raised in Chapter 6 the need for relationships at different levels. There we considered the asymmetrical nature of relationships with others. Here, in the discussion of the road toward wholeness I raise again the encounter with others. Wholeness cannot be achieved in isolation from others. Again from the Christian creation accounts we discover that solitary existence was not 'good' and a partnership was developed. So came with re-creation the development of kinship systems with all the intricacies of relationship. Biblical accounts demonstrate that the provision of God for support and encouragement often came in the form of horizonal relationship between the individual and others (Irvine, 1984). It is as relational beings that a totality is discovered that moves beyond individual subjectivity to objective discovery.

We noted in Chapter 6 that relationships for ministers often remain at a Level 4 which centres around the work of ministry and that often there is a mentality of insulation which intentionally prevents these from being deepened. Walls of protectionism prompted by insecurity and the desire to lessen the risk of hurt block out others. There is a resistance to intimacy.

It is in the context of seeking wholeness that these difficulties begin to be overcome. From the basis of a growing intimacy with the Divine and with the self comes the capacity for intimacy with others. The mistrust of others, the spirit of competition, the power-motivated action and all those things which develop from ego inflation begin to take proper perspective in a larger and whole context. Relationships develop between persons as opposed to bearers of 'roles'. The self now relinquishes a central position, be it ever so fragile, to take its place in a greater harmony in relationship to the Divine and to others. The Divine is no longer alienated. Others no longer appear as threatening. A sense of harmony begins to develop which allows encounter in all dimensions. Isolation from self, others and God decreases and with it the tension of alienation.

I will in the next chapter consider developing networks of support. These become possible as the glass walls of resistance and fear are lowered and a greater degree of interaction is allowed.

Notes

1 Mary Anne Coate (1989) refers to this in her section on inclusive language as developing from what she calls the *power of women* within each of us and affecting both feminine language and presence in liturgy (pp. 134–6).

2 This concept is developed in ch. 6 of Irvine (1989), entitled 'The composite "self" and the process of redemption'.

11

━━━━

Models of support

Clergy and their spouses experience the same kind of joy, pain and
brokenness as their parishioners. Where do they turn when faced with
personal problems? . . . Do they find the support they need?

(Gilbert, 1987, p. 1)

There is always a risk in the analysis of a subject that the practical
implications are somehow lost in the depth of the subject. Throughout
this book I have indicated that the intent is to be of some practical value,
be that simply through identifying the problem or in attempting to
provide some options for resolving it. It is recognized that no single
solution is possible or exists. There is the need, however, having
presented an analysis to ask 'What can we do about the problem?' and
'How do I apply it personally to my situation?' These I will consider in
the next two chapters.

It is important to stress that the development of support is not a
single act nor can it occur only at one level if it is to be effective. A single
source of support, because of our diverse needs and demands, may fail
to live up to our expectations. An example is the ministerial professional group which, when expected to be the primary support for
clergy at all levels, fails at the levels of personal and pastoral support.
We have recognized in the preceding chapters that isolation, relationships, expectations and needs exist in different forms and at different
levels. Each is important and each requires different dynamics of
support in order to satisfy the need. A generalist solution to specific
needs is so imprecise that it is of no value. Equally, to seek support too
narrow and precise will not satisfy the diversity of needs.

Support, therefore, must develop and be available on multiple levels.
This places the responsibility on all, from those at the professional,
denominational, local community and church level to the individual
minister, to assure such support structures are available. The onus,
however, is ultimately on the individual to utilize the support available.

System support models

Ministerial/professional systems support

As with all professions there is a need to develop and provide support at this the broadest of levels. Doctors, lawyers, teachers and others in professional careers have, in most cases, clearly established professional groups. These are groups which provide inclusive (as opposed to exclusive, based on exclusively specific philosophy, theory or perspective) training, set standards, determine professional ethics, provide criteria for entrance to the profession and deal with concerns of the group in general. These are the groups, as in the previously cited BMA document, which are concerned with the overall health of the profession.

Such a structure has not existed within the profession of ministry. There are valid reasons for this not occurring. The first is that the ministry has been seen as a 'calling', not a profession. This is still the case among many who would frown at the use of the term profession as applied to ministry. Secondly, the fragmented nature of the profession among various ecclesiastical structures, denominational groupings and national and regional judicatory bodies, each of which has various levels of control, has been one of several reasons for the lack of a professional code of ethics around the issue of sexual behaviour among clergy. Thirdly, the ambiguity of the nature of ministry makes such a broad-based supportive structure difficult. Finally, the lack of clear entrance criteria to the ministry has created great diversity.

It may well be that the establishment of such a body is difficult if not impossible in the foreseeable future. However, this is not to negate the value of the support gained at this broadest of levels and to recognize that to some degree the support is there in a variety of forms.

Non-denominational based training

There is available, in many areas, the opportunity to engage in training that is based on the profession in general rather than the specific denomination served. It is natural and right that each denomination will want considerable input into the training of a candidate for entrance to their ministry. I am referring here, however, primarily to the post-ordination training of the clergy. Such training becomes supportive in that it deals with the profession from a perspective free of denominational and theological encumbrance. (It is recognized that there is always some bias.)

A good example of this is the rise of postgraduate professional degree programmes such as some of the British Master of Theology in Ministry degrees, like that offered at New College, Edinburgh, and the North

American Doctor of Ministry. In the programme currently directed by the author, enrolment of ministers of some eight to ten denominations, from the charismatic to traditional Roman Catholic, has provided opportunity for strong professional support in an open-minded and healthy way. Recognition of diversity has enabled the acceptance of the individual, thus creating a strong supportive network which transcends theological understanding, denominational tradition and other barriers which often exist to lessen support and isolate. This has also been transferable back to specific ministry situations, overcoming the bias often created by our stereotyping of others.

Such training opportunities, as with other professions, may exist around specific areas of the work. Inter- or non-denominational training is often available in such speciality areas as pastoral counselling, clinical and chaplaincy ministries and preaching and worship. Those interested and involved in these areas often establish their own associations, establishing entrance criteria, setting standards and providing helpful dialogue and interaction. Once again this establishes a supportive network in the professional arena and provides the opportunity for meaningful interaction and relationships at other levels. As with the advanced professional degree programme, common interest and participation overcome the barriers which can exist in the face of diversity.

Cross-denominational agency support
There exist, nationally and internationally, professional agencies which have come into existence around specific needs or to support clergy in special areas of ministry. Some of these have developed as privately funded institutes or groups while others are more loosely defined by association membership. Examples of these are such bodies as the ecumenical group around rural church ministry at The Arthur Rank Centre, Coventry, and the British Church Growth Association, Bedford, to name just two. In North America the Alban Institute, Washington DC, the Association for Clinical Pastoral Education (ACPE) and its Canadian counterpart, the Canadian Association of Pastoral Practice Education (CAAPE), provide this type of resource. The support offered by these associations of professional resource, consultative help and interpersonal networking is significant. Many of these organizations also provide written material on a broad range of subjects not available through denominational groups. The Alban Institute with its wealth of printed material is a case in point. Both of the above mentioned professional resources are often overlooked when a minister considers his/her support system. Both, however, provide a level of support which offsets some of the problems such as trust and competition, often

found in other more direct professional support mechanisms.

Denominational support system

Denominations and national church bodies need to be seen as providing support for their clergy. Clergy are their most costly and essential investment. This support may be direct or indirect in the providing of the service through various levels of the church's system. It is often the denomination, as a system, which is accused of not providing adequately for its clergy.

Although this appears to be a likely source of support it is also the one which is probably most problematic. The church, as a system, usually has the best access to its clergy and resources, but it also often wields the most power over the lives of its clergy. This power may be real or perceived but it does influence, directly or indirectly, the career of the minister. It can influence placement, movement into other spheres of ministry, involvement on denominational committees and policy making bodies and, ultimately, it controls issues of ordination standards and removal from office. Because of this vested interest, ministers are often reluctant to utilize the support networks provided by the denomination for fear of the influence this may have on their future in ministry.

This not only relates to major issues such as moral failure or crisis of physical or emotional health. There is a real sense in which any seeking of support, or the admission of the need of it, is often viewed by clergy as a matter of failure. The seeking of external help, in the minds of some ministers, is seen to deny the sufficiency of the Grace of God to overcome, somehow, all difficulties. One minister interviewed expressed the seeking of help as 'acknowledging the Grace as sufficient for salvation, but not adequate for sustaining'.

Regardless of some limitations, and recognizing once again that support must occur on multiple levels, there are some effective support mechanisms which can develop at the denominational systems level.

Supportive agency

Each denomination must demonstrate desire to be supportive of its ministry by being a primary provider of care services. Departments within the denominational structure that are responsible for the oversight of clergy need to be seen as concerned not simply with the financial dimension, as is sometimes the case, but also with the whole needs of the minister.

This care needs to be proactive in nature rather than reactive. In the past care has often been available after the individual has experienced difficulty. Providing a support system which is sensitive and proactive may well prevent many difficulties from occurring. In order to do this the denomination needs to deal consultatively with its clergy, hearing and responding to the pressures that are being experienced on the front lines of ministry. Response from the top down is often futile and misses the mark. Response, as initiated by the needs of the user, will face real problems, and at least make resources available which are appropriate.

Continuing education support

The opportunity to engage in continuing education with others in ministry is an effective way to provide support for clergy. Some denominations provide for their clergy a range of educational events which are often focused on the advancement and integration of both knowledge and experience. A good example of this is the continuing conference scheme utilized by the Church of Scotland. Within this plan, ministers are invited back periodically during their years in ministry (18 months; five, eight and 15 years) to participate in three-day conferences at the expense of the denomination.

Continuing education provides support in two primary ways. First, *content* can respond to the needs of the clergy as well as the changing trends in society and culture. Stress experienced by ministers, as I have indicated, is often prompted by the tension between faith tradition and a modern, progressive society. These ongoing events, as well as special offerings, provide the forum in which to consider issues relevant to the needs of the moment. It is also in this continuing education phase that ministers are able to deal with issues, not simply from a cognitive or theoretical perspective, but also with the application of experience and professional knowledge. The wealth of resources that is made available as experienced ministers share in these events is enriching and supportive.

Secondly, there is the opportunity for supportive *interaction*. Often the comments heard at the end of a continuing education event relate to the value of being with others who share the same demands and problems in life. Many clergy live in isolated worlds, especially alone at the levels that are required to meet the inner needs of their personhood. Being with others is important. Much of the merit in these events is the interaction that occurs outside the class or seminar room. No continuing education event should undervalue the place of the 'off' time within the activity.

Sabbatical support structure

The sabbath year concept is not foreign to the religious world (Lev 25), but is one which has been forgotten to a great degree. There is a place for extended rest for all creation. The hectic pace of today's world and the forced productivity of both soil and soul make this ever more a necessity. Clergy often recognize and admit lack of sufficient time for both personal and spiritual nurture. The activism of daily church routine prevents sufficient time for reflection, meditation and growth.

Some denominations have attempted to initiate this with varying success. Clergy, for a variety of reasons, have seemed reluctant to take the opportunity. It may well be that this form of support, with its opportunity for rest and renewal, needs to be given higher profile and promotion by denominations. This may include the provision of interim replacement for the minister, financial support, planning guidance and the modelling of sabbatical leave by those in the leadership of the denomination. The time of sabbatical rest and renewal will assist greatly in refocusing attention from task orientation to personal awareness and in so doing will assist in the (re)establishment of balanced identity.

Peer support structures
It may well be that denominations can play a role in the establishment of peer support groups within their structures. Although much of this type of support usually comes from the regional or local level of the church the denominational structure does allow for the providing of support vehicles across the broad range of the church's ministry. For instance, clergy with speciality ministries such as rural, music or chaplaincy may benefit from groups established to support and provide resources for such interest and/or calling. Additionally the structural establishment of peer groups based on regions or districts can provide the means for interaction of those who share similar ministry settings.

There has been a growing concern in recent years relating to the assessment or evaluation of the individual's ministry. A denominational structure such as this can provide peer groups or partners as mutual assessment teams. A number of years ago the Baptist Union of Great Britain introduced a Senior Friend system to support new entrants into ministry during their initial years. This programme attached new ministers in their first charge to a senior pastor who served as advisor, mentor and friend. In a good number of cases this led to lifelong support and friendship. The problem encountered with this particular programme, according to comments given by a denominational leader, was that the senior friend, at the end of the 'official' period, was asked to give a reference for his/her 'friend' to the denomination. This changed, at least in the perception of some, the friendly intent of the programme to one of having some vested interest in the system leading to ordination and ministerial standing within the denomination. The programme, however, with modification, has great merit as a peer support and evaluation process. Similar structures may be used to provide assessment teams which supply the objectivity of another person without bearing the weight of hierarchial evaluation.

Gender-aware structure

As we have indicated in Chapter 5, women in ministry face not only the pressures common to the task of ministry, but also unique stress relating to gender issues. Denominations need to take seriously the support of women in ministry and educate all clergy in this area. Several things become evident here.

First there is a need to provide the opportunity for women ministers to engage in dialogue around their specific experiences of ministry and to find in one another role models. As has been indicated, tokenism has meant that there have been few role models for women. This is especially true in denominations where few women are in parish ministry.

Secondly, the research presented has indicated that women have more difficulty relaxing at the end of a day or a period of work because of family responsibilities. The stereotyping of gender roles in our society is difficult to overcome and, in the context of ministry, may take affirmative action to provide some solution. Support of women in ministry to allow time away from work for family matters as well as assistance in providing alternative care for intervals of retreat and renewal may be necessary. There is a recognition of the equality factor with male clergy, who may require similar support, but who would still maintain, as the research has shown, that the onus around issues of family care and child nurture predominantly falls to the female.

Theological education

In most settings theological education, even in denominational schools, has been seen as the domain of the theological educators. However, in a church and society demanding more from those in ministry, there is a need for a theological school to hear what is being asked of its graduates and to train persons to fulfil those demands. The denomination must continually assess the training requirements of its ministers and ask theological educators to provide training appropriate for the ministry of today. To allow the theological educators to assume they alone know the needs of clergy, and for that matter the church, in today's society, is to have training controlled by academia rather than by practice. Both must come into the equation to create an effective balance.

Denominations and church bodies can, and should, request that their training facilities provide an education for ministers which, by its nature, is supportive and assists in the decreasing of stress. Most clergy are trained in educational systems which emphasize the individualist nature of ministry. Ministers are trained as 'lone rangers' rather than team members and/or in the skills of team leadership. The very nature of education is often based on the development and accomplishment of the individual in competition rather than co-operation with colleagues in training. This translates into the same competition versus co-operation in the field.

Persons training for ministry need to explore more about who they are as persons. The experiential, psychological and emotional baggage needs to be unpacked or reinterpreted before it is carried into ministry. It is recognized that this is a lifelong activity. The process needs to begin early, at the training level. If not, a distorted self-understanding will affect the way in which the individual understands his/her relationship to the task of ministry. Such things as emotional insecurity and low self-esteem prevent open and full interaction with others who can and should provide the highest levels of support. Interpersonal relationships are affected, relationships are not allowed to reach their deepest level and isolation, with all its ramifications, dominates.

Classical or traditional theological education simply does not provide all that is required for a minister entering this complex age of ministry. It does not provide the training in and understanding of basic relational skills. This understanding is necessary not only for personal survival, but also for ministry among a generation more affected by relationships than institutional allegiance and tradition.

The initial training of ministers is probably the primary means of offsetting stress and isolation within the profession. Habits learned in the theological school and seminary will continue in the place of ministry. Learning co-operation, team ministry, and the need to provide self-care and care for one another through the development of healthy support structures during the years of training is the most effective means of influencing the continuance of these same supports within the field(s) of placement. Denominations investing in the training of their most essential and precious resource need to demand training that will affect the continued health of the clergy.

Auxiliary resources
Denominations may well provide auxiliary facilities to aid in the support of the clergy in their life and career. This may mean providing resources in a range of areas such as counselling, family and marriage enrichment, career management, retraining and placement, to mention but a few. It may be that these need to be made available through

private agencies or agencies sponsored by, but detached from, the authority structure of the denomination. This would assure confidentiality and trust, issues of great concern to ministers.

In Chapter 2 we considered Levi's concept of 'poor fit'. We recognize that there are times when ministers find themselves in situations, and sometimes a career, where they are not well fitted to the task. As Levi would indicate this is a cause of stress and affects the well-being of both clergy and church. To leave an occupation for which they have trained and to find an alternative and fulfilling career is difficult if not, for some, impossible. Issues of calling and of worthy service in another field add a greater traumatic dimension to the technical and financial dynamics of change. Many ministers feel trapped, escalating the already high stress index around any change. It is in these areas that denominations can provide effective support through career guidance, retraining and spiritual support.

Inter-professional support

Given that many clergy serving the same community as other professionals indicated a lack of professional support, there is a need for denominations to give assistance in developing networks in this area. Two primary foci seem evident: the collegial working alongside other professionals in the delivery of service, and the supportive basis providing mutual pastoral care among professionals.

In the first area it is important to make clergy aware of the need for such networks. Ministers often tend to function as solitary care givers. Secondly, providing the forum in which personnel of caring professions can dialogue will assist the clergy as well as others in understanding the nature and parameters of other professionals' domain. It is important to note here that some 46 per cent of the clergy in the survey felt they could not seek consultation on cases with other professionals because of confidentiality. This fails to recognize the ethics of confidentiality which exists within many other professions. Dialogue and a clear understanding both of this and of how professionals in other fields can best assist one another is essential. This will establish, at least to some degree, the foundations for interaction and dialogue at the local level.

The second area of inter-professional support is at the level of mutual care. Here the concern of the denomination should be specifically the care of the clergy. A joint clergy and other professional board has the potential to provide a wide range of care for clergy. To their credit some denominations such as the Church of Scotland have established such advisors' boards.

Community based support

It is at the community or local grassroots level that support is most often needed and directly experienced by the clergy. Here, among others who serve in the front-line ministry of the church, there is the daily requirement for support and the opportunity to interact with others. In this section on community based support we will look only at the formal structure of support, leaving the informal to the latter section on personal support structures.

Community based support structures, if they exist, usually occur in three different forms.

Denominational support

This is usually in the form of a fraternal or ministerial group among clergy of the same church tradition. The gatherings are usually scheduled periodically (often monthly) and are designed to be forums for considering the ministry of the church. Among the ministers surveyed a mixed response was obtained concerning formal denominational ministerial groups. Some indicated that because of homogeneity of theology and thought this gathering of their own denomination provided greater value as a support system. This was often in areas where other church groups seemed to dominate interdenominational associations. Others found that because the clergy in this group were all of the same church group 'one-upmanship' was greater. They reported a tendency to boast about successes and to avoid sharing areas of difficulty or seeming failure. Some found the competition in this group greater because all were assessed by the same set of standards. Because of the imbalance in numbers women felt marginalized in these professional groupings.

Denominational groups, however, can provide good opportunity for support. If competition is lessened and trust is allowed to develop, clergy who serve in the same tradition and in adjoining communities can find the commonality a supportive base. Rather than dismiss these groups because of their ineffectiveness in the past, there is a need to re-evaluate their purpose and to re-establish the group in a supportive manner. Such groups, properly established, can be a primary provider of support professionally, socially and spiritually.

Continuing education, in its role as a support structure, can be implemented at this level. The undertaking of joint study as a group over a period of time can provide the opportunity for shared learning and growth, an opportunity often missed at the pre-ordination training stage.

Interdenominational support structure

Much of what has been said at the denominational level can be applied here. In the group researched some 70 per cent said such an interdenominational group existed in their community although 10 per cent indicated they did not participate. The majority of those who did participate indicated the group was an informal fellowship designed primarily to discuss programming and problem solving. Although there were mixed responses to the effectiveness of this group, most ministers felt personal matters could not be discussed because of lack of trust and confidentiality. Many of these groups were dominated by one church group or theological perspective and were at times uncomfortable for others who felt marginalized. Again, because of the gender imbalance, women did not feel as though they fitted into this group.

Once again these groups can be a source of support if adequate levels of trust can be established. The opportunity to join with other ministers within community for professional, social and spiritual support fulfils a primary level of support. In a society where the religious and the clergy are facing decreasing importance and relevance, the solidarity of clerics is vital. The presence of the ministry within the community is strengthened, not by clergy functioning alone and/or in competitive fashion, but by unified action and harmony within the ranks. With the changing role of the church and clergy within society, the broad-based interdenominational structure provides the opportunity for continuing training and advancement of clergy relating to cultural transition and ministry, especially as it applies to the local community base.

Interdisciplinary support model

Clergy within the local community often feel separated from other professionals who serve, with them, the same group of people. Meaningful interaction with persons providing other services within community will provide mutual support and enhance service. This is especially true if the minister is to be seen as part of a team providing holistic care. An example of such an interdisciplinary support group was brought to my attention several years ago.

A minister in a community became sensitive to the fact that he often provided spiritual support for persons who were under the care of other 'care givers' within the community. On many occasions, because there was little or no communication between persons, or groups of persons, providing this care, lack of understanding between professionals and sometimes duplication of services occurred. After speaking with several other providers of care the decision was made to correspond with all identifiable care givers, inviting them to meet on a given evening at a central location (a pub) for a time of informal conversation. A room was set aside and on the first evening a dozen or so people were present. The conversation was informal and simply an opportunity to get to know one another. The decision was made to meet again informally a month later for another evening of conversation. The group grew as others attended and those present identified persons who should be invited. Informally the group explored areas of mutual concern, and ways in which they could assist one another. They developed a better understanding of what each had to offer through their specific discipline. From this friendships developed and deeper levels of mutual support came to exist. Communication in the delivery of service improved as professionals in different areas of speciality now knew one another and were able to phone someone they felt was a colleague. Doctors, community nurses, social workers, community care givers, ministers and others continued to meet informally, strengthening relationships and building community. For many, this became a highlight of the week or month and the support gained was invaluable.

Lest the sceptic say this may work in small clearly defined communities it is important to note that this model began and continues in a section of a large urban city.

Regardless of the specific model or approach used there is a need to establish communication and links between professionals within a community. Ministers entering a new community should make their presence known to other professionals. These liaisons, established early and apart from the crisis situation, become supportive networks as the stress of difficult situations arises.

Personal support structure

Given our understanding that there are various levels of support this, the personal support structure, is probably the one most effective and important to the minister. This is the one which is tailored to the specific and individual needs of the person. It supplies not the broad stroke, but rather the fine detail which completes the picture. Both are important. One cannot effectively exist without the other.

Often ministers will complain that the 'system' has not provided the adequate level or type of support. The ineffectiveness of the fraternal or professional group is used as demonstration of the lack of, and at times the impossible nature of, support for ministers. What is actually being voiced in these concerns is that the multi-level nature of support is not recognized and that the deepest level of inner needs are not being satisfied. This is where the need for a personal support structure comes into effect.

Between two worlds

The personal support structure is the one not provided by the system, be it at a denominational or community level. This is the one which is put in place by each individual minister and is of his/her own choosing and creation. The onus is on each individual to develop, create and sustain this most important level of support. This may occur through a variety of sources. It is important to remember here that no single source need exist or be utilized in detachment from others. An effective personal support structure will probably be strongest when it is a blend of several or all.

Community based

The community provides a rich source of support if we but identify and utilize what is available. Communities contain people of diverse age, background, experience, training, personality, interest and occupation. This is true even in small and rural communities as the historic population base merges its roots with the providers of services who are often incomers to community.

In the survey I conducted there was a difference noted in the levels of support, dependent on size of community and the specific type of isolation experienced. Professionally, persons in rural communities felt more isolated than their counterparts in larger or urban settings. In the interviews conducted the difference in educational levels between the majority of residents native to rural communities and the minister appeared more pronounced because of the limited number of university trained individuals actually living in the community. Socially, the nature of community, rural, village or urban, seemed to have little effect on support levels. Ministers in rural community did appear less affected by the demands of others and did not feel so 'trapped' by these expectations. In spiritual support there appeared to be little difference based on community size. The urban centres provided more opportunity, but the smaller population base seemed to afford a greater sense of community and support.

It is in this 'sense of community' that support can be developed. We need to be careful that we do not limit the definition of community to a geographical or territorial setting. Community exists at its most effective level when it moves beyond the physical definition to a bonding centred in a common fellowship or shared identity. It is in the sharing of this identity and fellowship that the sense of 'being one with' and 'belonging' develop, providing the opportunity for more meaningful relationship offsetting isolation.

It is the minister's responsibility to identify and to enter into this 'sense of community'. The incomer to community, at times, may attempt to find in the new community those things which were familiar and supportive in their former community. When they are not found as expected, there is the temptation to emphasize the differences and consider them as problematic rather than to celebrate the diversity which enriches and broadens life's experiences.

It needs to be noted here that, as stated in Chapter 6, the minister will, in many tight-knit communities, be considered an outsider. Entrance to the community may be limited by this perception of the life-long residents. This needs to be understood by the incoming minister and be handled with sensitivity and care. The incoming minister and family must appear to seek inclusion with community and recognize that attempts to move in too rapidly or to seek control will alienate. There is also the risk that incomers will form their own sub-community around shared experiences of coming to the community, education, broader world interest and other interests. An 'us' and 'them' dichotomy can quickly develop. This may provide a support base, but it is not one which is rooted in community and as such will change as incomers come and go.

In the urban settings continuing education, speciality organizations, theatre and other arts, recreational clubs and hobby groups are made available. All of these provide support opportunity. From these can develop the personal relationships which move beyond Level 4 into the more meaningful Levels 5 and 6, and possibly even the intimacy of Level 7.

Community of faith based

There is, or should be, a natural community base around those who share in the common basis of the Christian faith. This has often been distorted by denominationalism and labelling around matters of theology and faith. It seems impossible to accept others on the simple foundations of faith without attempting to identify them as 'conservative', 'liberal', 'evangelical', 'charismatic' or some such label. The terminology itself becomes divisive, building barriers that are arbitrary and detrimental. In this division created by labels, we lose the strength and support of persons who offer to us, as we do to them, a differing perspective which contributes to a holistic and rounded sense of being.

From the broad community of faith, ministers can draw deep and meaningful support. This may come from the laity of the Christian community or from those who are called to serve as ministers in other church groups. We have seen that there is sometimes a sense of distrust or competition between clergy of the same denomination. Although this lack of trust, which often develops from our own insecurity, needs to be addressed, the opportunity to form relationships with church leaders from other denominations appeared, in the thinking of some, to overcome this difficulty. This personal support, generating from others in the community of faith, is not to be confused with the traditional interdenominational ministerial group. There is the need to develop a personal basis of interaction beyond the formal structure of such a group. This will be, in most cases, with a limited and select group with whom there is mutuality of trust and sharing. In fact, such support may develop on a one-to-one basis and may, at least initially, be specific in focus, allowing for a sense of knowing and trust to develop. On one occasion in my own experience the original time together was to provide reflection on a specific need in the life of one of the individuals, but later developed into an ongoing agreement to serve as pastoral care providers for one another.

In the broad wealth of the community of faith there is opportunity for support to be developed, moulded to the unique needs of the individuals. We should never be limited by our own denominational or church structure.

Church (local) based

The question has often been asked: 'Should not the community of faith, in its local expression the church, be the support for its clergy as for all its members?' This is a valid question and one which finds its basis in the records of the early church in the New Testament. The church has a mutual concern for all, and especially those in the local communion, as part of the body of Christ. The truth is, if we go back to the quadrilateral of scripture, tradition, reason and experience, as presented in Chapter 1, the latter three parts have presented factors which contrast with the ideal of scripture. Therefore, the gulf between laity and the ordained has developed, and in some cases widened, creating the 'us' and 'them' concept within the church. Clergy are seen as apart from the normal flow of care within the community, being predominantly the care giver as opposed to the one in need of care. The asymmetry within the relationship has often prevented the mutuality of care developing within this framework.

However, given the levels and diversity of support which we have maintained as essential, there is a need for the minister to identify and to utilize the level(s) of support found within this most natural of supportive settings. It must be recognized that this level of support does not meet all needs. The support in the professional areas, which requires the deepest levels of trust around issues of confidentiality, cannot be found in this setting. In fact, the nature of confidentiality between parishioner and minister can only exist if it is maintained at this level. Issues of a professional nature will find their support at other points of intersection within the clergy's personal support system.

The local church can, however, provide deep and meaningful support for its clergy. This may be in the form of spiritual and personal support, as well as assuring them that physical needs are met. The caring nature of the community of faith needs to be all-inclusive, providing for the clergy and the clergy family equal support. There is a need to point out that the clergy and family must be willing to be supported. The wall of insulation referred to in Chapter 7 must be lowered, allowing the laity to realize that the minister and his/her family have needs similar to those of all others within the church.

The developing of support at this level can also take the form of sharing exploration and discovery. All, including the clergy family, struggle with common issues in life. The development of support groups around issues of marriage, child rearing, finances, stewardship, and grief, to name just a few, provides the forum for both enquiry and mutual support and care. The clergy may at points give leadership in these activities, while at others they may be the recipient of its support and care. It is not even necessary that the common basis of discussion always be an issue within the personal life of the clergy. The community, generated around the group in and of itself, can still become inclusive and supportive. For instance, a pastor may, with other church people, give leadership to a singles group. That group may generate a strong community base which is supportive of the minister as he/she engages in the broader ministry of the church.

The local church provides opportunity for mutual care and support at a variety of levels. The minister needs to be open to this support and prepared both to give and to receive.

CARE based support network

We have been considering the need to tailor a personal support structure for the minister. This is a structure developed by each individual, unique to his/her specific situation, which relates to the holistic needs of the person as an individual. Some have expressed the need to establish speciality support systems for clergy around such areas as singles ministers, women in ministry and special support for clergy in same sex relationships. While recognizing that the broader systems or community based levels must address these needs, the development of a CARE based personal support network allows each person to create the system which best suits their requirements. The proper design and selection of such a support group will present a balance sometimes neglected in single focus groups.

As has been stressed, it is the minister who must act to create this group. It is important that as persons enter ministry in their first parish or charge, and as they move between charges, early priority in the placement be given to searching out individuals and establishing a CARE based network. This will not, in most cases, be a pre-established group, nor will it be one which will immediately take form. Rather, it will be a long-term process of building up a personal network which may possibly change as needs and people change.

This network may connect at various points with other levels of support in all areas presented and the individual will have to determine the strength of the connections. At the core of the network, however, will be a smaller inner group which provides the stability of support for persons involved. This is not a one-way support network for the minister, but rather has the mutuality of the Intimate Encounter established at a Level 7 relationship. This group, like marriage, requires careful selection, courtship and commitment.

The term 'CARE' based is used to illustrate some of the components which must be part of the ethos of such a group. These ideal attributes are growing qualities present to varying degrees, although some are essential to the group.

Comfortable	There needs to be a level of comfort within the group. The security of being within a 'comfort zone' lessens the anxiety allowing for interaction without risk.
Confidential	The need to be able to interact with minimal risk of violation of trust is essential. The group must function on an expressed covenant of confidentiality.
Committed	Persons with the group need to be committed to one another and to the group and its process. The group will be ineffective if half-hearted participation is present.
Confident	Participants must possess mutual confidence in one another as valued partners within the group. Faith, not only in what each contributes, but in one another as persons is essential.
Compassionate	There needs to be a deep mutual respect and compassion for one another. There must be genuine care for one another.

Confrontative	The group is valuable as it has the trust which allows for objective assessment of one another. Confrontation which generates from trust is constructive by nature. (The constant soothsayer soon loses credibility.)
Available	The group must be available to one another. Ministers who often speak of college friendships, separated by both time and space, need the availability of support within close proximity and as need arises. The utilization of the group may vary in frequency, but to know of its availability is emotionally important.
Accommodative	The group, in its selective format, must accommodate the diversity within. The basis of the group must be such that the risk and fear of rejection is minimal. Becoming vulnerable at the levels of intimacy requires a group which is accommodating of all diversity.
Affirmative	There is a need for the group to be affirming in nature. This does not negate the confrontational nature of the group, but rather is in all actions affirming of the personhood of each participant.
Responsible	Each person in the group has a responsibility to the others. There is a sense of community which balances rights within the group with responsibility for the group.
Responsive	The group must be responsive to the needs of other participants. This involves the permission to be proactive in recognizing the needs of another and offering early support. For instance, the over dependency of a participant on a substance or another person may be recognized by others, and in the trust of relationship, remedial care offered.
Redemptive	The group must always seek to act in the redemptive nature of Grace.
Reconciling	All action must be reconciling in nature. By this is meant that it must continue in the establishment of relationship between the individual and the inner self, others and ultimately with the Divine.
Restorative	In the face of attitude, thought or action which may divide and isolate there is the need of the

	group to seek to unify and restore.
Equal	All within the group must be equal. Dominance or control by individuals or sub-grouping will destroy the balance and polarize participants.
Evaluative	The group can and should provide effective evaluation of one another. The 'success' factor discussed earlier needs the objectivity of a group to balance subjectivity.
Equipping	It is this group, tailored to the specific needs of individuals, which can effectively equip the minister, emotionally, spiritually and socially to face the separation and isolation experienced in ministry.

	Comfortable
	Confidential
C	Committed
	Confident
	Compassionate
	Confrontative
	Available
A	Accommodative
	Affirmative
	Responsible
	Responsive
R	Redemptive
	Reconciling
	Restorative
	Equal
E	Evaluative
	Equipping

This network is at the very centre of the support system for the clergyperson. Although we have referred to it as a group, it is anticipated that as it is established it may well begin as a one-on-one encounter. There is a need, however, for the sake of objectivity, to expand it to a group dynamic. Equally, there is a need to guard against it becoming too large, thus reverting to a broad sweeping support system rather than one which responds to the inner needs of individuals. As with the Intimate Encounter relationship, this group may well cross age, gender, educational, occupational and other barriers, and in so doing become effective and transformative.

Support, as we have seen, comes from different levels and from different sources. Although responsibility for supportive networks lies at all levels it must be the individual who avails her/himself of the resources available. In the end it is the individual who must actively seek or develop an environment in which they can find support and strength to continue in ministry in a complex and changing world.

12

Making it personal

Grace does not suddenly 'annihilate' fallen nature, inserting something totally new in its place. There is a restoration of lost balance, a return to full integration within ourselves

(Ramon, 1989, p. 89)

Tom listened intensely as the theme of stress in ministry was discussed. There were certain points in the discussion, such as the need to spend more time with spouse and family, where he experienced a twinge of guilt for he knew that this was an issue between him and his wife. The problem with these seminars, he thought, was that there was always analysis of what was and discussion of what should be, but little that a person could actually utilize in their own ministry. The session ended and, with a few joking comments to some fellow ministers about needing to get back to work before things got too out of hand, he was off.

Later in the week, after a little reflection, Tom dismissed the seminar as being relatively useless. This was confirmed in his thinking by the presenter's comment that the responsibility for change and control lay with the individual. That was obviously the comment of an academic who had never been, or could not remember what it was like to be, in real ministry. There were always so many demands placed upon ministers and this was especially true at St Mark's. There was just so much happening that to think that the response lay in the hands of the minister was simply not realistic. Let the presenter try and follow him for a day! The truth, he thought, was that he was busy, but probably not more so than others who were members of St Mark's. Besides, this was all part and parcel of ministry. No one said it would be easy and in reality he was handling it quite well.

How does all this apply in the real life of the busy minister? It is easy, as Tom did, to dismiss the problem and responsibility for action for a variety of reasons. Justification of busyness by comparing it to the lives of others makes the religious life as driven as all others and does not present a model indicative of balance and stewardship. The very fact that others, or the job itself, are blamed creates additional stress. As we have seen in Chapter 2, a major contributor to the feeling of stress is lack of control. If the control is vested in others, ministers feel trapped and stress increases. The other risk is to think, as Tom did, that he had it all in control. Rationalization which justifies busyness and promotes stress is destructive to the minister, to those closest to him/her and ultimately to ministry itself.

Each person is responsible for his/her own personal and professional well-being. Although there are expectations and pressures brought to bear by others, it is always the individual who responds. In the final analysis, responsibility lies with the person. If, however, the control is to be effectively exercised two things must occur. First, the individual must look at the reality of his/her situation in concrete terms. Secondly, there must be the will to act in ways which will move towards wholeness and balance.

Total assessment concept

The group of ministers had met to participate in a prototype of the questionnaire to be used in the survey I was about to conduct. They had been asked the question as to how many days they were allowed to take off in the context of the week. The next question required them to examine their diaries, the record of their activity, and to indicate how many days they had actually taken off in the past month (30 days). One minister showed signs of agitation as he thumbed through his book. Then with considerable anger he shouted 'I don't like this process! I thought we were going to talk about lessening stress!' He was discovering that in actuality he had not taken any time off in over 30 days and he was both surprised and upset by the revelation. We, more so than others, may be the most shocked by the way in which we handle our time.

There is the risk that we become so used to the routine of life that we lose our sensitivity to the imbalance within our daily and weekly routine. We function by responding to the demands of the task without recognizing that in continually so doing we have thrown off the equilibrium within our own life. Soon, like the minister above, we lose track of exactly how we have divided our time between the many requirements of life. We must take stock, in a concrete way, of our actions.

There is a need for a process of self-assessment. Much of what exists as self-assessment today, especially in the professions, is related predominantly to performance based appraisal. This calls for evaluation of how one has performed in the job up to the current point in time and provides the process to establish clear and workable goals for the future. Emphasis is placed on doing with little appreciation for being.

This is true in many assessment processes devised for clergy. Jacobs' (1989) helpful book acknowledges the need for consideration of the whole person, but then, as he specifies is his intent, directs the process predominantly towards the function of ministry. It is difficult to assess the outworking of the task of ministry if evaluation is not made of the health of the individual in all other areas of life.

The proposal for self-assessment presented here is intended to look at the self as a whole being, inclusive of the vocational dynamic. As we have seen the individual can only effectively function within ministry as he/she has a sense of their wholeness.

In the presenting of this assessment process it is recognized that there is no perfect procedure and that this one, like all others, will not meet all circumstances. This model, as with all models, is a construct, and as such is not real. The individual is asked simply to consider the process, to utilize it as appropriate and to modify it where necessary. The emphasis here is conceptual in that it attempts to cause persons to think about a broad and whole perspective of their life. In order to make the process work it is necessary to keep records or a journal. We will present the *total assessment concept* first and then look at the process of keeping a journal which will facilitate the process.

All components of an individual's life are important and equal. Although certain areas may seem to dominate more of our time than others, all are essential to the functioning of the total system. The Apostle Paul makes this clear in the terms of body life in his analogy of the church when he says 'those parts of the body which seem to be weaker are indispensable' (1 Cor 12.22). It is also recognized that it is impossible to define these components as we do here. There is a symbiotic flow between components and, again as the Apostle Paul points out, any action of a part affects the whole. Therefore, although we may examine specifically the component of the spiritual we recognize that this is a part of and affects all of being.

The pastor's physical being

That we are physical beings goes without saying. What, however, are we actually doing to care for the physical aspect of our being?

Let us be brutal here and suggest that many in ministry pay less than adequate attention to and provide less than adequate care for themselves as physical beings. There is the tendency to overwork, to be overly intense, to overeat, and to neglect exercise, adequate rest and the opportunity for the body to find time for an equilibrium and balance.

We have seen this in the context of our discussion as ministers take too little time off and constantly seem to be involved in the task and busyness of ministry in a way as McAllister says (1978, p. 53) 'that does not characterize any other profession or vocation'.

The pastor is a physical being. That demands stewardship of the physical being God has given us. We must recognize our physical limitations which can affect other capabilities. We cannot be or do all that is demanded of us. There must be time for renewal of the physical resource that is part of our whole being. This applies both to our days in ministry and in our training for ministry.

As physical beings there is a need to assess general health and well-being. It is also important that physical exercise be a part of the balance of the daily/weekly routine. The temptation following a hard day is to seek total rest from the hectic pace. Research has shown that a routine of exercise is a vital part of stress relief and a good means of restoring equilibrium to the body system. This affects all other facets of being.

The pastor's cognitive being

There is a need to assess those dimensions of being which relate to the mind. A healthy mind is an aspect of healthy being. I will consider this component in several different ways.

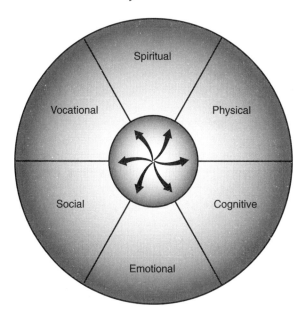

Total assessment concept

Figure 12.1   Total assessment concept

There is a need to be stimulated mentally. The expression 'use it or lose it' applies to our mental capacity. The demand, and capacity to respond, must always challenge our mental capacity thus stimulating it, or, as Levi (1987) would imply, stress will occur through 'poor fit'. First, we must ask, does what we do in ministry challenge us intellectually? Do we wrestle with the issues of life and faith as they become integrated in our action?

Secondly, have we continued to develop in the areas of cognitive growth? There must be growth in our mental capacity. There is a concept in the continuing education field called 'lifelong learning'. This means intentional planning around the ongoing mental/cognitive growth of the individual. The risk with clergy, as in all disciplines, is to concentrate on the area of speciality, for example the spiritual or theological. For a person seeking balance and wholeness in life this growth should reflect a larger and growing perspective especially as issues of faith and ministry strive to keep pace with a changing culture and society. The 'I'm too busy to undertake that diversity' may be the response of an individual who is not growing mentally and is content to try to function on yesterday's offerings.

The pastor's emotional being

The pastor, like everyone else within the church and community, is an emotional being. 'Well', you say, 'that is obvious.' But is it? As we have seen, due to many factors within the supposed 'tasks' of ministry, emotions become masked, often suppressed and even denied.

There exists the risk of the emotional impact of identification, or *over-identification*, by ministers with the problems of those they are called to serve. Ministers walk with their parishioners in their difficulties. These can become internalized in the ministers' thinking, especially as they recognize the same or similar problems faced in their life. Emotional energy is expended in the process of over-identification.

Feelings are often hidden because the minister also is human and he/she too possesses fears: fears of rejection, fears of the loss of love and respect, fear of the possibility of failure. There is no church (at least known to me) that is free from conflict. In the face of conflict all the fears which we have mentioned arise. How does the minister deal with these emotions?

This leads to a difficult area for many clergy to discuss and with which to deal. I believe, however, that it comes under this section and must be considered as part of self-assessment. Emotional difficulties may reach the level of acute distress. There is, at times, the constant suppression of emotions which fester underneath the surface and will erupt causing critical disruption and pain. The walls of insulation produced by past hurt in pastoral relationships may mask suppressed stress, anger and depression, but can usually only do so for a while.

We as clergy cannot handle this very well when it exists within ourselves. We assist others in emotional turmoil but deny the problem within ourselves. It is as though admission of emotional difficulties somehow denies the Grace of God within us and that we have failed. But it is there. It is part of our humanity.

There is a danger if we consider emotional difficulty, such as depression, as somehow indicative of our lack of spiritual strength. As integrated beings there are always contributing factors and the spiritual is no exception, but to make this the sole cause, as some are apt to do, leads to increased guilt, self-condemnation, sense of failure or, in the extreme, fear of demon possession. We may voice this warning to others seeking our counsel, but often in our own thinking we still believe that somehow we have failed God if we encounter such difficulties. Many of the saints of the church experienced deep emotional turmoil. Yet for them this deep night of the soul or desert experience was often a time of renewal, greater dependence on God, and new beginnings.

What about our emotional being? Can we identify areas where we suppress emotions or need specific help? If so, there is a need to seek help from other professionals. Emotional difficulties may manifest themselves in many ways. As we have seen from such reports as the BMA study on stress there are physiological reactions as well as behavioural responses. Among them are such things as over-dependence on substances such as alcohol and drugs. Ministers, like others, run this risk. The Ansvar Survey of English Social Behaviour (1994–95) conducted by Christian Research found that 52 per cent of ministers surveyed drank alcohol once a week compared to 28 per cent of churchgoers. The use of alcohol weekly is not indicative of a problem, but there is a significant difference here which could translate to later difficulties.

Consideration must be given to the emotional health of the clergy. Wayne Oates recommended as early as 1958 in a journal article entitled 'The healthy minister' that all in ministry would benefit from a period of therapy as part of their ministerial training.

The minister's social being

In this section of the assessment several factors must be considered. First, we include here interaction within a kinship system as it relates to the family and those closest to the individual. Close examination must be given to both the amount, quality and effectiveness of time spent within partner and family relationships. These, as we have seen, are the areas which can easily be neglected and reduced to required functionary events. Comments have been heard from ministers (often of the older generation) that the raising of children was left to the partner (usually the wife). Although this may not occur quite so openly today, there is a risk that primary decision making concerning family matters and child rearing is left to the partner most in the home, namely the spouse. Intentional interest, concern and participation should be evident in family interaction.

Assessment of the relationship between husband and wife is also necessary. This includes intimacy as expressed in sexuality. This, in its purest form, is found in the deep relationship of Level 7 or Intimate Encounter. However, as we have seen, even within marriage the intimacy may be absent and although physical sexual activity may occur, an equally and mutually satisfying relationship may not exist. Emphasis must be placed here on the equality within this level of relationship. This unsatisfied desire for intimacy makes the risk of unacceptable sex in the context of the profession greater. Openness and honesty around these issues in assessment and with a partner is vitally important.

Also, under this section, it is important to apply all the levels of relationships which were developed in Chapter 6. Although interaction occurs with many people in a broad range of events and situations it is necessary that the interaction span the range of levels and fulfil our multiple relational needs. The assessment should pay close attention to the presence of relationships in Levels 5, 6 and 7. At the Level 5 range care must be taken to distinguish between the social activity that is work related, and therefore really a Level 4 activity, and one which is genuinely a Level 5 relationship. Similarly it is important to recognize that asymmetry must exist, especially at Levels 6 and 7. Association which is always directed towards others may need to be more accurately classified as a lower-level activity.

The social assessment must also consider the means by which the minister expresses him/herself in a manner that provides opportunity for relaxation. There is the potential that all social 'outings' are in the context of the faith community or related to church events. In a recent conference with a group of lay church leaders, many in the group came to the realization that their whole life centred in the church community and that all of their activity was church related. For the minister, this means that he/she is always carrying with them the role of minister, never able to participate free from that identity. Does the assessment include opportunity to express oneself socially outside of the role?

The minister as vocational being

Much of assessment processes centre around evaluation of work and the way in which people perform their jobs. This is an important area of appraisal, but needs to be considered in the context of the whole.

For many clergy this is an area of over-identification. Often the role becomes the primary identity and most time and energy go towards its maintenance. We have looked at this at considerable length within this book. There is a need to assess the degree to which the vocation affects the balance within the whole being of the minister.

Care must be taken. It is natural that one's vocation or calling is a major portion of one's life and activity and therefore demands a considerable time commitment. However, we are not addressing here a simple quantitative division of time. This is no different for the clergy than it is for the doctor or the lawyer. The difficulty arises when it dominates all other activity and everything else is secondary in importance to work. We saw that time off by ministers still consisted of 'church talk' and family time was depleted by the emotional drain of the minister's work. The minister's social or church-acceptable image influenced his/her family life and child rearing. It is when all else is overshadowed or suffers because of the work that the balance is wrong.

Also, it is important to assess what is motivating the work activity, especially when it is excessive. Is it our concept of God, our desire for success, the need to prove self-worth, the expectations of others or some other driving force? Often, so it would appear, it is the desire to appease the expectations of others, thus demonstrating success, that drives the individual to overwork. Not only actual functioning, but the question 'Why?' must be asked. Does the vocational calling produce driven women and men?

Vocational growth

An aspect of vocational assessment relates to growth. There is a need to continue to advance in the profession. This advancement in the church is not predominantly a movement to bigger, larger or more successful parishes, although it is deemed such by some, but rather an advancement in understanding, perspective and, therefore, capability. There is a risk of becoming 'trapped' in 'doing ministry' by the perpetuation of known tasks and rituals. This, in and of itself, will lead to an irrelevance in attempting to intersect the faith message with today's perspective and world.

The assessment of growth, like success, is difficult to measure unless we fall into the trap of utilizing quantitative measures such as increase in baptism, church growth, financial stability. Growth needs to be assessed in ministry in terms of development, not only of performance competency, but in terms of conceptualization, of attitude, of spiritual maturity and other perceptual components. There is no such measurement available. However, the following model of skill acquisition has proven helpful to many in looking at vocational growth in its broader sense and is presented here with the suggestion that individuals, in the process of reflection, apply it to their own development.[1]

The Dreyfus model of skill acquisition
The Dreyfus model of skill acquisition (1980) is based on the work of two UCLA professors, Stuart Dreyfus, a mathematician and system analyst, and Hubert Dreyfus, a philosopher. The Dreyfus model suggests that the integration of knowledge and skill leading to a higher level of excellence is based on five levels of proficiency. Patricia Benner, who has utilized the model in training in the profession of nursing, reports concerning the two changes evident, one of performance and one of perception and understanding:

> The levels reflect changes in two general aspects of skill performance. One is a movement from reliance on abstract principles to the use of past, concrete experience as paradigms. The other is the change in the perception and the understanding of a demand situation so that the situation is seen less as a compilation of equally relevant bits and more as a complete whole in which only certain parts are relevant. (1982, p. 402)

The five levels of proficiency are as follows:

1. *Novice.* The novice is the beginner who has no experience relating to the situation in which they are expected to perform a task. Their training for the task which they perform is predominately in terms of theory. This theory can be applied having never experienced or utilized it before. The person at the novice level functions primarily on the basis of learned technical knowledge and is therefore bound by the rules and techniques that have been taught. Functioning is by the book. It is not expected at this point that they will make discretionary judgements, but rather that they will function according to the rules or manual.

2. *Advanced beginner.* The advanced beginner is one who has had some experience within the profession. From this experience base, they are able to distil some meaning from recurring patterns and events. These are not specifically learned precepts, but rather are more overall global characteristics that have been observed and have therefore become recognizable in current task functioning.

At the advanced beginner level, the person still requires assistance in setting priorities since they operate on general guidelines and are only beginning to perceive relevant recurring patterns within practice.

3. *Competent.* This level of efficiency relates to persons who have a number of years of experience and have some skill within a situation as a result of learned theory integrated with experience. The competent professional does not see their action simply as related to the specific situation, but rather as related to long-term goals and plans. The competent practitioner functions very well and does the job efficiently.

   It is interesting that Benner points out that this level is supported and reinforced by the institution. The function of the competent person is characterized by standardization and routine functioning and it is possible to predict with considerable accuracy how the person will function. For the system, there are no surprises, but rather good service within the parameters described by the controlling levels of management and administration. Supported by the institution, many persons remain at the competent level.

4. *Proficient.* Continued practice within the profession should move the practitioner into the level of proficiency.

   Whereas the competent practitioner saw action in relation to long-term goals, the proficient professional sees the dynamic in a more holistic perspective. He/she is able to determine whether the picture presented is a total picture or whether it is incomplete. Decision making is now based on a holistic perspective rather than dealing with specific aspects and trying to fit them into the picture as one would fit pieces into a complex puzzle.

   Maxims are used to guide the proficient professional. These are based on a deep theoretical understanding of the situation coupled with experience and provide guidance as to what is important to the whole picture allowing for a rapid 'intuitive like' response.

5. *Expert.* At the expert level the professional is no longer reliant on procedural knowledge (rules, guidelines, maxims) to connect his/her knowledge of the situation to action required. Intuitive response is automatic, based on a sensing of the whole.

   Because the expert's action is automatic and holistic it is difficult, if not impossible, for the person at this level to describe the action in procedural terms or incremental strategies. Description is in holistic outcomes. To expect a procedural description would be like asking the professional race-car driver, whose combined sensory and intuitive processes (let alone external factors) prompt thousands of gear shifts within the heat of a race, to describe the factors that prompted the decision that lead to a specific shifting of gears.

It is possible for the minister to assess where he/she is in the context of this skill acquisition model. Among clergy the third level, that which is characterized by competent action, is most prevalent. This is the level most supported by the institutional church, for it presents no surprises while delivering a good quality of service. The view of ministry at this level is predominantly task orientated and is characterized by the ability of the individual to do long-term planning and goal setting. All of this, however, is within the standardization provided by the system. The level of competence may tend to trap persons with its affirmation and awards within the institutionalized church.

Movement beyond the third level brings one into a more whole understanding of vocation, beyond the specifics of task, to an integration of doing and being. Action is a function of total being, lessening the tension between any compartmentalization or separation between thought, word and deed. This is consistent with the concept of intentional ministry generating from a central integrity as introduced in Chapter 1.

There is no precise science by which one can identify where one fits on the scale. Introspection and reflection on one's ministry as it relates to this scale can assist in determining where one is and what is helpful for continuing professional growth. In the context of a changing society, and with it a transition in the role and identity of the minister, it is essential to experience growth in the vocation. The foundation of yesterday, even that which contributes towards competency, is not sufficient for the demands of tomorrow.

The pastor's spiritual being

It is not possible to compartmentalize personhood or being. There is indeed a holistic nature to being which makes the individual, and in this case the pastor, an irreducible whole. The spiritual dynamic of being is not quantifiable and permeates all aspects of being. We have considered in Chapter 10 the need to re-establish or reaffirm a spiritual identity and have said that in so doing we create a space at the very centre of being to encounter the Divine, others and ourselves. Having said that, there is a need to examine and assess our spiritual lives as a very central part of being.

The continued discipline of spiritual growth and formation is a personal concern to all Christians and the minister is no exception. In fact, always immersed in the task of ministry, the minister may well experience little spiritual growth and renewal. Involvement in preparation of sermons, pastoral care of others, prayer as part of that care, and administration of a busy parish may prevent opportunity, and for some even mask the need, for personal spiritual nurture. The ministry of Word and Sacrament may well be an outward working preventing the Living Word from encountering the minister in a transformative and intimate way.

Assessment calls for an evaluation of what actual spiritual nurture and growth is being experienced in one's life. What time is taken for personal prayer, meditation and spiritual exercise? There is a need to separate that which is done as 'expectations of the role' and that which is personal and internal. It is vital here that spiritual growth not be equated with proficiency in the task. As Hitchcock (1991, p. 27) clearly indicates, although mastery of a discipline may bring spiritual benefit, spirituality is not a thing that can be measured in terms of performance excellence.

A second part of spiritual assessment relates to the presence of spiritual support and guidance. As we have considered, spiritual isolationism is prevalent and at times intentional. However, to seek to function without guide and input from others is indicative of a naivety of need or an arrogance of self-sufficiency. Regardless of cause there is a need for the spiritual intersection of others in our lives, not only in the crisis, but in the lifelong endeavour for growth and spiritual maturity. Who provides this spiritual care for the minister?

The spiritual assessment will be the most difficult of all. Supposedly objective assessment processes like Fowler's *Stages of Faith* or Benson and Donahue's *Faith Maturity Scale* do have some merit. However, the process being suggested here is more pragmatic, asking simply 'What occurs in your life to nurture you spiritually?' and 'Who provides for your spiritual guidance and nurture?' 'Do you have a spiritual director, soul-friend or some such resource person in your life?'

The space at the centre

At the centre of the total self-assessment figure is a central space from which all else emanates. The question is 'What occupies this space?' What is it that drives all action and around which the person lives his/her life? It is from this integrated centre of being that all life is held together in wholeness.

The credal response is that the chief end is found in a commitment to humanity's love and worship of God. Therefore, the central driving force of all life for the Christian is to do all things to the glory of God. This is the ideal and it is right and proper that such should exist.

However, what is it in reality that becomes the central focus of life and from which all else flows? This is not to raise controversy, prompt denial or create guilt. It is helpful, and indeed necessary, for each person to ask the question for and of themselves. Freud would say that the driving central force for all humanity is a 'will to pleasure', Adler a 'will to power', Frankl a 'will to meaning', but is it as universal as that? For each of us there is a personal driving force which may consist of a central desire for advancement, careerism, pleasure, economics, service and fulfilment of the divine will, to name but a few.

Each individual must assess what is his/her motivation and driving force in life. To understand and acknowledge this is to recognize and interpret what is happening in other aspects of life. It is from this central integrating force (or the lack of it) that all action occurs.

Keeping a journal

The concept of keeping a journal is not a new one. It has obviously been around since the early apostles who kept records of their journeys, encounters and conversations, some of which made their way into the New Testament story. The early church leaders kept diaries, not only of their actions, but also of their spiritual thoughts and journey. The *Confessions* of Augustine present an excellent accounting of both records of doing and the corresponding feelings of being. Record keeping for many early Christian leaders became the means by which they could record their lives and monitor their spiritual progress.

Morton Kelsey (1989) states 'Keeping a journal is one of the most helpful practices in our working towards human fulfilment' (p. 116). In a process of self-assessment intended to move us towards wholeness it is absolutely essential. It becomes the tool of self-measurement which, when properly used, chronicles for us the place of beginning against which we measure progress and, ultimately, ending. Without this measure, movement becomes indiscernible except in broad terms and predominately external components. For instance, we can recall early years of ministry in terms of major events and movement, but lose much of the sharpness of the cutting edge of our thought which motivated those actions during that time period. So soon we forget the impact of the moment with all its joys and pain.

Journal keeping assists in other ways. There is always a discrepancy between what we think we do or have done, and what actually has transpired. For instance I may think I balance my time well on sabbatical between the research, writing, speaking engagements, conference presentations, goal setting with colleagues and the sabbath rest badly needed. My journal records soon revealed that my tendency towards being a workaholic has short-changed the sabbath rest and that there is need for readjustment. Journal keeping, as was evident in the minister who checked his diary, can be brutally revealing, but absolutely essential.

Journal keeping also records significant thoughts, emotions and reactions as one interacts with the diversity of life. Written in the aftermath of such actions it records how one's life and faith interacted. It is in that interaction within our own lives that depth of understanding comes, enabling us to provide care and concern for others. It is the record of our journey, common with all humanity, which allows the empathy to interface with the lives of others.

Setting up the journal

Probably one of the greatest deterrents to keeping a journal is the time that it takes. In the rush of a hectic day and the routine of a busy life it is hard to imagine where one can find the time to do yet another thing. Several things are important here. First, the habit of journal keeping and reflection will pay dividends both as an organizational process and a means of determining the way forward. Secondly, the keeping of a journal fits in well with daily spiritual exercise as it encourages reflection and meditation. Thirdly, although difficult to maintain in the beginning, like all discipline, it soon becomes a habit which proves invaluable. Finally, the simpler the journal process is, the easier it is to maintain.

Since we are really looking at this, in these writings, as an assessment process, we will suggest a way conducive to evaluation. The outline suggested is designed so that one can easily determine the areas of strengths and weaknesses within the whole picture presented in the total assessment concept. Each person may find ways of modification to suit his/her needs, but care should be taken to make the components defined above readily identifiable.

In order to give a maximum overview as an assessment process, it is recommended that the journal be kept in three different time frameworks: daily, weekly and monthly. The first is a daily recording which chronicles the day and conveys the sense of the events in closest proximity. The second is a weekly reflection which allows for a 'flavour of the week' overview, summarizing predominant events or emotions. The final is a monthly reflection process which permits the determining of trends and ongoing directions. There will be the desire on the part of the person keeping the journal to evaluate a series of months, such as an annual review, as part of determining what has transpired and in the setting of future goals. Continuing periodical reviews will give opportunity for a valuable longitudinal assessment often missed or made only in generalities.

Simplicity and a process that is user-friendly is the key to sustaining a journal. For the computer literate such records can be recorded and stored by that means. The more traditional method of utilizing a notebook works for some while for others the ease of writing on a computer and the tangible form of the hardcopy has led to the use of ringbinders for computer print-offs. Whatever works for the individual is best.

Whatever the process used, confidentiality and security of the document is essential, for it will contain very personal records. Associated with this is the final disposal of such records. One of the growing concerns of many journal keepers is how to keep these confidential records secure after death. Once again, each person will need to determine their own process for this. Some have commissioned a trusted friend to dispose of the documents in the case of death while others have recorded their request in a will along with all other dispersal of property. This is personal, but needs to be considered.

For our purpose, rather than keeping a general journal, it is suggested that each time period be considered in the light of the following guided questions. These will assist in identifying the matter of balance in each time period. Individual journal keepers may want to expand on these questions making them more personal. Such development is fine, always keeping in mind that the simpler the process the greater the likelihood you will maintain the activity. For some it may be helpful to set the journal up on a form basis with designated space for a response to each question as illustrated here. This, either in hard form or on computer, calls for succinctness, thus making the review process much easier. It is recognized that not all questions will prompt a daily response. However, a continued absence in response to a given question may demonstrate a need in that specific area. The limited space on the form may be seen by some as too restrictive and a separate journal section with cross reference may be advisable for expansion on specific events or responses. Similarly, specific sections of the journal may be kept for theological insights, biblical reflections, goal setting or any such area as is deemed helpful by the recorder.

The journal will contain both the record of the task of ministry and the personal journey of the individual. It should be remembered here that the assessment is of balance and a sense of wholeness of being. The record of doing is important, but equally so is the record of reflection and inner discovery.

Finally, it is important that the recorder be frank and honest in the writing of the journal. There is always the temptation with each of us to record our journal to reflect our cherished self-image, with a bias which portrays us in the most positive light. This is not very helpful for self-assessment and personal growth. Record as accurately as possible. This will mean the ventilation of emotions and the feelings we have towards others as well as other things not often expressed. This calls for a moving beyond social acceptability or spiritual piety to what is happening in reality at the centre of our being. Remember this is your journal for your benefit. Any sharing of the journal, should you opt for it, will be by your personal choice and at your discretion.

DAILY JOURNAL
(Record under separate headings)

[1] What occupied most of your time today?
[2] What is/was your predominant feeling as the day came to a close?
[3] What provided you with the greatest sense of satisfaction?
[4] What was the greatest source of frustration/anxiety?
[5] Describe time spent with family and in personal relationships.
[6] Did you find time for your own personal space for relaxation, exercise and rest?
[7] What challenged your thinking?
[8] What was your source of spiritual renewal today?
[9] Other comments or observations on the day:

WEEKLY JOURNAL
(Record a short weekly review at the end of each week)

[1] What seem to be the predominant factors/issues of the week?
[2] What, upon reflection, was the greatest accomplishment of the week?
[3] What provided the greatest sense of frustration?
[4] What building did you do during the week of relationships with family, friends and others?
[5] What spiritual renewal/strength did you receive during the week and from what source did this come?
[6] What stewardship was exercised over your physical being?
[7] Were there aspect(s) of your life neglected during the week? If so, which? Why?
[8] Other comments or observations on the week:

MONTHLY SUMMARY

Using the weekly summaries for reflection, complete a short monthly review using the guide questions as outlined under the heading for WEEKLY JOURNAL.

The questions provide only the broad-sweep framework for the self-assessment process. This is only one level of evaluation and individuals may want to take a closer look at specific components. This may be done by seeking out specific assessment tools or finding individuals who may be of assistance. For instance, a closer evaluation of vocation may use the helpful 'Agenda for appraisal' as presented in Chapter 7 of Jacobs' book (1989, pp. 136ff.), or spiritual nurture may be assisted by finding a spiritual director. The needs identified by the journal process will determine the remedial action to be taken by the individual. Each person must be proactive, however, in seeking that action. Part of that process may be assisted by the objective reflection of the CARE support group as described in the last chapter. Again, this is a personal matter and one which develops as trust and confidence in the group develops. It is important, however, having entered into continuing self-assessment, and having identified areas of need, that we act upon them.

A final comment on balance

I have a growing concern that in the seeking of balance there is the temptation to create further imbalance. We find a certain ease in doing the familiar or entering into the same thing, but under a different format, with the assumption that a change is as good as a rest. There is a recognition that there is a need in life for R and R or *rest and recuperation*. This is a term often used in the military to allow personnel an opportunity to find relaxation and compensation from the intensity of battle service or military posting. Such action is required in the life of the minister.

R and R is needed not only in rest and recuperation, but in the form of *response reversal*. By that is meant the need to compensate for our responses within ministry by seeking, within reason, a reversal of action bringing balance. For instance, the following examples of responses find balance in the reverse reaction:

Response	Reverse reaction
Doing	Being
High adrenaline	Low adrenaline
High intensity	Low intensity
Exterior focus	Interior focus
Ministering to	Ministered to
Work/task	Play/party
Church life	World life
Sacred	Secular
Action	Reflection

High profile	Anonymity
Talking	Silence

It is possible to go on and list other areas of responses and reverse reactions. The risk is, as we have indicated, that we find comfort in doing the familiar and are threatened by the reverse. It is difficult for the person who is always in the presence of communication and noise to face silence. The high-adrenaline character of a stockbroker may find yet another adrenaline fix in a daily five-mile run. Although this may provide for the physical, the question must be asked as to what activity compensates the body system by lowering adrenaline output and reducing stress on the system.

For the clergyperson there is the risk of time off being a busman's holiday. Coming from immersion in the world of the sacred, vacation time and off time may be found in the comfort of another sacred body, such as a biblical or theological conference or a spiritual retreat centre. Although this may provide, as is needed from time to time, spiritual renewal, it does not alone provide the balance required. Similarly ministers, as do many Christians, find most, if not all, relationships within the church world. Does this provide balance of perspective, understanding and relationship?

The raising of this issue is not to decry any of these functions or activities. All have a place in the balanced life. Care must be exercised, however, that such balance does exist. As the writer of Ecclesiastes has said: 'There is a time for everything and a season for every activity under heaven' (3.1). Later, balance is again addressed in a warning not to be 'overrighteous', 'overwicked', 'overwise' or a 'fool' culminating in the statement:

> It is good to grasp the one
> and not let go of the other. '
> The man [person] who fears God will avoid all extreme
> (7.15–18 NIV)

Note

1 This model is used with ministers entering advanced professional studies in the Doctor of Ministry programme directed by the author. It is valuable in helping the individual to determine how they are performing in actual practice.

Epilogue

In the maturity of the second half of life, we, as human beings, cease creating a new ego identity and begin to rediscover the depth of our intrinsic being. So say the analytical psychologists. So we often hear in the great literature of our time. T. S. Eliot in *Choruses From 'The Rock'* eloquently alluded to this when he indicated that all of life consists of a searching which ends in returning to the place of beginnings to know it for the first time.

This has always seemed, in one sense, tragically profound in its understanding and portrayal of life. It is only as we explore the complexity and diversity of life that we come fully to understand and appreciate the beginning and each new beginning along the journey. The tragedy is that there are parts of the journey that upon return, even with a new sense of understanding, can never be recaptured in all of their fullness and richness. A new appreciation does not necessarily offer a renewed opportunity to relive.

So in ministry and all of life, opportunities are missed. We live with the stress of proving our adequacy, of establishing relevance, of seeking advancement and in fulfilling what we believe are the expectations of others and maybe even what we consider the demands of God. In so doing we may miss the special intrinsic moments of intimacy with others, especially with husband or wife and children. We neglect the development of deep friendships and enter into task-based relationships. We may impede the moments of moving inward to a deeper spiritual meaning to life, failing to find times of intimacy with the Divine. In coming to a fuller understanding of this, often only in the second half of life, we have allowed to escape many an opportunity. Children reach adulthood and leave home, potential friends move on and, indeed, we ourselves pass our prime.

This book has led us into many areas of enquiry. We have considered issues of shaping, culture, theory and of doing and being. We will not have satisfied the quantitative vocational researcher who seeks descriptive statistics, sometimes without asking the 'why' question of such responses. We have sought, however, to raise issues, to understand the subject better, to heighten awareness, and even to be so bold as to suggest a self-assessment process and remedial action.

The research of the book has forced the writer to re-examine his own life and in so doing to seek to apply it personally by seeking a better balance in life. In so doing it is hoped that along the journey more moments can be more fully appreciated while the opportunity is still possible. If in some small way this happens for the reader then the book has fulfilled its purpose.

Bibliography

Adler, A. (1928) *Understanding Human Nature*. New York: Greenburg Press.

Angus Reid Poll of Religious Life in Canada (1993) 'God is alive', *McLean's Magazine* (Toronto), 12 April.

Barr, J. (1977) *Fundamentalism*. London: SCM Press.

Barr, J. (1984) *Escape From Fundamentalism*. London: SCM Press.

Benner, P. (1982) 'From novice to expert', *American Journal of Nursing*, March.

Benson, P. and Donahue, M. J. (1993) *Faith Maturity Scale: A Conceptualization, Measure and Empirical Validation*. Minneapolis: Search Institute.

Bibby, R. (1990) *Mosaic Madness*. Toronto: Stoddard Publishing.

Blizzard, S. (1956) 'The minister's dilemma', *Christian Century*, vol. 73.

Bowman, C. (1996) Preliminary report to the Diocese of Southwell on a portion of his research for MA degree, University of Nottingham (unpublished).

Brierley, P. (1995) *UK Christian Handbook, 1994/95 Edition*. London: The National Bible Society and Christian Research.

Brierley, P. and MacDonald, F. (1995) *Prospects for Scotland 2000*. London: The National Bible Society and Christian Research.

British Medical Association (1992) *Stress and the Medical Profession*. London: BMA.

Brunner, E. (1937) *The Divine Imperative*. Philadelphia: Westminster Press.

Brunner, E. (1962) *The Christian Doctrine of the Church, Faith and Consummation* (*Dogmatics*, vol. III). London: Lutterworth Press.

Burgess, W. J. (1911) *John Smith the Se-Baptist, Thomas Helwys and the First Baptist Church*. London: James Clarke and Co.

Carr, W. (1994) *Brief Encounters*. London: SPCK.

Church of England (1995) *Something to Celebrate: Valuing Families in Church and Society*. The Report of the Working Party of the Board of

Social Responsibility. London: Church House Publishing.

Church of Scotland (1995) 'Report to the General Assembly'. Edinburgh.

Coate, M. A. (1989) *Clergy Stress: The Hidden Conflicts of Ministry*. London: SPCK.

Coger, M. (1985) *Women in Parish Ministry: Stress and Support*. New York: Alban Institute Publication.

Concise English Dictionary (1982) Ware, Herts: Omega Books Ltd.

Davidson, M. and Cooper, C. (1983) *Stress and the Woman Manager*. Oxford: Martin Robertson and Co. Ltd.

Davies, G. (1990) 'Believing without belonging', *Social Compass*, vol. 37, 4.

Devine, P. (1989) *Relativism, Nihilism and God*. Notre Dame, IN: University of Notre Dame Press.

Dewe, P. J. (1987) 'New Zealand ministers of religion: identifying sources of stress and coping strategies', *Work and Stress*, vol. 1, no. 4, 351–63.

Dreyfus, S. and Dreyfus, H. (1980) 'A five-stage model of the mental activities involved in skill acquisition'. Berkeley: University of California (unpublished).

Eadie, H. A. (1970) 'A study of health and illness in the experience of Church of Scotland ministers'. University of Edinburgh, PhD thesis (unpublished).

Eadie, H. A. (1972) 'The health of Scottish clergymen', *Contact*, 42.

Eadie, H. A. (1973) 'Stress and the clergyman', *Contact*, 42.

Eadie, H. A. (1975) 'The helping personality', *Contact*, 49.

Eayers, G. (1926) *Wesley, Christian Philosopher, Church Founder*. London: The Epworth Press.

Ecker, R. (1985) *The Stress Myth*. Herts: Lion Press.

Edinger, E. F. (1991) *Ego and Archetype*. Boston: Shambhala Press.

Edwards, T. (1980) *Spiritual Friends: Reclaiming the Gift of Spiritual Direction*. New York: Paulist Press.

Fairhurst, E. (1975) 'Expectations, change and identity-stress' in Gowler, D. and Legge, K. (eds) *Managerial Stress*. London: Gower Press Special Studies.

Fanstone, M. (1993) *The Sheep That Got Away*. Crowborough: Monarch Publishers.

Fisher, S. (1986) *Stress and Strategy*. London: Lawrence Erlbaum Associates Press.

Fletcher, B. (1990) *Clergy Under Stress: A Study of Homosexual and Heterosexual Clergy in the Church of England*. London: Mowbray.

Fowler, J. (1992) *Stages of Faith in Religious Development: Implications for Church, Education and Society*. London: SCM Press.

Frankenhaeuser, M. et al. (1989) 'Stress off and on the job as related to sex and occupational status in white collar workers', *Journal of Organizational Behaviour*, vol. 10.

Gibbs, E. (1993) *Winning Them Back: Tackling the Problem of Nominal Christianity*. Crowborough: Monarch Publications.

Gilbert, B. (1987) *Who Ministers to Ministers*. New York: The Alban Institute.

Gilligan, C. (1982) *In a Different Voice: Psychological Theory and Women's Development*. Cambridge, MA: Harvard University Press.

Goodling, R. (1980) 'The clergy and the problem of professional impotency', *The Duke's Divinity School Review*, vol. 45, no. 3.

Hands, D. R. and Fehr, W. L. (1993) *Spiritual Wholeness for Clergy*. New York: Alban Institute Publication.

Harbaugh, G. (1984) *Pastor as Person*. Minneapolis: Augsburg Publishing House.

Hart, A. (1984) *Coping With Depression in the Ministry and Other Helping Professions*. Dallas: Word Inc.

Hauerwas, S. and Willimon, W. (1989) *Resident Alien: Life in the Christian Colony*. Nashville: Abingdon Press.

Herald (The) (1995) 'Perspectives'. Glasgow, 28 September 1995.

Hitchcock, J. (1991) *Web of the Universe*. New York: Paulist Press.

Hulme, W. (1985) *Managing Stress in Ministry*. San Francisco: Harper and Row.

International Labour Office (1992) *Preventing Stress at Work*, vol. 11:2. Geneva.

Irvine, A. R. (1984) 'Isolation and pastoral ministry'. Wolfville, MDiv (Hon) dissertation (unpublished).

Irvine, A. R. (1989) 'Isolation in the parish ministry'. St Andrews, PhD dissertation (unpublished).

Irvine, A. R. (1990) 'Report to the Church of Scotland on isolation and the parish ministry'. Edinburgh (unpublished).

Jabay, E. (1967) *Search for Identity*. Grand Rapids: Zondervan.

Jacobi, J. (1976) *Masks of the Soul*. London: Darton, Longman & Todd.

Jacobs, M. (1989) *Holding in Trust*. London: SPCK.

Jung, C. G. (1953) 'The relations between the ego and the unconscious' in *Two Essays on Analytical Psychology* (*Collected Works*, vol. 7). London: Routledge and Kegan Paul.

Kanter, R. M. (1977) *Men and Women in the Corporation*. New York: Basic Books Inc.

Kelsey, M. (1989) *Reaching: The Journey to Fulfilment*. Minneapolis: Augsburg Publishing House.

Kutash, I. L. and Schlesinger, L. B. and Associates (1981) *Handbook on Stress and Anxiety: Contemporary Knowledge, Theory and Treatment*. San

Francisco: Jossey-Bass Publishers.

Levi, L. (1987) 'Fitting work to human capacities and needs: improvements in the content and organization of work' in Kalomo, B., Batawi, El. and Cooper, C. L. (eds) *Psychological Factors at Work*. Geneva: World Health Organisation.

Levison, M. (1992) *Wrestling With the Church*. London: Arthur James Ltd.

Lewis, C. S. (1955) *Mere Christianity*. London: Fontana Books.

Lumpkin, W. L. (1969) *Baptist Confessions of Faith*. Valley Forge: The Judson Press.

Lyall, D. (1995) *Counselling in the Pastoral and Spiritual Context*. Buckingham: Open University Press.

McAllister, R. (1965) 'The emotional health of the clergy', *Journal of Religion and Health*, vol. 4.

McAllister, R. (1978) *Journal of Religion and Health*, vol. 9.

McFadyen, A. (1990) *The Call to Personhood*. Cambridge, UK: Cambridge University Press.

McGinnis, T. (1969) 'Clergy in conflict', *Pastoral Psychology*, vol. 20, no. 197.

Marsh, P. (ed.) (1990) 'How people interact' in *The Marshall Cavendish Encyclopedia of Personal Relationships and Human Behaviour*. London: Marshall Cavendish.

Methodist Church in Britain (1991) *Some Elements of Pastoral Practice: A Discussion Paper*. Peterborough: Methodist Church Publishing House.

Merton, T. (1961) *New Seeds of Contemplation*. New York: New Directions.

Merton, T. (1971) *Contemplation in a World of Action*. London: George Allen & Unwin Ltd.

Naisbitt, J. (1982) *Megatrends*. New York: Warner Book Edition.

Oates, W. (1958) 'The healthy minister', *Pastoral Counselling*, vol. IX, no. 84.

Oden, T. (1983) *Pastoral Theology*. San Francisco: Harper and Row.

Ogilvie, L. (1984) *Making Stress Work for You*. Waco, TX: Word Publishers.

Oswald, R. (1981) 'Severely isolated clergy research project'. New York: Alban Institute (unpublished).

Oxford, Diocese of (1995) *Code of Ministerial Practices*. North Hinksey, Oxford: Diocesan Church House.

Paterson, M. (1995) 'Perspectives', *The Scotsman*, 5 October.

Powell, J. (1978) *Why Am I Afraid to Tell You Who I Am?* London and Glasgow: Fontana/Collins.

Pratt, D. A. (1987) *Stress in the Ministry*. London: The United Reformed Church.

Ramon, Brother (1989) *Soul Friends*. London: Marshall Pickering.

Rassieur, C. (1982) *Stress Management for Ministers*. Philadelphia: Westminster Press.

Rediger, C. L. (1988) 'Supporting clergy systematically', *Church Management – The Clergy Journal*, vol. 65.

Rediger, C. L. (1990) *Ministry and Sexuality*. Minneapolis: Augsburg Press.

Rutter, P. (1989) *Sex in the Forbidden Zone*. Los Angeles: Jeremy P. Tarcher.

Sanford, J. (1980) *The Invisible Partners*. New York: Paulist Press.

Selye, H. (1950) *Stress: General Adaption Syndrome and the Disease of Adaption*. Montreal: ACTA Inc.

Selye, H. (1981) 'The stress concept today' in Kutash, I. L. and Schlesinger, L. B. and Associates (eds) *Handbook on Stress and Anxiety: Contemporary Knowledge, Theory and Treatment*. San Francisco: Jossey-Bass Publishers.

Shapiro, I. (1990) 'The benefit of the doubt', *Saturday Night*, vol. 103.

Shipley, P. and Coats, M. (1992) 'A community study of dual role stress and coping of working mothers', *Journal of Work and Stress*, vol. 6, no. 1.

Sipe, A. W. R. (1995) *Sex, Priests and Power*. London: Cassell.

Sutherland, V. and Cooper, C. (1990) *Understanding Stress: A Psychological Perspective for Health Professions*. London: Chapman and Hall.

Theodorson, G. A. and Theodorson, A. G. (1969) *A Modern Dictionary of Sociology*. New York: T. Y. Crowell Co.

Thornton, M. (1984) *Spiritual Direction: A Practical Introduction*. London: SPCK.

Tillich, P. (1968) *Systematic Theology*. Welwyn, Herts: James Nisbet and Co. Ltd.

Tournier, P. (1964) *Escape From Loneliness*. Philadelphia: Westminster Press.

Vanier, J. (1986) *Man and Woman He Made Them*. London: Darton, Longman & Todd.

Wills, T. A. and Langner, T. S. (1981) 'Socioeconomic status and stress' in Kutash, I. L. and Schlesinger, L. B. and Associates (eds) *Handbook on Stress and Anxiety: Contemporary Knowledge, Theory and Treatment*. San Francisco: Jossey-Bass Publishers.

Index

accountability 68
alcohol/drugs 185
Ansvar Survey of English Social
  Behaviour 185
authority 6, 29, 54–6, 67–8

balance 196–7
  activity 127, 196–7
  relationships 197
  time 127, 133, 152, 181
Benner, P. 188
Benson, P. and Donahue, M.
  J. 191
Bibby, R. 57–8, 60, 70
Blizzard, S. 66, 74
Board of Social Responsibility of
  the Church of England 119
boundaries 98, 120–1
Bowman, C. 126, 134
Brunner, E. 145, 155, 158
British Medical Association
  (BMA) 20–1 , 22, 24, 161, 185
burnout xiii
  see also stress, excess

call of God 37, 43–5, 49–50, 63,
  131, 136, 138
  see also paradox, calling–career
Carr, W. 56
change
  church reaction to 6–7, 63
  personal reaction to 28–9, 59,
    63, 168
children (pastor's) 137–40
Coate, M. A. 56, 78, 159
Code of Ministerial Practice 120
Code of Professional Conduct 120
Coger, M. 77, 79–80

competition 37, 61–2, 76, 167,
  169, 174
contemplation 156–8
control
  see power; stress
Cummings and Cooper 22

Davidson, M. and Cooper,
  C. 78–84, 126
Davies, G. 67
depression 83, 123, 138, 185
Devine, P. 59
Dewe, P. 27
Dreyfus model of skill
  acquisitioni 188–90

Eadie, H. A. 20, 24, 32, 52
Ecker, R. 21
Edinger, E. F. 106, 109, 149
Edwards, T. 157
encounter
  with Divine 155–7
  with others 158–9
  with self 158
expectations
  clergy 35–6
    external 8–9, 13, 34–9
    imagined 33, 34, 129
    internal 27
  clergy family 129–33
  spouse 131–4, 135, 136

failure 13, 75
  see also success
Fairhurst, E. 64
faith, rooted in antiquity 6, 53–4
family 36–7
  see also expectations; image;
    isolation; relationships; time

205

Fanstone, M.   54
Fisher, S.   40–1
Fowler, J.   191
Frankenhaeuser, M.   79, 89
fraternal   76, 160, 169
    see also ministerial

gender   78, 83–4, 148–9, 166
Gibbs, E.   69, 72
Gilbert, B.   160
Grace of God   185
guilt   32–3, 34, 39, 83, 116–17,
    123, 131, 154, 185

Hands, D. and Fehr, W.   155
Harbaugh, G.   51
Hart, A.   138
Hauerwas, S. and Willimon,
    W.   6, 49, 65
Helwys, T.   57
Hitchcock, J.   191
homosexuality   122–4

identity   28, 63–4
    character   109
    false   108
    role   109
    spiritual   145
    spouse's   134–5, 136–7
image
    family's   129, 131, 133, 137,
        141
    imaginary   129
    minister's   29, 51, 52, 54–5, 63,
        74–6, 93, 102, 131, 135, 139,
        150–1, 187
inclusivism   60
individualism   57, 59, 70–1
insulation   110–12, 185
integrating perspectives,
    exteriority versus
    interiority   150–1
integration   11–13, 62, 107, 148
    non-integration   12
International Labour Office   15,
    21
intimacy
    negative   134–5
    sexual   93, 86
Irvine, A.   xiv–xv, 74, 75, 100,
    103, 159
isolation
    definition   99–100
    professional   101

social   101–2
spiritual   102–3, 191
spouse's   134
types of   100–2

Jacobi, J.   125
Jacobs, M.   182, 196
journal keeping   192–6
Jung, C. G.   xii, 22, 28, 31, 104,
    108, 158

Kanter, R. M.   80
Kelsey, M.   98, 122, 146, 147, 192

Levi, L.   43, 168, 184
Levison, M.   77, 81
Lewis, C. S.   154–5
loyalty
    to denomination   70
    to relationships   70, 129–30,
        167
Lyall, D.   viii–ix, 120

McAllister, R.   28, 35, 183
McFadyen, A.   52, 118, 151
manse   131–2
masks   xiii, 28, 104–8, 109, 116,
    135, 139–41
Merton, T.   151, 156, 158
minister as outsider   40, 94–6,
    100, 103, 173
ministerial   76, 160, 169
ministry
    code of ethics   97–8, 112,
        119–20
    models of integration   12
    nature of   13
        intimacy   136
        relational   35, 38, 89
    personal/professional   13, 14,
        49, 68
models of support
    community based support
        169–71
    denominational
        support   169
    interdenominational support
        structure   170
    interdisciplinary support
        model   170–1
    personal support structures
        CARE based support
            network   175–8
        church (local) based   174–5

community based   172–3
community of faith
  based   173–4
system support models   161–8
  inter-professional
    support   168
  ministerial/professional
    systems support   161–8
  auxiliary resources   167–8
  continuing education
    support   164
  cross-denominational
    agency support   162–3
  denominational support
    system   163
  gender-aware
    structure   166
  non-denominational based
    training   161–2
  peer support
    structures   165–6
  sabbatical support
    structure   164–5
  supportive agency   163–4
  theological
    education   166–7
Moral Majority   55, 67
  see also religious influence,
    political
Myers–Briggs Type Indicator
  (MBTI)   75

Naisbitt, J.   53
negative intimacy   134–5

Oates, W.   185
Oden, T.   43
Oswald, R.   79, 100
overwork   187–9, 193

paradox
  calling–career   147
  doing–being   146, 148, 152
  secular–sacred   146, 148
parsonage   131–2
perfectionism   33, 154
persona *see* mask
personal space   38–9, 61
  see also time, personal
Powell, J.   91
power
  dynamics   148
  invisible   130–1
  visible   130

see also authority; religious
  influence
Pratt, D.   133, 138, 146
Prospects for Scotland 2000   54,
  55, 57–9
public ownership
  of clergy   56
  of clergy family   132–3, 137

Ramon, Brother   153, 180
Rassieur, C.   81, 82
Rediger, L.   51, 114, 116, 118,
  123–4
relationships
  asymmetrical   94
  family   128, 186
  levels of   91–4, 99, 100–1, 103,
    106, 109–10, 123, 134–5, 139,
    147–8, 158–9, 173, 176, 186
  spousal   186
  spouse's   134
  violation of   93, 95–6, 113–14
  see also ministry, nature of
relativism   59, 68–70
relevance   62–4, 71–2
religious influence   5–6, 61, 67
  political   5, 55, 67
Rutter, P.   84, 96, 114, 116, 118,
  120, 149

Sanford, J.   149
self-assessment   181–96
  central space   191–2
  cognitive   183–4
  emotional   184–5
  journal keeping   192–6
  physical   182–3
  social   185–6
  spiritual   190–1
  vocational   187
  vocational growth   187–90
sexual misconduct *see*
  relationships, violation of
sexual orientation   31, 122–4
sexuality   30–3, 121–2, 148
  see also theology
Seyle, H.   24, 25, 43
Shapiro, I.   58
Shipley, P. and Coates, M.   83
Sipe, A. W. R.   69, 96, 116, 119,
  121
social action   6
*Some Elements of Pastoral
  Practice*   120

spiritual director 156–8, 165, 191, 196
spouse, career 136–7
stress
  control 39–41
  defined 16, 20
    phenomenological 21–2
    process 22
  excess–distress 25–7
  external 34–9
  internal 27–34
  models of 16–20, 22
    interactive 18–20
    response based 17–18
    stimulus based 16–17
  poor fit 43–5
  real versus ideal 41–3
  vital–villain 22–5
success 13, 29, 37, 61, 71
Sutherland, V. and Cooper, C. 16, 20, 21

theological quadrilateral 9–10, 174
theology 33–4
  of ministry 14, 36, 97–8

of personhood 117–18
of self-denial 107
of sexuality 118–19
Thornton, M. 157
Tillich, P. 155, 158
time
  balance 152, 181
  family 186
  personal 61, 83
  spousal 186
  stewardship 127–9, 133
total assessment concept 181, 183
Tournier, P. 102, 152
traditions 7–8

Vanier, J. 113
vicarage 131–2
voluntary structure 40

women in ministry
  dual role 83–4
  in organizational structure 82
  tokenism 80–1
workaholism 187–9, 193